Spiritual Disclaimer

Notice is hereby given:

BY CONTINUING BEYOND THIS POINT, the reader acknowledges and agrees that the state of Spiritual Enlightenment discussed herein conveys upon the seeker-aspirant-victim no benefits, boons, blessings, or special powers and bears little or no resemblance to assorted New Age or Eastern varieties widely dispensed under the same name. Orgasmic euphoria, orgiastic bliss, obscene wealth, perfect health, eternal peace, angelic ascension, cosmic consciousness, purified aura, astral projection, pan-dimensional travel, extra-sensory perception, access to akashic records, profound wisdom, sagely demeanor, radiant countenance, omniscience, omnipotence, omnipresence and opening of the third eye are not likely to result. Tuning, harmonizing, balancing, energizing, reversing or opening of the chakras should not be expected. The kundalini serpent dwelling at the base of the spine will not be awakened, poked, prodded, raised, or otherwise molested.

NO PROMISE OF SELF-ADVANCEMENT, self-esteem, self-aggrandizement, self-gratification, self-satisfaction or self-improvement is made or implied. Likewise, self-indulgent, self-involved, self-centered, self-absorbed, and self-serving persons will not find satisfaction herein. The reader should construe no assurance of reward, rapture, empowerment, deliverance, salvation, enrichment, forgive-ness, or eternal rest in a heavenly abode. No raising, altering, transforming, transferring, transposing, transfiguring, transmuting, transcending or transmigrating of consciousness is to be expected.

PURCHASE OR POSSESSION OF THIS BOOK does not grant admittance to idyllic or mythical realms including but not limited to: Atlantis, Elysium, Garden of Eden, Heaven, Never-Never-Land, Nirvana, Paradise, Promised Land, Shambhala, Shangri-la, or Utopia.

THIS BOOK MAKES EXTENSIVE USE of analogy and symbolism. The terms vampire, zombie, caterpillar, butterfly, dreamstate, Maya, and others are used metaphorically. Likewise, any suggestion that the reader should leap from a skyscraper, step into a blazing inferno, perform ritual self-disembow-elment, or bathe in a vat of corrosive acids are not to be taken literally. The reader is advised that cutting off his or her hand, plucking out his or her eye, or chopping off his or her head, may result in bodily injury.

THE PURSUIT AND ATTAINMENT of Spiritual Enlightenment may entail loss of ego, identity, humanity, mind, friends, relatives, job, home, children, car, money, jewelry, respect, specificity in time, solidity in space, strict adherence to accepted physical laws, and reason for living.

THE SPIRITUAL ENLIGHTENMENT REFERRED TO herein is a process and product of will and self-determination. It requires no reliance on or cooperation with God, Goddess, Satan, discorporate entities (angelic or demonic), gurus, swamis, seers, sages, holymen, priests, teachers, philosophers, faeries, gnomes, pixies, sprites, (wee folk of any sort), or any other agent or agency of non-self authority.

HEART-CENTERED APPROACHES AND QUALITIES generally considered to be of the essence of Spiritual Enlightenment, such as love, compassion, tolerance, grace, tranquility, and pacifism, will be viewed herein as antithetical, misleading, and irrelevant.

THE SEEKER-ASPIRANT-VICTIM has no need of any spiritual practices or belief systems including but not limited to Buddhism, Kabbalah, Hinduism, Sufism, Taoism, Gnosticism, Mohammadism, Judaism, Christism, Paganism, Occultism, Zoroastrianism, Wicca, Yoga, Tai Chi, Feng Shui, Martial Arts, Magick, or Necromancy.

THE SEEKER-ASPIRANT-VICTIM has no need of any so-called spiritual or New Age paraphernalia, trinkets or amulets including but not limited to crystals, gems, stones, seeds, beads, shells, incense, candles, aromas, bells, gongs, chimes, altars, images, or idols. No special clothing, jewelry, adornments, tattoos, or fashion accessories are necessary to this endeavor.

THE SEEKER-ASPIRANT-VICTIM need not avail him or herself of any of the myriad enlightenment-inducing procedures and techniques including but not limited to meditation, candle-gazing, mantra intoning, subjugation to guru, standing on one leg, pilgrimage on belly, unaided flight, drugs, breathing techniques, fasting, wandering in deserts, self-flagellation, vows of silence, sexual indulgence or sexual continence.

THE SEEKER-ASPIRANT-VICTIM has no need or use for any spiritual powers, arts or sciences including but not limited to astrology, numerology, divination, tarot or rune reading, mandala making, fire-walking, psychic surgery, automatic writing, channeling, pyramid power, telepathy, clairvoyance, lucid dreaming, dream interpretation, ESP, levitation, bi-location, psychokinesis, or remote viewing. Furthermore, tricks, stunts or feats such as shooting arrows from horseback, endurance of cold, live burial, materializing ash or jewelry, walking on fire or glass, laying on glass or nails, piercing of face or arms, conjuring and rope tricks, have no bearing or merit as regards the Spiritual Enlightenment discussed herein.

CONFRONTATION WITH PERSONAL DEMONS, the facing of deep-seated fears, and the step-by-step dismantling of personal identity may result in elevated pulse, high blood pressure, loss of equilibrium, loss of motor control, loss of pallor and skin tone, loss of hair and teeth, loss of appetite, loss of sleep, loss of bowel and bladder control, tremors, fatigue, shortness of breath, dry-heaves, acid reflux, dyspepsia, halitosis, diarrhea, seborrhea, psoriasis, sweating, swelling, and swooning. The emotional upheaval attendant upon the discovery that one is oneself a fictional character in a staged drama may result in forlornness, weltschmerz, intolerance, anger, hostility, resentment, hopelessness, despondency, suicidal despair, morbid depression, and a suffocating awareness of life's meaninglessness.

THE SEEKER-ASPIRANT-VICTIM is hereby advised that study of ancient cultures, travel to distant lands, or learning of foreign languages avails not in the least, and that, for the purposes of understanding and attaining the Spiritual Enlightenment discussed herein, there is no better place than here and no better time than now.

THIS BOOK IS NOT INTENDED for human consumption. If ingested, induce vomiting and seek immediate medical assistance. Avoid inserting this book into bodily cavities. Repeatedly plunging this book into the mouth, eyes, ears, nose, vagina or rectum may result in unsightly bulges and a painful burning sensation. If symptoms persist, consult a qualified metaphysician.

ALL CHARACTERS, PLACES AND EVENTS depicted in this book are entirely fictional insofar as this book and the universe in which it exists are entirely fictional. Any resemblance to actual people, places and events is purely the result of resemblance to actual people, places and events.

NO DOLPHINS WERE SWUM WITH in the making of this book. Removal of this warning is illegal where prohibited by law. Batteries not included. Be careful what you wish for. Jed McKenna action figure sold separately.

SPIRITUAL WARFARE

Jed McKenna

Spiritual Warfare

www.WisefoolPress.com

Cover Photo: U.S. Department of Energy photograph.
XX-33 ROMEO: 11 megatons. Fired near Bikini Atoll on March 26, 1954.

"Now I am become Death, the destroyer of worlds."
Robert Oppenheimer recalled these lines, spoken by Lord Krishna
in the Bhagavad Gita, while witnessing the first nuclear test.

Printed in the United States of America

ISBN: 978-0-9714352-2-3

Library of Congress Cataloging-in-Publication Data

McKenna, Jed
  Spiritual warfare / Jed McKenna.
     p. cm.
  Includes bibliographical references.
  ISBN 978-0-9714352-2-3 (pbk.)
  1. Spiritual life. I. Title.
  BL624.M39738 2007
  204'.2--dc22

                                        2007016329

This book is dedicated to
KEN KESEY

Contents

Truly, I have attained nothing

from total enlightenment.

— Buddha —

1. Great Moments in Enlightenment History

When we remember we are all mad, the
mysteries disappear and life stands explained.

—Mark Twain

OW MANY SPIRITUALITY BOOKS START with a chase scene? And how many where the enlightened guy writing the book is being chased by the cops?

I mulled these questions over as I watched more squad cars arriving to join in the pursuit. A few of the patrol cars were driving slowly through the dark neighborhood streets behind me, using their spotlights to scan the houses and small yards.

This was a New England vacation community in the off-season. The town had two resort hotels with marinas, restaurants, bars, pools, golf courses and all the rest. There were a few ski hills within twenty miles, but they didn't bring in big winter crowds. Anyway it was almost April and it was getting warm and they were closed now. The town had a lot of bars and that's what the local cops mostly worried about; handling alcohol-related incidents and drunk drivers.

I was close enough to hear about half of what was being said by the cops in their staging area where the whole production had begun nearly an hour earlier. I could hear some of what they said into their radios but not the staticky replies. There was a kind of empty urgency that had many of them confused. Urgency of any kind up here was quite a novelty. I doubt any of the local cops had ever drawn their weapons in the line of duty. They were basically a security force for the resorts and the hundreds of summer houses and estates packed along the lake's surrounding hillside.

They wouldn't find anything on me; no watch, no wallet, no money. I was just out for a walk so I hadn't stocked my pockets. I didn't lock the house I was renting, so I wasn't carrying a key.

I like renting houses in resorts during the off-season. You get the best of everything with low prices and few people. No jet skiing or sailing, but I'm not big on recreation anyway. I've had good luck with ski communities in summer and water resorts in winter. That's what I was doing here. I had a beautiful house for the last three months that would have cost eight times as much in-season. Few neighbors, little traffic, not many kids or dogs, just quiet and privacy. In the sleepy town, a short and pleasant walk away, there were good restaurants that were open but not busy. I was an hour from a medium-sized college town if I needed anything the small town couldn't provide. My lease was going to expire in two days, at which time I would throw my stuff in a backpack and a garment bag and move on. A girl came in to clean twice a week, so I didn't even have to worry about that.

So, all well and good, nothing to complain about. Where I would go next was just a matter of whim. I had my passport and had a very interesting invitation to a place in Mexico, but I could go anywhere in the world and park for a few months. I hadn't decided yet.

So that's where I was now, sitting in the dark, leaning on a tree near the town's hilltop memorial park, watching the cops bustling around in their agitated condition. They were in the parking lot where this whole thing had started, looking at maps, trying to determine who they were chasing and why. They had no answer to either question.

It was a Thursday night. Friday morning actually, around 1:00 a.m. I had been out for a walk, just like many other walks on many previous nights. Down to the marinas, along a stretch of sandy beach, then over a fence and a bit of wandering through the town, window shopping in the deserted streets, then up into the neighborhoods, avoiding houses where I knew dogs would start barking or motion-sensing lights would come on. Then it was downhill, back to the lake path that would take me back to my own neighborhood and the house I rented. There was a popular bar nearby, then a strip of lakeshore road with boat landings and sheds, then the parking lot and small field. As I made it through the field I saw a couple of young guys standing on the small footbridge that connected the parking area to the lakeshore path. They were smoking a joint and got a little nervous as I approached. I waved and smiled. "Just passing through, guys," I said and they relaxed. Then they got tense again. I turned and saw why. Two squad cars were pulling up fifty yards away, obviously coming this way.

"Shit!" exclaimed one of the stoned guys. "Ditch it."

The two cops were now out of their cars trotting toward us, flashlight beams bouncing crazily around. In a flash of inspiration that is the hallmark of the enlightened master, I shrieked like a girl and ran away.

It wasn't planned, it just seemed like an amusing thing to do. I really thought they'd have me within fifty steps and that would be that. I figured I could savor the taste of freedom for about another thirty seconds before a winded and seriously unamused copper had me chewing the turf. I was just out walking, I have no record, there was nothing in my pockets or in my system, so they'd tell me what a jerk I was and let me go. If I was thinking at all, that's what I thought. It didn't work out that way, though. No one came after me. Not yet.

I trotted up the cement stairs, into the memorial park. I was a little disappointed to find I wasn't being chased so I hooked back to see what was happening below. Already a third squad car was arriving. They had the kids and they were talking animatedly with them and pointing to the stairway I had climbed and the area from which I watched them. Maybe they were still interested in me. I decided they were when two of them came back across the footbridge toward the stairs, flashlights out and scanning. Time to go.

I got to the road and started jogging back to my house. Then I decided to get clever and try to have some fun with it. I was curious about how serious they were about finding me. I hooked back around some hedges into a secluded driveway. There was a van backed in so I used the bumper and a rock wall to get on top of the flat-roofed garage. I crossed that, went over a four-foot cyclone fence, and climbed onto the side deck of another house. Everything in this area was tiered up from the lake, two rows of houses, a narrow street, then two more rows of houses and so on. Garages and sheds were low and flat and trees were sparse to allow unobstructed lake views. Buildings and wood fences were all painted white and it was a bright moonlit night. Once I was up one street and three houses above the lake, I stopped to see what was going on. At this point, I assumed the cops were right behind me, and the fun, such as it was, would be over. I'd be completely unable to explain my juvenile antics. They might threaten me with a psych-eval or something, warn me sternly, and we could all go on with our lives. Instead, I saw that the cops were still down by the lake searching bushes and boathouses with their flashlights. They were nowhere close.

Fun's over, I thought, a bit disappointed. I hadn't really meant to get away and wasn't sure what to do with my freedom. I could walk back to my rented house in three minutes. Instead, I started heading back toward town on a high street that gave me a good view of all below. As I came around a bend in the road leading to a nice high vantage point, headlights were suddenly blazing in my eyes and an amplified voice barked out an order I couldn't quite make out, though I guessed it was a suggestion that I not run away.

So I ran away. What can I say? The lights startled me, I thought the whole thing was over, and frankly, I'd been a little bored of late. Calling upon my only superpower, gravity, I went sailing downhill into a short driveway, through a yard, over a retaining wall, along a fence, across a deck, across a street, then, getting clever, along the street, back up the hill, across another street, along hedges for several houses, up a driveway, around a house, over a low fence, through a dormant garden, across another street, and then leaned on a kid's tire swing to pant like a dog for a few minutes.

I still hadn't done anything wrong, technically. I'd never heard any order to stop from a police officer. The car with the headlights ordered me to do something, I think, but I couldn't see that it was the police because of the blinding lights. I doubt anyone would be too impressed with that defense here in Mayberry-on-the-Lake, but it amused me to think I was the victim in all this, an innocent man, wrongfully accused, driven to ground and mercilessly hounded by Johnny Law.

This is all going somewhere, by the way.

I could hear activity; voices, cars, intermittent radio static, but I had no idea what was happening. I was very surprised that a car had been parked, lying in wait for me. I had thought the escapade was winding down, and here they were running a dragnet operation on me. I wondered how many others were involved. I didn't think the town even had six police cars and probably only two or three out patrolling on a Thursday night. Had I just stumbled into the only one dispatched to find the mystery runner, or were there more? I was still close enough to my rented house that I could cross a few streets and yards and be running a bath in five minutes, but that had a sort of open-endedness that didn't feel right.

There was a fairly nice treehouse in the yard where I was playing ninja. I tested the nailed two-by-four ladder and climbed to the lowest platform where I was well concealed. I heard crunching gravel and saw a patrol car with its lights off slowly creeping along, windows open, watching, listening. I thought of the old throw-something-in-the-other-direction-to-make-your-pursuers-go-the-wrong-way trick, but I wouldn't fall for it and I doubted they would either. Anyway, he wasn't even using his spotlight, just creeping and listening.

I knew my way around all these streets pretty well from my walks. I knew which houses had motion-sensing lights and which had good views. I was only a couple of hundred yards from a large house with some of the best views of the neighborhood, the lake and the town from its main deck. I alit from the tree, jogged the short distance on the street, then up the main street that fed into all the neighborhood streets from the town, up to the house with the views. From the back door near the driveway I climbed a circular metal stairway to the deck and crouched behind the railing to see what I could see.

I could see one police car creeping along the streets and another parked down near where the lake path left the summer houses and ran along the pricier estates, blocking that escape route. Down near the parking area where the police had originally pulled up I could see glints of light and metal through the trees, but nothing specific. It was around this time that the thought occurred to me, somewhat belatedly, that I had no idea what I was doing. I relaxed onto a teak lounger that was comfortable even without its cushions and pondered the silliness of my situation. I laughed and watched the stars and let a deep feeling of contentment wash over me. This is my life, I thought. I talk and write about spiritual enlightenment, I move around and live in interesting places, I run from coppers and trespass on people's decks and gaze out at a million stars. This is my life and it's goofy and delightful and the best life anyone could ever have.

I lay there for fifteen minutes, maybe dozing off a bit; contented, amused. The night had been fun, a nice note to end on since I'd be leaving the area soon. I decided to walk back to the house, have a shower and go to bed. I stood up and stretched, pleasantly chilled and eager to get home and get warm, when a spotlight hit me, wobbled a bit, and locked on.

"Silly people," my lulled mind thought, "don't they know we're done playing? I just want to go home now. All done. Thanks for the nice time, fellas."

Apparently, they didn't know that. They thought we were still playing and they didn't really seem too playful about it. They actually seemed kind of serious. Orders were shouted and adult language employed. My delicate state of inner harmony was disturbed and the chase was rejoined.

I followed the deck around the side of the house, crossed a small patch of yard, scrambled up over a retaining wall and onto the highest street. Once on the road I stopped and listened for the police car. The way it was facing they would either have to turn around or go the longer way to the ascending hairpin to get to the street where I was. Either way they were coming up here so I turned around and retraced my steps along the side of the house, across the deck and down to the bottom of the circular staircase where I was very exposed. My jacket was light tan and practically radiant in the moonlight, so I took it off and stashed it in a roadside hedgerow where I could pick it up tomorrow, should tomorrow ever come.

Now I could hear radio chatter and I could see and hear that more cars were approaching the area. I realized that some of the radios I was hearing were from patrolmen on foot. I peered through the night and was able to make out flashlight beams closer than comfort allowed.

I jogged along the road staying close to the edge of driveways and hedges. The running thing wasn't that much fun and it wasn't part of any sensible plan so I stopped and considered my choices. I was cut off from my house now, so the bath and bed plan was no longer an option. I could just stop playing; sit down and wait for them to arrive and hope to be in my nice warm bed before sunrise. I stood there and mulled my options, waiting for rightness to make itself known, when one of the cops on foot appeared from around a bend sixty feet away and rightness made itself known.

He didn't see me, so I tiptoed into a driveway, crept up the stairs along the side of a one-car garage and then onto the flat, tar and pea-gravel roof. There was a foot-high wall around the perimeter so I was able to stay low and watch activity below. The cop came into view, waving his flashlight from side to side, up driveways, under bushes, up into trees. There was some radio talk I couldn't hear but I made out the word "county" and got a little worried. It occurred to me now that they were waking up local cops for this and calling in county cops. That seemed a bit much to me, but I hadn't been consulted.

I liked my little garage perch, but I was clearly exposed from above and behind, so I couldn't stay. Once the cop was past I went back down and followed along behind him. That seemed like a good idea until, not realizing he had stopped, I got too close and made a scuffing noise in the gravel. His flashlight swung toward me, he barked a command and once again, I bolted. I crashed through a hedgerow, along the side of a house, and along a railroad tie retaining wall between houses. The copper caught me in his beam from ten yards away, I ducked down to the next street and came out near the top of a toboggan slide; a two-hundred foot wooden chute for riding down and onto the lake, when frozen, with a parallel stairway for walking back up. Wondering which way to go, I received inspiration from a bumper sticker on a nearby car. "What would Jesus do?" it asked, and the answer came in a flash. He'd grab a lid off a garbage can and ride it down the wooden toboggan slide to the lake and freedom. Of course, Jesus would probably have a much better medical plan than I do.

Instead, I trotted back to the hilltop park to watch events unfold and decide what to do. I got there safely and settled at the base of a tree overlooking the scene below and caught my breath.

Maybe you're thinking that the enlightened master is supposed to be a sterling example of composure and serenity, a person of exquisite poise and understated elegance radiating love and compassion, exuding an air of calm and imperturbability, a transcendent being who lives untouched by the petty challenges and annoyances of daily life. That's what I was thinking too as I leaned up against a tree and contemplated the absurdity of my situation.

"Well," I muttered, "this doesn't seem very enlightened."

✧

When I don't know what to do, I don't do anything, so that's what I did. I sat and watched, making no particular effort to conceal myself or continue the game.

The whole adventure had started about an hour ago. There were four police vehicles down in the lot; others came and went. County was in on it now, and I'd overheard talk of calling in state, but they clearly didn't want to let it turn into a bigger fuss without knowing who they were after or why.

I was curious and a little saddened to see that the cops weren't enjoying themselves. I know myself to be ridiculously uninformed when it comes to people, but I didn't understand why they seemed so upset. It was a beautiful evening; starry, pretty moon, a bracing little chill in the air. They were out doing police-y sorts of things; stalking dark streets with flashlights and guns, searching for some mysterious wrong-doer, playing with maps and microphones, organizing search patterns. A real live manhunt. A pleasant departure from the usual grind of bar brawlers and drunk drivers. I couldn't see what wasn't nice about the whole thing, but, as I say, I don't really understand people. Anyway, they didn't seem amused.

After a few minutes of watching and puzzling, I realized I'd had enough and silently asked the universe what I should do. The answer came clearly and immediately. I heard the ranking county cop decide that it was time to call in the dogs. One of his men went off to radio it in. There was my answer. I had no interest in letting this thing go that far, so I got up, brushed myself off, and walked down the hill to introduce myself.

"Hi guys," I said, interrupting their map huddle, "I think I'm the guy you're looking for."

Suddenly, guns. Lots of 'em.

I was ordered to put my hands on the hood of the police cruiser nearest me. A middle-aged, overweight cop with sergeant stripes appeared to my immediate right, leveled his pistol at my head from one foot away and said with trembling sincerity: "Make no mistake, motherfucker. If you move one motherfuckin' inch I will blow your motherfuckin' head off."

You don't get an offer like that every day.

And here's the funny part: I didn't move. That's actually the part that I find most interesting and worth relating about this whole episode. The urge to move was certainly there. The laugh part of the urge actually made it out, but I cut off the actual motion part somehow. I didn't laugh at the cop or the melodrama or the absurdity, I laughed because here it was, unexpectedly but quite clearly, the exit. No muss, no bother, less effort than flicking a switch. Just snap my head around and yell *Boo!* and a deliciously amusing end would be instantly and painlessly delivered.

Is this what tonight was all about? Was it time? I saw the perfection of the circumstances and I watched as the impulse to accept the cop's generous invitation raced up from the depths and made it so near the surface that the first manifestations of it, the laugh, actually broke free, but then, curiously, inexplicably, some agent or mechanism of intercession aborted the imminent snapping around of the head that I could already feel in my shoulders. Instead, I simply said:

"Okey-doke."

✧

How many spiritual books start like that?

2. Timeless Time & Spaceless Space

The universe seems to me infinitely strange and foreign. At such a moment I gaze upon it with a mixture of anguish and euphoria; separate from the universe, as though placed at a certain distance outside it; I look and I see pictures, creatures that move in a kind of timeless time and spaceless space, emitting sounds that are a kind of language I no longer understand or even register.

—Eugène Ionesco

THE REST OF THE EVENING and early morning were anticlimactic but not unpleasant. No one seemed to harbor any ill-will toward me and no one treated me like the reckless dipshit you might suppose. The sergeant wasn't pleased, mainly because he had to get the city attorney out of bed so they could figure out something to charge me with. The tricky part was that, to everyone's surprise, I hadn't done anything illegal. That didn't matter; there was no way they were letting me go without charging me with something. I saw that they were having a hard time thinking up a charge, so I assured them that I was leaving the area soon and wouldn't be returning for a court date. That seemed to relax them a bit.

Still, I ended up spending four hours in the cop shop while they put it together. It was all pretty informal; cuffs off, a light pat-down, taking some information. No fingerprinting or photographing. I didn't have my wallet so I couldn't prove who I was, which they weren't too thrilled about.

"Drive me to my house and I'll grab my wallet," I suggested. "You're probably gonna wanna set a fine, so I'll need my credit cards anyway."

"We don't take credit cards," grumbled the sergeant.

"Then you'll have to run me by the ATM over on Lakeview, too," I said. Then, to make sure they didn't overtax my munificence, I added: "But my daily limit is a hundred bucks. If it's more than that I guess I'll be your guest for awhile."

That little fib worked and the fine would eventually turn out to be a hundred bucks. Go figure.

"Don't you have some one-size-fits-all charge to suit every occasion?" I asked. "Disturbing the peace, interfering with official acts, disorderly conduct, something like that?"

That just caused more grumbling. Whatever the charge ended up being, we all knew it was just a formality; they had to charge something and I had to pay something, and it had to be done in such a way that I was set loose that night and that would be the end of it; no court appearance, no lawyers, no scrutiny.

Fine with me. I was getting snoozy.

They told a big young cop named Ben to take me to my house, to the cash machine and back. I rode in the front seat, no restraint. He waited while I ran in for my wallet. He was a polite kid, a former highschool linebacker type, who was eager to do a play-by-play reenactment of the evening's chase.

"I almost had you there by the sled-run," he said proudly, meaning the toboggan slide.

"Oh, that was you? Yep, that was darn close. What was it you yelled? I couldn't make it out."

"Yeah," he laughs good-naturedly. "I started to yell *'Freeze!'*, but that seemed like TV stuff so I changed it to *'Stop!'* in the middle but didn't get it all out. I think I yelled *'Free-stab!'*"

"Yeah," I agree, "that's what it sounded like. Free stab."

"Where'd you get off to? I thought I was right behind you."

Time to lie. Everyone in the police station had been doing this sort of excited retelling of the chase and their own role in it. In a town like this, tonight would be talked about and recounted for years to come; guns had been drawn, county was involved, dogs and helicopters were almost called in, deadly words had been spoken in earnest. It turned out that the runner wasn't a real criminal, but no one knew that when it was happening. Coulda been a real desperado.

"You *were* right behind me," I told him. In truth, I had ducked behind some hedges, watched him lumber by, and went back the way he had come.

"I thought you had me easy, but I just ran flat out and hid in a kid's tree-house till it was quiet."

That pleased him. That was a tale he could tell.

✧

"The sergeant aimed his gun at your head and threatened to shoot you if you moved?" asks Lisa, setting down the pages she'd just read. It's a month after these events and we're sitting at my poolside desk on a small estate in Mexico where we are both living.

"Yeah, why?" I look up from my laptop at the lake and mountains and rub my eyes. "Is that weird?"

"I don't know," she says, "it sounds a little theatrical."

"He had to reach across himself and lift his stomach up with one hand so he could pull out his gun with the other. It wasn't that theatrical."

"Were you scared?"

"Of what?"

"Oh, I don't know, uh, being shot in the head?"

I shrug.

"That's about the least scary thing I can think of."

"Jesus, you're a strange man."

I shrug again.

✧

Over the course of the few quiet months I spent living in that resort town in New England, the idea began forming in my head that there might be a need for a third book; that there were still important things left unsaid and other things that had been said but not fully explored. When I finished the first book, *Spiritual Enlightenment: The Damnedest Thing*, it was a relief to have it out of my system and be done with it. But not for long. The second one, *Spiritually Incorrect Enlightenment*, began making its presence known, so we got that one out. Again, I felt that I had it out of my system and no more writing would be necessary, meaning, in effect, that I was done with teaching, corresponding, writing, and all things spiritual. Then, over the few months before the thing with the cops, there it was again. I didn't nurture it, but I understood from those earliest stirrings that it would survive and that a third book would need to be written. I didn't do anything to encourage it. I just let it sit there in my head to live or die on its own.

The argument against doing a third book was that I was out of the teaching mode and spiritual mindset, and happily so. I was no longer communicating with anyone on these topics and they were no longer lively in my thoughts. They were out of my system and environment, and there was nothing to suggest that I would be re-entering the world of human spirituality. Where would a third book come from?

More than that, my own connection to the pre-awakened human experience was now so tenuous that I doubted a third book was even possible. The paradigm gap had grown too wide. I could no longer remember what life was like on the other side. My own experience was now so far removed from what most people called reality that there was practically no overlap. I see humans the way humans see chimps; from the same evolutionary remove. My memories of my own pre-awakened state were now as remote and impersonal as my memories of the second grade. I mentioned this gradual erosion of my dreamstate personhood in both books. I had been making an effort to maintain a connection, but after *Incorrect* I let it go, and now it was all but gone.

One of the arguments in *favor* of a third book was that it would provide a framework within which I could function; a context in which I could have something to do and a reason to do it. All context is artificial, of course, but what do I care? I like being alive, but it's more fun when there's a game to play. Writing with an audience in mind is one such game.

So I made the standard deal with the universe. If you want the book written, lay it out in front of me and I'll write it. I'm not going to chase it, I'm not going to struggle to come up with stuff to write about. That would be artificial and egoic. I couldn't do it and it wouldn't work. I knew nothing like that was being asked of me, but I wanted a clear understanding between us: If you want a third book, I'll do it, but the only way it's going to happen is if you orchestrate it. Drop it in my lap.

Dealing with the universe this way is nothing new to me. We understand each other pretty well. I know how to speak and I know how to understand what I'm being told. Patterns, signs, subtle variations in rightness and not-rightness, flow and obstruction; this is how it works. I make it sound as if the universe and I were two separate things, but it's actually the absence of that artificial distinction that I'm talking about. This is one of the things we'll be taking a closer look at in this book. This is the thing that everyone wants to know about and tap into; effortless functioning, direct knowing, the manifestation of abundance, health, prosperity, happiness. Understand how the universe works, merge back into it, learn to operate in alignment with it, and you'll blush to recall that you once thought that Albus and Obi-Wan had cool powers.

There are plenty of books about how to manifest our desires from within the segregated state of Human Childhood; to use prayer or wishcraft or affirmations or laws of attraction to get a better house, a faster car, the perfect mate, and so on. What we'll be discussing in this book is making the transition to the integrated state of Human Adulthood and developing within it, so that prayer, wishcraft, affirmations, and laws of attraction become superfluous, the way cheating becomes superfluous when you know the answers.

Once that initial agreement with the universe about the third book was in place, other things started lining up and the project started coming into focus. For one thing, a third book just felt right. There was more to say, important stuff, maybe the most important stuff of all, and leaving it unsaid would have kept the project from ever feeling complete.

Another thing was that the book was already dropping into my lap. I knew what the main themes would be within the first minutes of contemplating it. Also, at about the same time, I became aware of a folder full of emails I had received from a college professor, now retired, who had, I would discover, a very courageous mind and a very specialized library. He lived in Mexico and, in every email he wrote, he invited me down to visit and to avail myself of his views and his books. Most recently he wrote about his daughter and her marriage that was on the rocks. The professor's name was Frank and his daughter's name was Lisa. Frank had recently lost his wife and Lisa had recently lost herself. She's one of the people helping me write the third book. She's the one who thinks I'm a strange man.

✧

"All this universe talk," says Lisa after reading an early draft of the preceding few pages, "it just sounds so, I don't know, I guess I don't see this perfect order you're talking about. All I see is randomness and chaos everywhere. I don't see any real order to things."

Strange that what's so simple and obvious to me can be so foreign and incomprehensible to others.

"When you are asleep within the dream we call reality," I say, "it appears that there is chaos and randomness, as if anything could happen at any time. When you awaken within the dreamstate, when you open your eyes and begin to see it directly instead of imagining it from behind closed eyes, then you begin to understand how it really works; that there is a flawless, perfect intelligence governing every detail of the dreamscape of being, from the smallest to the largest. There is order, consistency, intelligence; there can be no violation or mistake."

She gives me her piercing attorney stare.

"And *you* are more attuned to this perfect universe than most people?"

"I'm not artificially walled off from it. Most people are."

As I sit there at my *al fresco* workspace with Lisa and two other people who are assisting me at the moment, it amazes me, as it often does, how bizarre and unlikely people are. It's as if I'm dreaming these two-dimensional characters into existence and it's weird that I'm not doing a better job of it. They're like fleshy robots running on outdated software, unable to adapt and evolve and develop along lines that, to all appearances, are fully open to them. They possess immense stores of knowledge and full capacity for thought. They competently handle all the complexities of life—family, health, finance, career, spirituality, household—day in and day out, year after year. They are intelligent, mature, clever, kind, honest, and fairly representative, in the broad strokes, of people anywhere in the Western world. And yet, whenever I talk to them about the most basic and essential facts of life, all I get is dubious stares and incoherent skepticism. Growth, adulthood, energetic patterns, flow and obstruction, desire and manifestation; these should be topics in which we're all completely immersed by the age of ten, like our mother tongue, and yet here we are, a group of supposed adults, and we can barely cobble together a serviceable lexicon of true adulthood.

On the face of it, I'm not the most likely candidate for this role. I'm not the guy you look at in high school and say: "Oh yeah, this guy has spiritual enlightenment written all over him." I have qualities, the ones I need, but nothing to indicate that I would be one of the few to find the answers man has sought since the beginning of wonder. But truth and enlightenment aside, I am a well-developed and still-developing Human Adult. I have a working knowledge *of* and integrated relationship *with* the universe that is so fluid and easy, so magical and endlessly delightful, so natural and seamless, that whenever I look at bright, capable, outwardly honest people, I have to remind myself that my reality, my safe, happy, co-creative universe, is completely alien and unknown to them. My living reality is as absurd to them as theirs is to me. What I now consider normal daily functioning would be considered by most people as something out of a B movie, having nothing to do with "real" life. Even though these people I'm sitting with look like me, walk and talk like me, and appear to occupy space only a few feet away from me, we inhabit completely different and largely unrelated realms of being.

We'll do a bit of a re-cap and a pre-cap in the next few chapters, but for now I want to introduce this distinction. It has nothing to do with enlightenment or truth-realization, it has to do with being a naturally developed human being instead of a spiritually stunted, developmentally retarded human being; a Human Adult instead of a Human Child. Virtually everything and anything worth knowing or pursuing in terms of growth, spiritual or otherwise, is about making this transition, and then continuing a lifetime's development. That's what life really is, and no one knows it. I've said that the greatest men and women who ever lived were just children on a playground from my perspective, and this is what it means. This should and seemingly *could* be everyone's perspective. You're reading this book so you should certainly be assuming it could be yours. For anyone in the state of Human Childhood, except a human child, there should be no topic of interest other than freeing oneself from spirit-smothering emotional shackles and resuming one's right and proper life. To put our attention on anything else is to cower away from the real journey of life.

Lisa, who sits with me and who will be with us throughout this book, began her unshackling recently, involuntarily, and as a complete spiritual neophyte. Bob, who we will meet later, is a longstanding spiritual expert and author who can speak knowledgeably on everything from Advaita to Zen. By the end of this book, Lisa will have completed the transition to Adulthood and be continuing her development within it, while Bob will still be mired in all his books and knowledge and spiritual egohood.

If, that is, they exist at all, and aren't just shadowy apparitions inhabiting my own dreamscape environment, as to which I have no opinion.

3. The Whole Truth

> Well, I am certainly wiser than this man. It is only too likely
> that neither of us has any knowledge to boast of; but he thinks
> that he knows something which he does not know, whereas I
> am quite conscious of my ignorance. At any rate it seems that
> I am wiser than he is to this small extent, that I do not think
> that I know what I do not know.

> *—Socrates*

WHADDA YA KNOW?

Really. What, with absolute certainty, do you know?

Put aside all opinions, beliefs and theories for a moment and address this one simple question: What do you know for sure? Or, as Thoreau put it:

> Let us settle ourselves, and work and wedge our feet downward
> through the mud and slush of opinion, and prejudice, and tradi-
> tion, and delusion, and appearance, that alluvion which covers the
> globe... through church and state, through poetry and philosophy
> and religion, till we come to a hard bottom and rocks in place,
> which we can call reality, and say, This is, and no mistake; and
> then begin...

In other words, let's cut the crap and figure out what we know for sure. The cogito does exactly that, and it's very simple. The question is: What do you know?

The answer is: I Am.

All other so-called facts are really non-facts and belong in the category of consensual reality and relative truth, i.e., *un*real reality and *un*true truth.

Cogito ergo sum is the equation that proves the fact. But first, before we go on, let's ask what *else* we know. What else can be said for certain?

Nothing. We don't know anything else. And that's the real point of the cogito. The importance of I Am isn't that it's a fact, but that it's the *only* fact.

I Am is the only thing anyone has ever known or will ever know. Everything else, all religion and philosophy and science, can never be more than dream interpretation. There is no other fact than I Am.

The cogito is the seed of the thought that destroys the universe. Beyond the cogito, nothing is known. Beyond the cogito, nothing *can* be known. Except I Am, no one knows anything. No man or god can claim to know more. No god or array of gods can exist or be imagined that know more than this one thing: I Am.

✧

We can't avoid letting this topic drift briefly into the Old Testament. When Moses asked God His name, God answered, "I am that I am." The name God gives for Himself is I Am.

Note that I Am is unconjugatable. It allows of no variation. God doesn't say, "My name is I Am, but you can call me You Are, or He Is." The cogito, the I Am pronouncement, does not extend beyond one's own subjective knowing. I can say I Am and know it as truth, but I can't say you are, he is, she is, we are, they are, it is, etc. I know I exist and nothing else. Understood thusly, I Am, aka God, truly is the Alpha and the Omega; the entirety of being, of knowledge, of you.

The cogito is the line between fantasy and reality. On one side of the cogito is a universe of beliefs and ideas and theories. To cross the line is to leave all that behind. No theory, concept, belief, opinion or debate can have any possible basis in reality once the ramifications of the cogito have fully saturated the mind. No dialogue can take place across that line because nothing that makes sense on either side makes sense on the other.

Everyone thinks they understand the cogito, but nobody does. Descartes himself didn't. If professors of philosophy truly understood the cogito, they wouldn't be professors of philosophy. Alfred North Whitehead said that all philosophy is a footnote to Plato, but all philosophy, Plato included, is rendered obsolete and irrelevant by Descartes. Nothing but the subjective I Am is true, so what's the point of prattling on? There's simply nothing else to say.

The cogito isn't a mere thought or an idea, it's an ego-eating virus that, if we are able to lower our defenses against it, will eventually devour all illusion. Once we know the cogito, we can begin systematically *un*knowing everything we think we know, and *un*raveling the self we think we are. To understand the cogito at the surface level takes a minute or so. To let it devour you from the inside out can take years.

Life is but a dream. There is no such thing as objective reality. Two cannot be proven. Nothing can be shown to exist. Time and space, love and hate, good and evil, cause and effect, are all just ideas. Anyone who says they know *anything* is really saying they don't know the *only* thing. Any assertion of truth other than I Am is a confession of ignorance. The greatest religious and philosophical thoughts and ideas in the history of man contain no more truth than the bleating of sheep. The greatest books are no more authoritative than the greatest luncheon meats.

No one knows anything.

Disprove it for yourself. Anyone wishing to deny these statements about the meaning of the cogito need merely prove that something, *anything*, is true. By all means, give it a try; smash your head against it, but it can't be done. The cogito is like a Molotov cocktail with which we can firebomb our own mind, safe in the knowledge that truth doesn't burn. This, however, is not the end of the journey of awakening.

It's just the beginning.

4. A Brief Review

The single biggest problem in communication
is the illusion that it has taken place.

—George Bernard Shaw

Y OU CAN SKIP THIS CHAPTER, but if you get confused later
about the terms and concepts we're using and the relationships
between them, come back here to find it all explained. If you didn't read
Damnedest and *Incorrect*, you should definitely spend a few minutes here.

THE DREAMSTATE PARADIGM

Reality is merely an illusion, albeit
a very persistent one. *—Albert Einstein*

The reality we seem to be experiencing and sharing is consensual
reality. In no respect can it be distinguished from a dream.

SPIRITUAL ENLIGHTENMENT

If you have the choice between enlightenment and a
million dollars, take the million dollars! Because if you
get the million dollars, there will be somebody there to
enjoy the million dollars; but if you get enlightenment
there's no one there to enjoy the enlightenment. *—Ramesh
Balsekar*

The first thing to understand about the term Spiritual Enlightenment
is that it's a clunker. (The term, not the state, though the state has nothing
to recommend it either.) No one actually in this state would ever have
decided to call it Spiritual Enlightenment, yet no other state merits such a
title.

Some would argue that certain non-ordinary states, such as Cosmic Consciousness and God Consciousness, are worthy of so illustrious a designation, and if they were any more abiding than Guffaw Consciousness I might agree. As it is, my former bond broker had more than thirty experiences of direct, timeless union with the God-mind, and now he's just another John Q. Schlubb pushing product and riding the train, so the way I see it, if it ain't abiding, it ain't shit—just another ride in the park.

Spiritual Enlightenment is the state in which the self is free of all delusion, including self itself. Truth-Realization is another useful term to describe this state. *Untruth-Unrealization* is more accurate, but less wieldy. Abiding Non-Dual Awareness has its good points too.

The process of becoming enlightened is a deliberate act of self-annihilation. It is the false self that does the killing and the false self that dies; a suicide in all but the physical sense. Because there is no *true* self to fill the vacancy created by the passing of the *false* self, no self remains. Hence it is rightly said that No-Self is True Self.

It is not possible to knowledgeably choose or want Spiritual Enlightenment. To desire it is to misunderstand it. Ego cannot desire egolessness. One does not undergo the process of awakening out of love for the true but out of hatred for the false; a hatred so intense that it burns everything and spares nothing.

MAYA: ARCHITECT OF DELUSION

> As soon as man awakens for a moment and opens his eyes, all the forces that caused him to fall asleep begin to act upon him with tenfold energy and he immediately falls asleep again, very often dreaming that he is awake or is awakening. *–Gurdjieff*

Maya might best be understood as the intelligence of fear. She is the keeper of the kept, the warden of the Dreamstate. It is Maya who bestows upon us the miraculous and life-giving power to see what's not and to not see what is. It is Maya who makes the Dreamstate possible and escape from it nearly *im*possible. She enables the Dreamstate to exist, and if you wish to awaken from it, then it's her you must destroy, layer by layer. But don't live in metaphors; she's not a she and she's not external to you. She's inside you and those layers are the stuff of which your ego is made.

Maya is the structural integrity of ego. Observe ego at work, make a study of it, dissect it, reverse-engineer it. Maya is not a person or a concept or a goddess. There is no way to understand what Maya is except to grapple with her. There is no way to know how deep she goes until you have gone that deep.

In this war Maya has every advantage but one; truth. Maya doesn't exist. Truth does.

HUMAN ADULTHOOD & HUMAN CHILDHOOD
(INTEGRATED STATE & SEGREGATED STATE)

> There is nothing in a caterpillar that tells you it's going to be a butterfly. –R. Buckminster Fuller

> There came a time when the risk to remain tight in the bud was more painful than the risk it took to blossom. –Anais Nin

Human Childhood is the ego-bound state. It is, in human children, a healthy and natural state. In human adults, however, it's a hideous affliction. The only way such an affliction could go undetected and unremedied is if everyone were equally afflicted, which is exactly the case. No problem is recognized and no alternative is known, so no solution is sought and no hope for change exists.

We live our entire lives under false pretenses, in a case of mistaken identity. We subscribe fully and without reservation to our false selfhood, mistaking these two-dimensional roles we play for who and what we really are. In fact, we should be discarding these juvenile disguises in our early teens and embarking on life journeys of such superiority that, by contrast, the ego-bound life is not life at all.

Think of a grasshopper caught in a spider's web, injected with a non-lethal poison and then cocooned in layer upon layer of silk thread, kept alive for freshness but tightly bound to prevent thrashing or escape. It is still alive, but bears no resemblance to its authentic grasshopper self. That state of immobilized, narcotized stupor fairly represents the state of the chronic Human Child, misapprehended worldwide as a normally developed adult.

And the spider fairly represents Maya.

✦

Most human beings cease to develop at around the age of ten or twelve. The average seventy year-old is often a ten year-old with sixty years time-in-grade. Our societies are of, by, and for Human Children, which explains the self-perpetuating nature of this ghoulish malady, as well as most of the silliness we see in the world.

The Human Child who has spent years at the same developmental stage understands growth as a process of solidification; of slow hardening into a rigid mass. In our world of Human Children, this mortification of the spirit is considered normal, healthy and respectable.

If we gauge societies in light of the developmental maturity of their citizens, we see very little difference, even between extremes. One society may be, on average, slightly further along than another, but the reality is that no society has advanced beyond the stage where girls play dress-up and boys torture frogs. If we lived in a society conducive to healthy, normal development, everyone would outgrow childhood in the personality struc-ture at the same time we outgrow it in the physical structure, but there is no such society, and no reason to think there ever will be. We are trapped in a state of self-aware simian consciousness. That is the human condition.

Any of the negative things we might say about people in general—that we're greedy, corrupt, apathetic, stupid, hateful, violent, etcetera—are not symptoms of the human animal or the self-aware being, but of Human Childhood. Human Childhood, though, is itself just a symptom of the one core disease from which all others radiate; fear. Fear is the natural and certain state of one who lives with eyes closed. Ignorance is the condition of thinking one's closed eyes are open and that the world of one's imagining is the world as it exists.

For a person to transition into Human Adulthood at an appropriate developmental age would require an actual rite of passage, rather than a merely symbolic ceremony as is sometimes observed, but it would take much more than that. It would require a society of Human Adults in which to occur, so it won't. That's the bad news. For a person to transition into Human Adulthood at an *in*appropriate developmental age, however, can and does occur. That's the good news. The individual who wants to achieve change and growth in his own life, who wants to move beyond the state of developmental retardation imposed by a developmentally retarded society, can probably do so. There's no saying what's possible for whom, but I feel pretty confident in saying that anyone who can understand their captivity and desire their freedom would find it possible to bring about a dramatic change in their condition.

✧

This is where the sincere seeker must make the most rigorous and concentrated effort. If we don't get this, we don't get anything. It's not enough to *kind of* get it. We have to grok it, live it and breathe it, make it our own personal religion and become fanatic about it. We must learn to see the difference between a Human Adult and a Human Child as easily and unmistakably as we see the difference between a sixty year-old and a six year-old.

This may sound a little weird, but your ego is smarter than you, *way* smarter, and if you don't recognize that and respect it, you stand very little chance against it. I've seen many very insightful books by very brainy men and women who were experts on the subject of ego transcendence but who, I could easily tell, had not transcended their own egos. The spiritual/religious marketplace, which should be dedicated entirely to ministering to this all-important developmental advent is, in fact, arrayed almost entirely against it.

Ego doesn't need to be killed because it was never really alive. You don't have to destroy your false self because it's not real, which is really the whole point. It's just a character we play, and what needs to be killed is that part of us that identifies with the character. Once that's done—*really* done, and it can take years—then you can wear the costume and play the character as it suits you to do so, now *in* the character but not *of* the character.

HUMAN ADULTHOOD VS SPIRITUAL ENLIGHTENMENT

> What is the greatest thing ye can experience? It is the hour of great contempt. The hour in which even your happiness becometh loathsome unto you, and so also your reason and virtue. *–Friedrich Nietzsche*

The difference between Adulthood and Enlightenment is that the former is awakening with*in* the dreamstate and the latter is awakening *from* it. Shallow, early-stage Adulthood is often mistaken for, and sold as, Spiritual Enlightenment, but it's not. It's just the first real glimpse of life, the death/rebirth transition from womb to world.

The most important distinction to be made between these two states is that Human Adulthood makes sense and Enlightenment doesn't. The main benefit most spiritually inclined people can derive from having a clear understanding of what it really means to be truth-realized is not so they can achieve it, but so they can dispense with it and reset their spiritual sights on something worthier than enlightenment, which is, literally, the biggest nothing of all time.

Human Adulthood is what everyone really wants, not truth or enlightenment. This is where you find all the good stuff and a lot less of the bad. You have to grow into it, of course, continue to develop and mature, learn and expand, but that's where all the perks are; profound and abiding contentment, the ability to manifest desires and shape events, the ability to do less and accomplish more, find your true calling, connect with your higher self, never stub another toe, and so on.

And Human Adulthood is what everyone, spiritual or not, religious or not, atheist or not, should be setting their sights on. This is what I've come to understand in my years of teaching and writing. If I were to give advice, I would recommend Adulthood to everyone and Enlightenment to no one. Human Adulthood is life-positive, Enlightenment is life-negative. Human Adulthood is the real prize. Spiritual Enlightenment is pointless and meaningless, and should only be sought by those who have absolutely no choice in the matter.

SIMPLICITY

> *Veritatis simplex oratio est.*
> The language of truth is simple. *—Seneca*

The journey of awakening is, despite our endless desire to complicate it, perfectly simple. Anytime we get muddled, disoriented, feel weak in heart or clouded in mind, get our heads turned around by some spiritual sales pitch or philosophical argument or guru *de jour*, we need only return to simplicity. There is nothing to learn, nothing to know, nothing to practice, nothing to become.

FOCUS & INTENT

> It is impossible to imagine Goethe or Beethoven
> being good at billiards or golf. *—H. L. Mencken*

The vast majority of spiritual seekers are motivated by desire, so the failure of their search is a foregone conclusion, as is amply evidenced by mankind's history of near-total inability to find the one thing that can never be lost.

How is it possible that something as simple as seeing what is manages to elude even our most devout seekers and our greatest minds? Because no one really wants what awakening really is. We may express a vague sort of desire to awaken, but we want a very specific kind of awakening; the kind that doesn't require us to leave our cozy dreamstate or, better yet, makes it even cozier. We don't want to awaken from the dream; we want to dream that we are awake.

The true desire that drives the process of awakening is more akin to a psychotic madness. It is a wickedly profound and protracted crisis, not the dreary little dark night of the soul the hucksters pawn off on the tourists.

Many people hear the ringing alarm in life, the call to awaken, but what we really want, more than sex, power, fame, love, immortality or money, is to hit the snooze button and go back to sleep. When life calls, all we want to do is pull the covers over our head and roll over and, above all, keep our eyes closed.

The last thing anyone really wants, whatever they might say, is to have their slumber disturbed.

SURRENDER

> One thing only I know, and that
> is that I know nothing. –*Socrates*

To surrender is to relinquish the illusion of control, which initiates the death part of the death/rebirth process, which is the transition from the bondage of the womb-like Segregated State to the freedom of the ever-expanding Integrated State. No faith or belief is required to accomplish this act of surrender, only clear-seeing. When one begins to understand ego and fear for what they really are, then this process becomes as easy and natural as dropping a heavy weight.

Sadly, owing to the faux-surrender popularized by pop Christianity, jailhouse conversions and twelve step programs, this vital and necessary growth stage has fallen into disrepute and is widely scorned as the desperate act of the stupid, the frightened and the weak. This is a clear example of how Maya operates in the world.

THE PRICE OF TRUTH

> A taste for truth at any cost is a passion
> which spares nothing. –*Albert Camus*

The price of truth is everything. The price of truth is nothing. This is another way of stating the gateless gate paradox. From the unawakened side, the gate blocking one from enlightenment is enormous and impassable. Delusion fills one's entire field of view because it resides prior to perception. Once delusion has been destroyed, we can see that it never really existed.

IGNORANCE

> The greatest obstacle to discovery is not ignorance,
> it is the illusion of knowledge. *–Daniel Boorstin*

There are two kinds of ignorance. One is the relatively benign kind where we don't know or understand something. This kind is not usually a big troublemaker. If you don't know how to change the oil in your car, you hire someone to do it. If you don't know how to make lasagna, you buy a cookbook. If you don't know how to skydive, you don't jump out of airplanes.

The other kind of ignorance is the perniciously debilitating kind. It's the kind where we think we know something we don't know, or that we understand something we don't understand.

The former type of ignorance is what most spiritual aspirants waste their lives trying to address, never realizing that it's the latter that enslaves them.

SPIRITUAL AUTOLYSIS

> Thought must be divided against itself before it can
> come to any knowledge of itself. *–Aldous Huxley*

> To hold a pen is to be at war. *–Voltaire*

Spiritual Autolysis is a writing process that allows us to utilize the fullest potential of our intelligence by bringing the mind into the sharpest possible focus. Autolysis means self-digestion, and that's the purpose of this technique. Unlike journaling or keeping a spiritual diary, it's all about finding and illuminating the next obstacle to our progress. It is not concerned with finding answers, but questions. There are no answers to be found, only the questions that define our limitations. Understand the question, and you destroy the limitation. It is through courageous thought and clear-seeing that delusion is destroyed.

Everyone thinks they think, but when someone begins to truly think—surgically, unemotionally, destructively—they quickly see that it's not something they've ever really done before. It is by writing, by external-izing the thought process, by depersonalizing it, by standing back from it and representing all sides in an organized and objective manner, that we are able to unleash an intellectual ferocity of which we are normally incapable and unaware.

A good way to start is to write down a statement you're sure is true, and then try to figure out exactly why the statement is false, which, unless you have stated a negative (No belief is true.), made a subjective observa-tion (My foot hurts.), or wrote the only true thing you know (I am.), it is.

FEAR

> Taking a new step, uttering a new word, is
> what people fear most. –*Fyodor Dostoevsky*

Fear is the prime emotion of the eyes-closed state. All emotions are attachments and the energy source of all attachments is fear.

Fear of what? Fear of no-self. The nameless, faceless dread of non-being. Not just fear of death, which anyone can deny or explain away, but fear of nothingness, which no fairytale can fix.

GRATITUDE

> If the only prayer you say in your whole life is
> Thank You, that will suffice. –*Meister Eckhart*

Gratitude of a non-specific, all encompassing quality and tinged with a not-unpleasant sadness, might be said to be the primary emotion of the truth-realized person and the mature Human Adult. It is this gratitude that comes in as fear goes out.

FURTHER

> When you reach the top,
> keep climbing. –*Zen proverb*

The word Further is like a talisman, a power object. We must pull it out and gaze upon it after every battle, every time we think we must be done, that we must, at last, have arrived. As much as it may seem otherwise, there's always Further. Get up, dust off, and gird thy loins for the next fray.

Carl Jung said he had to descend a thousand ladders to arrive at the little clod of earth he really was. At each landing, he must have thought himself done until his eyes adjusted and he saw that there was yet another ladder to descend. If Dr. Jung had command of the word Further, he would have known that there were more ladders still, and that a little clod of earth was infinitely more than he actually was.

Whenever you're sure you've arrived, there's always Further. The day may come when there is no more Further and you will recognize that fact not with fanfare and tickertape, not with radiant backlighting and choirs of angels, but with the bemused and unenthusiastic observation that you are...

DONE

Done means done.

5. A Brief Preview

'Tis the good reader that makes the good book; in every book
he finds passages which seem confidences or asides hidden
from all else and unmistakenly meant for his ear; the profit of
books is according to the sensibility of the reader; the
profoundest thought or passion sleeps as in a mine, until it is
discovered by an equal mind and heart.

–Ralph Waldo Emerson

YOU CAN SKIP THIS CHAPTER, but if you get confused later
about the three houses or the two women or the two men or the girl
or the dog or the locales, come back here to find it explained. If you're still
confused, it's my fault. I overwrote the book by a few hundred pages and
in cutting it down we lost some of the narrative detail and a lot of local
color, but saved most of the substance. This chapter replaces four chapters
of exposition that provided some clarifying backstory that Lisa, my editorial assistant, has urged me to boil down to one short chapter, so here it is.

Lisa didn't start out as my editorial assistant. I met her through her
father Frank who told me a little about the crisis she was undergoing and
suggested that it might have something to do with my books. Intrigued by
her walking wounded demeanor, her thousand mile gaze and her tightly-
clutched dayplanner, I invited her and her daughter Maggie to come live in
the guesthouse on the estate I'm renting. After some discussion she grate-
fully accepted. It was only later that she started helping with the book.

Lisa is the grown daughter of Frank. She's also an attorney, the wife of
a dentist, the mother of two kids, Maggie and DJ, and a reluctant spiritual
journeyer. She's in the final stages of a very hairy existential meltdown that
has been slowly consuming her for three years.

Frank, her dad, is a retired university professor who invited me down
to visit him at his retirement home in the Mexican state of Jalisco. He lives

in a community called Lakeside, which is actually made up of several towns along the north shore of Lake Chapala. Frank's wife Isabel died the previous year, leaving Frank at somewhat loose ends. I decided to accept Frank's oft-repeated invitation to visit him in Mexico for two reasons. One was the content of the thirty-one emails he wrote to me and the free access he offered to his uniquely stocked private library. The other was my grandfather.

My grandfather, actually my grandfather's brother, now long dead, had a twenty acre ranchito a few miles outside the Mexican town of San Miguel de Allende. That's where he retired after a long and successful career in law. He wasn't Mexican and didn't speak Spanish, he just wanted to *fully* retire and have some horses and live out his life quietly. I spent a few summers at his hacienda as a kid and it had impressed itself upon me as the ideal home. He was a cantankerous old bastard who didn't like anybody, his more direct relations least of all, but he liked me well enough, possibly because I enjoyed fishing with him, could memorize long passages of Byron, his beloved poet, and because I was mostly quiet.

"What happens when two snakes start eating each other's tails and keep eating," he asked me when I was formally introduced to him at the age of eight.

I thought about it for a moment before answering.

"I don't know, sir," I said.

"Goddamn right you don't," he said, and that was that. We met once a year after that. "Figure it out yet?" he'd ask. "No sir," I'd answer. "Still working on it?" he'd ask. "Yes sir," I'd answer. "Good man," he'd reply, and that was the full extent of our relationship until, at twelve, I was invited to spend a month with him in Mexico over the summer break. I accepted and went that year and for the next few until other interests and commitments forced me to decline his invitation. Despite the fact that there was never anything like a conversation between us, or because of it, we got on very well.

I've lived in a bunch of places in the last two decades, some for a few years, many for only a few months, but none where I felt like I'd want to settle in for good. It was when I asked myself where I *did* want to live that my grandfather's hacienda came clearly to mind. I never thought of actually buying it, but it was the overall feeling I remembered from his place that I was always trying to rediscover in others. That was what I thought a home should be.

So, while wintering in the off-season New England resort community wondering where I'd like to go next, and with it starting to look like I'd be writing a third book, I came across a folder full of Frank's archived emails and thought fondly of my grandfather's house and realized that Mexico could, for many reasons, be a good place to settle down. It is my personal preference to be near people but not among them. I am most comfortable living on the edge of a community but with a certain degree of alienation from it. Anything in Asia, for example, would be too alien, and anything English-speaking wouldn't be alien enough. Mexico was perfect; just the right amount of cultural and lingual barrier. I made the arrangements and that's where I was heading a few days after declining the fat sergeant's gracious invitation.

Once in the Lakeside area, through an interesting chain of events, I ended up renting a house that was exactly four times over my stated budget, but which turned out to be perfect. It was a small estate owned by a pretty famous symphony conductor from a pretty major American city who seldom came down. It was on a hillside, completely walled, and consisted of a main house and a guesthouse, a pool and poolhouse, and all sorts of small buildings, a few gardens and terraces, half a dozen satellite dishes and two fountains, all packed into just over an acre. It was well out of any town, a five minute drive to anywhere. It would be correct to say that I did not wish or choose to live in a place like this, things just unfolded that way.

The property came with a maid and a gardener, a married couple who had been with the estate for years. They had rooms in the main house but lived elsewhere. The main house also had a beautifully appointed home theater room fully stocked with music and movies because the owner received free copies of everything from the major labels and distributors. I thought I'd get more use from the theater than I ever did. Down from the main house was a casita, a guest house, that was small and comfortable and adjacent to the pool. By the pool was an open pavilion-type building with kitchenette, a combination changing room/bathroom, and comfortable seating area and fireplace. The long wall that ran along the pool was made of floor-to-ceiling glass panels that could be rolled aside, converting the pavilion to an exceedingly pleasant indoor/outdoor space overlooking Lake Chapala below and the enfolding mountains beyond. A pergola-type roof extended about ten feet out over the pool deck, so I moved the dining table to the open wall and turned it into a large desk and that's where I spent most of my time and wrote most of this book.

The views were spacious and often gorgeous, especially at sunrise and sunset. In addition to these views, the area was blessed with a near perfect climate; the extremes weren't extreme and the usual temperatures were right in the comfort sweetspot. The area was green and lush and bursting with color. The towns were wonderful places to shop and dine and stroll, and lacked little I could want, certainly nothing I couldn't get in Guadalajara, less than an hour away. Before I knew it, I began house-hunting in the towns along the north shore of the lake.

In my first week in the area, I found the house I wanted to buy near Upper Ajijic. I made an offer and it was accepted, which, for a variety of reasons, left me scrambling to put together the entire buying price in cash. This was quite an endeavor, especially in the tight timeframe in which I had to do it, but through some tricky maneuvering, some unpleasant tax consequences, and with some good help, I managed it and I had a local account stuffed with virtually every dime I could scrape together, ready for closing on this lovely home.

And then the seller backed out.

I found that to be a curious turn of events, but I knew it was for the best, whatever that might be. I waited to see why it happened and was rewarded less than a week later when I received word that a distant cousin of mine was in need of fast cash and was selling my grandfather's hacienda; the one I wanted more than any other but had never seriously considered. Now the seemingly inexplicable action of the seller backing out of the first house after my mad scramble for cash made perfect sense. If it had not been for that, I would not have been in a position to buy my grandfather's house, which I liked much more than the one in Ajijic and was able to buy at a reasonably reasonable price. It was also through the action of finding and trying to buy the Ajijic house that I demonstrated desire and intent which the universe recognized and rewarded. Lisa, still new with me and still in lawyer mode, couldn't fathom the fact that I signed away all my worldly wealth to buy a house I hadn't seen in more than thirty years without visiting it, inspecting it, getting appraisals, making counteroffers and all that. My response of "the way is clear" didn't seem to relax her.

Okay, so there's that. We're almost caught up here.

The several weeks I spent trying to liquidate my small portfolio of assets for the house purchase was a very jumbled and confusing time. That's when I met Lisa and her daughter Maggie and invited them to move in. That's when I acquired the dog of my heart's desire, and that's when I found out that someone I knew, someone like me, had died.

✧

The Lakeside area has a lot of American and Canadian expatriots who move here for the ideal climate and low cost of living. Whereas a town like San Miguel is more artsy and young, Lakeside is more elderly and sedate. There are very good medical services available and Guadalajara is close, so it makes for a popular retirement choice. Frankly, I'll be happier to be living on the edge of a more artistically and spiritually-oriented community.

Anyway, I wasn't in the area for long before I met a dog named Mango. She was a four month-old Border Collie. She was being walked by her frail looking owner, a seventy-ish woman who had recently retired to the area with her husband. As soon as I saw the dog I knew it was the one I had been slowly tracking in on for the last year; that we had both been travelling paths that brought us to this meeting. It was a simple recognition on my part, not an impulse or a desire. I knew as soon as I saw her that she would be my dog and an hour later, she was. In very short order I paid the woman what she had paid the breeder, though in her relief she'd asked for much less. The dog now had a new owner and her new name, I perceived rather than decided, was Maya.

This woman and her husband had been very ill-advised in their choice of dog, as she now understood. Border Collies are working dogs and can make very poor pets, especially if their circumstances deny them the amount of daily energy expenditure they require. This woman and her husband just thought they were pretty. They are. They're also fiendishly smart and indefatigable and can go seriously nuts if they don't get the exercise they need. I had started thinking about dogs more and more over the last year; reading books and magazines, gaining knowledge and refining my desires, and had arrived at the realization that I would have a Border Collie. That was where rightness lay. Once I realized it, I released the whole thing, knowing the details would sort themselves out.

Okay, I can't keep this as short as I'd hoped, but all this stuff has to be mentioned. Actually, the dog thing and the house thing are both far more complex and involved and illuminating than I've shown them here, and both, in their fullness, are such clear, intricate and elegant examples of the processes of manifestation, of the workings of the Integrated State, of trust and surrender, of clear-seeing, of intent and desire, of the subtle machinations of the universe, of, in fact, the nondual nature of the I-Universe entity, that if I ever decide to write a book specifically on the living reality of the mature Integrated State, these two episodes would feature prominently, alongside many other such episodes that irrefutably support my long-standing conviction that the universe is, in fact, a big, playful puppy.

❖

I mentioned that it was in that same hectic week that I was informed of the death of someone I knew, someone like me. Her name was Brett and she was truth-realized, enlightened, whatever. She taught a small group that met in her riding arena on her Virginia farm once a month, members of which brought my books to her attention and got me invited for a visit. She and I became cohorts and I visited several times and participated in her group meetings. She died, I learned, on her way home from running some errands. The driver of an oncoming car was distracted with a cell phone, veered off onto the shoulder, over-corrected and ran head-on into Brett. Brett was killed instantly, the other driver was okay.

✧

That catches us up pretty well. The book might still be a bit rough in spots, but it was that or spend another year smoothing it out cosmetically without improving it in substance. At Lisa's insistence, we removed most of the Spanglish that we all sprinkled throughout every conversation and that I originally thought would be fun to include here. Also gone is a lot of the texture of life in Mexico, good and bad, mostly good. The material about Frank's library and the time he and I spent together and the discussions we had has been cut from this book, but might be made available elsewhere. We'll see plenty more of Lisa, her daughter Maggie, Brett, and the two Mayas in these pages, and we'll end, fittingly with Lisa and me travelling to Virginia to deliver Brett's eulogy.

There. Less than seven pages. Not so bad.

6. Living the Dream

Af-flu-en-za n. 1. The bloated, sluggish and unfulfilled feeling that results from efforts to keep up with the Joneses. 2. An epidemic of stress, overwork, waste and indebtedness caused by dogged pursuit of the American Dream. 3. An unsustainable addiction to economic growth.

I'M SITTING AT MY DESK working on my laptop, fumbling through papers, and pausing once in a while to enjoy the magnificent view spread out before me and the piano and cello music piping in through indoor and outdoor speakers. Lisa appears and stands uncomfortably in front of my desk. In the few weeks that she and her daughter have been living on the estate with me, we've had almost no conversation beyond matters of arrangements and daily greetings. I had started to think that the entire summer might pass without us ever really saying more, though I encouraged her to bring her daughter down and take advantage of the pool whenever they wished.

"May I?" she asks, pointing to a chair.

"Please," I say.

She sits and fidgets. I point the remote at what I assume to be a communication node connected to the stereo in the main house and I lower the volume of the music. Maya sticks her head out from behind the couch to see if anything exciting is happening and slips back behind it.

"Drinks, food, help yourself," I say, indicating the kitchenette, "there's limonada. Water, ice, all fine."

She nods.

"How's the house?" I ask.

"It's very nice, thank you," she replies. After her dad introduced us I learned that she was looking for a place for her and Maggie, so I offered her the guesthouse on the small estate I was renting. As an afterthought I realized that I'd be much happier in the casita and that they could have their own rooms and baths in the main house, so when they arrived I put them there instead. Between the casita and the poolhouse I was very comfortably situated. If I wanted to use the theater room I still could, but that was the only thing I liked about the main house. The maid and gardener had their own rooms there too, by law, I think, so it had a less private feel to it.

Instead of paying rent, Lisa agreed to handle utility payments and other household functions involving the rental agency and the staff and a whole host of little details that need taking care of. Her Spanish is much better than mine and she has an easy way with the locals that I haven't developed yet. On her own initiative, she expanded her duties to include all-round guardian of my time and privacy, which was great for me and seemed soothingly purpose-giving for her.

When we met at her father's house, Lisa was clutching a dayplanner; an uncommon sight down here. I remarked on it at that time but got no response. Now I try again.

"Still got your dayplanner, I see."

Her hand is resting on it. She doesn't reply. I return to my reading. After a few minutes she releases a torrent of words.

"I could be working as a waitress with big hair and a fat ass, living in some fleatrap apartment in Corpus Christi when I'm sixty, you know."

That was unexpected.

"Divorced," she says, "alone. Maybe I'd get a Christmas card from Maggie and DJ, with a picture of their families. Maybe I'd have some trucker boyfriends. Make good tips."

"I thought you were a lawyer."

"So did I," she says, "I thought I was a lot of things."

"Okay, so how do you end up with a big ass in Texas?"

She nods and grins as if that were the really funny part.

"All the king's horses and all the king's men," she says cryptically.

Lisa is in crisis. She has gone through a protracted meltdown that has uprooted her from her well-established life and deposited her unceremoniously here in central Mexico with her daughter and no idea of what's going on or why. I know where she's at, I know what she's going through, but I'm not her shrink or her drinking buddy. I'm not going to play the role of drawing her out. I turn back to my laptop and continue reading.

Sensing that she might have lost my interest, she tries to regain it with a more direct appeal.

"I don't know what to do," she says.

"About?"

"About my life," she says forcefully. "I had a life and now I don't and I don't know what happened to it or how to get it back."

I wait.

"I can't just hurl myself into a life of reckless spiritual abandon, you know. I have responsibilities. I have my children to think about. I had a career, standing in my community, friends, relationships. I guess all that's gone now. I still have my credit rating to think about. If I start missing payments even by a few days my credit score will go down and they'll raise my rates. That's serious, you know. I have to think about my future and the future of my children. You joke about living out of dumpsters, but that really happens. I mean, I'm not afraid it would come to that, but who knows what could happen?"

I don't say anything. Frank mentioned that she'd read my books. Now she's trying to get me to defend her decisions while she rails against them, which is not a service I provide.

"I can't just let go of everything and hope for the best," she continues. "It doesn't work that way. I mean, maybe it works for you, you seem to be happy and have a nice life and everything, but who knows what the deal is with you? I mean, you're obviously an exception, to say the least. You look like a human being, but I think that's very deceptive. It is, isn't it? You're really not like the rest of us, are you? It's one thing to read about you, to read your books, but when I'm here with you, and Maggie is here, and my father, well, then it's very different."

I wait.

"I think you may be a very dangerous person, Mr. McKenna. No offense."

"None taken. Call me Jed."

"I don't mean to be rude, but I'm sitting here looking right at you and I don't really know what I see. You're more than just dangerous; I have to keep reminding myself of that. You're like this weird corrupting influence that sits by the pool and offers me limonada and lets me live in his house and says call me Jed."

"And listens patiently," I add. "Take a breath."

She takes a breath.

"Well, yes, and listens patiently. Sorry. Thank you."

"So what's with the dayplanner?"

She looks down at it and I can see that she's drifting out of focus a bit so I go back to my work. She doesn't speak for several minutes.

"I got a good night's sleep last night," she says, her mood more settled. "I haven't had a good night's sleep in years. I forgot what it was like. We were living in a motel room for the last month so Maggie could finish out her school year and I've been bouncing off the walls. No sleep." She pauses to consider. "I feel good, I think. Sorry to go off on you like that."

Minutes pass as she sits quietly and I return to my work. Jorge walks past on his way down to the dolphin fountain. Lisa watches him, then gets up for a glass of limonada.

"I used to watch the Mexicans doing the yardwork," she says with an air of longing. "I'd be so envious, such a simple life. I fantasized about being a homeless person; living under a bridge, going to the library and just reading all day, begging for coins so I could have my raspberry-banana smoothies. I guess I thought living out of dumpsters sounded okay. That's how bad it was; I dreamed of being homeless."

"That's how bad what was?"

"Life. My life."

"Still in a bit of shock?"

"Oh yeah," she says, nodding, "that's how it feels; numb, like I just got out of jail, like the last fifteen years are just this blur where I was always tired and worried and busy, and now it's suddenly over and I don't know what to do or where to go or who to be. I guess I'm rambling. I might be a little nervous talking to you. I hope I'm not being rude. I'm very grateful to be here with you, *very* grateful. I think I might have to declare bankruptcy, too. That's really freaking me out. Believe me, I'm about the last person anyone would expect to declare bankruptcy."

"Between a dentist and a lawyer you must have been doing well," I say. "Two professionals, kids, house in the suburbs. Living the American dream."

She barks out a disturbed laugh.

"Some dream. We were drowning in debt. It was terrible. The American dream was like being slowly suffocated; like an elephant sitting on your chest. That was normal, but now it seems completely insane. No escape, no way out. No wonder I went nuts. Thank God I did. How else can you get out of something like that?"

"Friends weren't any help?"

"What friends?" she scoffs. "You know, I don't even know what that word means. I always thought I did, but I don't, not really. Anyway, all the people we knew were just like us; careers, kids, debt. Half the people I knew were self-medicating. A lot of them were medicating their kids, too. That's how the whole thing holds together instead of just flying apart. Everyone's got their pills or booze or both; you have to. And then massive doses of caffeine to kickstart each day."

She pauses and sips her drink.

"I spent three hours and twenty minutes a day commuting; car, train, bus, walking and in elevators. I timed it." She's looking at me like I'm supposed to be doing the math, but I know she already has.

"Over eight hundred hours a year," she says. "More than a solid month of every year just travelling to and from work. More than fifteen months I spent just commuting. All we really have is time, and that's how I spent mine; just flushed it away, wished it away in small pieces, being eager for the time to pass, for the trip to end. Then the same thing in the office from eight until six; watching the clock, wishing the morning away so I could go to lunch, wishing the afternoon away so I could go home. Never happy where I was, always busy and tired and preparing for the next thing. Weekends were actually worse because that's when everything that didn't get done during the week had to be done. Cleaning, shopping, kid stuff. What are you gonna do with kids? Take them to some fastfood dump with a playground, feed them some cheap sugary crap you know is no good for them and head off to the mall. You try museums and ballgames, but junk-food and malls are the reality. Dennis plays golf and watches sports on the weekends because he has to unwind after his long work week. He didn't even commute. His practice was in town. He thought having all that free time commuting sounded nice."

She takes a long, deep breath and slowly releases it. She has her back to the beautiful view.

"I was like that little girl in your first book," she continues. "I started seeing this whole human transport system; me and the same few hundred people I saw every day but never spoke to, just shuttling back and forth like mindless sheep, all with our newspapers, laptops, headsets. I'd think about it, of the whole world stuck in this same huge machine, getting endlessly, pointlessly processed. Old ones falling out and new ones replacing them. Every morning these steel tubes all around the world, carrying millions of people, pumping them like fresh blood into graveyard cities and pumping them back out at night, dirty and tired. Like a brotherhood of sheep, of captivity, of mindlessness, of lives unlived, of empty activity. Everyone, though; not just commuters. Clerks in stores, cops, bus drivers, everyone you see. You get inserted into this machine when you're four or five and you don't come out the other end until your sixties. Once you start seeing this place for the madhouse it is, you can't *stop* seeing it that way. It's everywhere, everyone. It doesn't make any sense. That's not life. It *can't* be. I don't know what it is, but it's not life."

✧

This is what Chief Broom calls the Combine in Ken Kesey's *One Flew Over the Cuckoo's Nest*, but it's what Kesey was calling the cuckoo's nest itself. Protagonist Randall P. McMurphy flips out when he discovers about his fellow inmates what Plato tells us of those shackled in his cave: Our captivity is voluntary. No one is being held against their will.

There are no locks keeping anyone chained in their seats in Plato's cave, and the patients in Nurse Ratched's ward are there voluntarily and can sign themselves out whenever they want. That's what freaked McMurphy out. We are enslaved by our own fear and ignorance and we can be free as soon as we can will it. The patients on Nurse Ratched's ward are happy there.

They don't want to go out into the big scary world. They are paralyzed by fear and soothed by constraint. In Kesey's book, Chief Broom made a break. In Lisa's life, Lisa made a break.

✧

This book, by the way, is dedicated to Ken Kesey, not just for *Cuckoo's Nest* or the bus or the pranksters or the acid tests, but for the courageous and visionary spirit behind all of them. Ken Kesey *was* Randall P. McMurphy and sixties America was his madhouse, and he takes a rightful place beside Walt Whitman and Herman Melville in the American pantheon of heroic explorers.

Of McMurphy, Chief Broom narrates:

> He goes to getting ready for bed, pulling off his clothes. The shorts under his work pants are coal black satin covered with big white whales with red eyes. He grins when he sees I'm looking at the shorts. "From a co-ed at Oregon State, Chief, a Literary major." He snaps the elastic with his thumb. "She gave them to me because she said I was a symbol."

✧

"And for what?" Lisa continues. "This wasn't for a few months or even years, this was our whole life! We were trapped! Fifteen years of it! Isn't that nuts? And for what? To raise kids? That's just an excuse. Anyone can raise kids; you don't have to live in constant soul-crushing servitude to do it. One day I asked DJ what he really wanted out of life and he said he wanted to be a dentist just like daddy. It was like being kicked in the stomach." She shakes her head sadly. "And you know, it's not just that it's a terrible way to live; it's not really life at all. It's not something you choose, it's what you get when you *don't* choose. We just marched ourselves into these damned idiotic, impossible lives without ever stopping to think about what we were doing. High school, college, post-grad and then straight into the workforce. Get married, have a kid, borrow money, buy a house, fill it with junk, have another kid, borrow more money, bigger house, more junk. It's completely insane, but that's how everyone I know lived. Affluenza, they call it, like a disease. That's what it is. For the last seven years we've been struggling just to make the minimum payments on our debt."

"And this was all pretty normal?"

She laughs bitterly. "Everyone I knew was the same way. Some at a higher income level, some lower, but I think practically everyone we knew was dangerously over-extended in every direction. Money, time, work, responsibilities. We were doing everything right and we didn't really have any misfortune; no tragedies or health issues. We've been members of the local country club for ten years. Yes, we were living the American dream. Exhausted, broke, not good parents, not happy, and now split up."

She pauses.

"I didn't really have a nervous breakdown you know."

"I know."

"I had a moment of clarity, that's what it was, but I knew it wouldn't last, I knew I'd get swallowed back up into this state of marginal consciousness where years fly by like minutes, so I made a vow to myself during that moment of clarity. I swore that I would end it. Whatever it took, I promised myself that I would get out. I had to break the cycle and grab the kids and run like hell. I reminded myself about my vow every day, but I was slipping back anyway. I was forgetting the vow and why I made it. It's like anesthesia, like when they make you count backward from a hundred. You think you're okay at ninety-seven and then there's no ninety-six."

"And?"

"And it all just came flooding back when DJ told me he wanted to be a dentist. It was like being slapped awake and I knew it was now or never. I knew it was my last chance to make a break. My mistake was trying to figure out how to do it cleanly and take both kids with me. Way too ambitious. I packed for myself and Maggie, wrote a note, jumped in the car and got out of there. I made a terrible shambles of everything, of course, at home and work, but I knew that was the only way it could happen and that it was now or never, now or never. There was no nice way, it was just too fucked up and I'm sorry but there it is. Jesus, it was that or be stuck in that deathtrap forever; me and my kids. I think of it as a breakdown sometimes because that makes it sound excusable. If I was sane, then doing something that horrible could only be called evil. I don't think I'm evil."

She's red-eyed, but not crying. I can see she's cried out.

"You are sane and you're not evil," I say. "I guess you know that."

"It's nice to hear it," she says, "especially from you. It's just so hard to reconcile. The proportions seem so, I don't know, disproportionate, but that's how it had to be. Anyway, it's done now, for better or worse, and here I am. Here we are, Maggie and me."

"Rock and roll," I say.

She smiles and nods solemnly.

"Rock and roll," she says.

"Good," I say. "Good spirit. That's everything."

"There was no other way."

"I know."

"Please tell me I haven't made the worst mistake anyone could ever make," she says. "Tell me I haven't ruined my children's lives, that's all I want to hear."

"How do you feel now?"

She closes her eyes and sighs heavily.

"I can't describe what a relief it is to be out of that situation. I can breathe now, I can sleep." She gestures to indicate this garden paradise in which we sit. "You don't know how amazing this all is. I can't believe I lived like that, I can't believe I considered that to be happiness and success. I can't believe I thought that was life."

"So, was getting out the worst mistake you could ever make?" I ask.

Her face breaks into a huge smile.

"It was the best thing I've ever done," she says jubilantly, "I don't know what's coming next, but I am so glad to leave that world behind. This has been the whole death-rebirth thing you talk about. I know I'm scared and confused right now, that's okay, I'll get through it, but I'd rather die than go back to that life, or whatever the hell that was."

7. Imago

Perhaps the deepest reason why we are afraid of death is because we do not know who we are. We believe in a personal, unique, and separate identity—but if we dare to examine it, we find that this identity depends entirely on an endless collection of things to prop it up: our name, our "biography," our partners, family, home, job, friends, credit cards... It is on their fragile and transient support that we rely for our security. So when they are all taken away, will we have any idea of who we really are?

Without our familiar props, we are faced with just ourselves, a person we do not know, an unnerving stranger with whom we have been living all the time but we never really wanted to meet. Isn't that why we have tried to fill every moment of time with noise and activity, however boring or trivial, to ensure that we are never left in silence with this stranger on our own?

–Sogyal Rinpoche

I T'S EVENING. LISA HAS PUT Maggie to bed. She opens a bottle of wine and pours us each a glass. She hands me mine and sits down across from me, glass and dayplanner in front of her. She'll be going to bed after this but I still have to go out and walk the dog and have my nightly nightcap with Frank and then come back here and try to get in another hour of work.

Lisa sits quietly and sips her wine. She needs to be pushed and she wants to be pushed, so I give her a push.

"Why are you carrying your dayplanner?"

As if it requires a burst of resolve, Lisa takes a deep drink, then opens the leather-bound book to a page near the back and places it in front of me. It's a photo from a magazine, black and white, grainy, laminated and hole-punched, buried deep amid the calendar and contact pages. It's a body falling from the World Trade Center on September 11th, 2001. You can tell by the shape of the hair and clothes that it's a woman. Her face is just barely visible, just enough to imagine features, to wonder.

I look up at Lisa and find her deeply entranced by the photo. She removes it from the dayplanner and holds it. She rubs it with her fingers. She speaks in a very quiet voice.

"It was a Tuesday," she begins in a quavering whisper. "She got up just like a thousand times before, showered, woke the kids, got her husband going. She took time to notice that it was a beautiful September day and to share that with her family, trying to make the daily grind a little easier, to make the day seem special, but it was just another Tuesday. By six-thirty her house was awake and everyone was grumbling through their morning routines. Once she had everyone going she returned to dress and do her face and hair, standing in front of the mirror in her slip, thinking about work, about the day ahead, about family schedules and upcoming events, about the lines in her face, the extra pounds on her body, bills, her parents' health, just like any other morning."

Lisa's eyes are shimmering with tears now. Her fingers rest on the bottom of the photo.

"When I first saw this picture, this woman, seconds from death, I couldn't take my eyes off it. It held me, like a trance, and this whole back-story, this woman's life as I imagined it, her house on Staten Island, the ferry ride to work every morning, it all just flooded over me. I taped the picture to my bathroom mirror, one just like this, and every morning as I went through my own daily rituals, I'd look at it and think about how she started her day just like I am now, just another day; brush teeth, floss, worry about little things, thoughts full of details and concerns."

She pauses, sips her wine. I don't say anything.

"That first picture got ruined. Dennis didn't like it; he said it was morbid. He didn't want to have to look at it every morning. I didn't want anyone else looking at it anyway. I got this one and protected it and put it here where only I would see it. I sit with her on the train ride in the mornings. I talk to her, I guess, and she talks to me. That's how it happened. It started out as this sense that the life I was living was all wrong. I resisted that thought, tried to push it away, but it wouldn't go away, it just stayed there at the periphery, always there just at the edge; office, car, dinner parties, grocery shopping, club, meetings, always there. Then your books," she laughs and looks at me, "your books just threw on the houselights, exposed everything, made everything raw, and that's when it built to the bursting point. It had to do with your books, but it had been slowly building for the three years she'd been talking to me."

"The woman in the picture talks to you?"

We sit in silence for a long while.

"'I was nobody.' That's what she says to me. 'I was this way for my boss, this way for my co-workers; I was this person for my parents, this person for my children. I was this person on the phone, this person with store clerks and staff. I dressed for other people, spoke and behaved for other people, spent the minutes, hours and days of my life for other people, and there was never anything left for me. I read books and magazines to help me be all these different people, I spent what little time I could spare shopping and at the gym to keep thin and well-dressed, always struggling to be these people I needed to be.'"

Lisa speaks in a whisper and holds the picture in both hands.

"'I worked ten hours a day and commuted two. I cooked, cleaned, shopped, paid bills, and was lucky to get four hours sleep a night. I told myself it was all for the children, but I always knew that was a lie. We could have done much better for the kids. We were just stamping out more versions of ourselves because that's all we knew how to do. We became just like our parents because we didn't know who else to be. That's what I'm thinking as I fall, that it's hard to be sad because I don't know who's dying. What does it matter that I'm gone if I was never really here? I'm two seconds from the end of a life that was never really mine. I was all these people but I was never me, and now it's a beautiful September morning and my life is over and I don't know who to be.'"

I don't say anything. Lisa sniffles and smiles at me and laughs.

"Then she starts blubbering about how she wishes she hadn't been such a prude in school and how she should have tried more drugs and toured for a summer with the Grateful Dead and maybe spent a month in a nudist colony." She laughs self-consciously and puts the picture away. "That's usually when I start tuning her out."

✧

She takes a break to freshen up. Despite her pain, I can only be happy for her. What's dying in her is something that should die. What most people call life is really just the fearful protraction of a pupal state, like butterflies too scared to emerge from the cocoon. The butterfly stage of development is called *imago*; adulthood. That's what we are meant to be, imago. If we lived in a society of *imagines*, we would be well prepared for metamorphosis; it would occur when it's supposed to and be easier by magnitudes. Not easy, but not cataclysmic either. But we don't live in such a society, and when the transition happens, if it happens, it is more likely to result in catastrophic upheaval than a coming of age ceremony.

Nevertheless, I'm happy for her. No one visiting a coma patient suggests that they look peaceful and are better off spending their life in that state just because waking up from it might be unpleasant.

Lisa pours herself another glass of wine and returns to her seat.

"The photograph is what started the whole thing for me," she says, "but who knows? It wasn't a big event, it was like a tiny pinprick, just a little jolt, but right from that instant, you know it's fatal, like a poison has been injected into your system and there's no antidote, no hope. I think I knew right from the very beginning what it really meant, what would have to happen. I fought against it for three years, tried to keep it pushed aside, tried to bury it under all the minutiae of life, work, family, home, but all that time it kept growing in me, growing like a cancer. What was it, really? A thought? A realization? A glimpse? I really don't know, but it's definitely a point of no return. I knew all my denial was just a temporary solution. I knew I was heading toward my own ruin by staring at the picture every day, but I couldn't help it. It would have felt like a betrayal not to. That was a painful time. I felt like a stranger in my own home, like an alien in human disguise. I had this secret thing growing inside me; as it got bigger, the other me, the mom, the wife, the attorney, all the rest, got smaller. I was looking out through the same eyes, but behind them I was an imposter, a pretender, trying to hold on to a world that was no longer mine. I knew from the first chapter of your first book that the time had come, that whatever was happening to me would soon be born after this uncomfortable three year gestation. That this thing that had been growing inside me would burst out and ruin everything."

"And now here you are, sitting in conversation with me," I smile. "Ain't that a piece of luck."

"I guess you and I wouldn't be sitting here talking together if I were just normal, the way I was; if I wasn't in this goddamned meltdown. I mean, it's not like we're, you know... I don't know. Never mind."

"What would we be talking about if you weren't in this meltdown?" I ask. "Your retirement plan? A shoe sale at Bloomingdales? The war on terror?"

"I guess not. Never mind."

"So you're asking me, if you weren't on fire, if your life wasn't in flames, could we be having this conversation, and the answer is no. Our voices could never bridge the gap. But because you're in this crisis, and because you are here with your death by your side, we can talk."

"My death?" she asks quietly.

I laugh, but gently.

"Certainly," I say. "Who do you think that is in the picture? Who do you think you've been talking to on the train and in the bathroom? Who do you think is trying to slap you out of your coma?"

✧

We take our glasses out to the loungers by the pool and watch the play of moonlight on the lake below and mountains beyond. The conversation settles into a more relaxed mode as she makes some effort to understand who or what she's talking to.

"I was just reading some New Age book in Dad's library that said there were probably several million enlightened beings alive right now."

"Is that what you think?"

She thinks.

"No, not enlightenment the way you talk about it, which is the only way it makes sense. I guess the book was talking about something else."

"Me too. I'd be very surprised if there've been a thousand ever, or if there'd ever been more than there are now. I know there are other things out there that are called enlightened or awake, but if you stick with Truth-Realization, it's hard to get fooled."

"And these other states?"

"I don't know, not my field. In Maya's house are many mansions. They're all just dreamstates within the dreamstate, so who cares? From what I've seen, they're usually about happiness, goodness, compassion, beauty, heart crap, that sort of thing. Does that sound like what that book was talking about?"

"Heart crap?"

"Sure, all the ways we have of putting a pretty bow on our fear so we can be happy in the dungeon instead of smashing out of it."

"You're not into happiness?"

"I'm not into anything."

"You're into truth."

"Not really. No one's into truth. I used to be into not living a lie, but that's over now. Now I'm into writing books, but that's almost over too. Soon I'll be into something akin to sitting in a rocking chair on the front porch, me and my dog, watching the world pass by."

We sit in silence for a few minutes.

"We moved into a hotel at first so Maggie could stay in her school and I could stay at work, but it was the same thing, I could feel it, still too close, the old life was sucking me back in. I knew if I went back that would be it. I'd be lost, my kids would be lost. I was so scared."

She looks away.

"And now, here you are," I say because it seems like my turn to say something. The pool had some weird thing where it changed colors at night, but I figured out how to turn it off and now it just stays cool blue.

"You have to go somewhere," she says with a bit of heat, still looking off into the night. "You can't just run off and join a commune or a nunnery. So I ran back to daddy, is that your point?"

"It's not, actually," I say, "I'm on your side, even if you're not."

"I'm very tired," she says, "please don't talk in riddles."

"You *can* just run off and join a commune or a nunnery, or something of the sort," I say, "but you didn't. Most people do. They do it to avoid the crisis you're now in. They bend like circus contortionists so they don't break like you're breaking now. They make parallel or backward leaps into new systems and ideologies where they can keep themselves distracted indefinitely. They think they're breaking out when they're only tunneling from one prison cell into another. In Maya's prison are many cells."

"So where could I have gone?"

"There are plenty of solutions in place for someone who comes to that crisis; safety nets put out by Maya to catch the jumpers. You could have called yourself a born-again Christian. People throw themselves on Christ's mercy these days if their latté is under-foamed or to shave a few strokes off their golf game. You could have stayed in your old life and gone the Jesus route, it's pretty mainstream now. Or, you could have gone to a shrink and talked and medicated your way through life. You can stay medicated from cradle to grave these days, I guess."

She glowers at me.

"Or, you could have gone to the New Age and self-help aisles of your local bookstore and bought into one therapy or modality or ideology after another while the years flowed placidly by. You could have gone to Buddhism and run out the clock; that's what it's there for. Or, you could have flown off to India or Japan on some self-absorbed spiritual quest to discover your inner whatever. There are plenty of places for people to go when they're trying to hide from the answers, but I would think a shrink or Jesus would have been your best bet."

"I could see myself doing any of those things. I can definitely understand the temptation. That would have been the end of it right there, I guess."

"Maya hath power to assume a pleasing shape."

"I thought that was Satan."

"Is that what you thought?"

"But I thought people were trying to *find* the answers," she grumbles.

"The answers are all in plain sight, the difficulty is in *not* finding them. That's what people are trying to do. That's what religion and spirituality are for; to help us not see what's perfectly obvious."

"To stay asleep, you mean. To stay in the dreamstate."

"Mankind is completely addicted to staying asleep. More than food, sex or survival; delusion. How do you break a habit like that?"

"How?"

"The way you're doing it. Explosively. Messily. Self-destructively."

"Great."

"In fact, what you've done, getting someplace safe and not too demanding, someplace where you can step back from your life and take an objective look and regroup, is the best possible thing. It might feel like running home to daddy, but what you're really doing is running *into* the crisis, not away from it. With a kid, no less. This is war, if you haven't noticed, and you haven't shirked. I know it doesn't feel like it, but you should be very proud of how you've acquitted yourself so far. I mean that on a human-wide scale, by the way. You're a good soldier."

"Thank you," she says, "I guess."

✧

Heaven, salvation, compassion, mindfulness, self-awareness, inner tranquility, peace on earth, good will toward men; these are all safe, no-muss, no-fuss spiritual objectives. They're undemanding, low-impact, lifestyle-friendly and easy on the pocketbook. None of these terms really means anything, so no one gets too caught up in success and failure. They don't lend themselves to fanaticism—no one blows up a bus in the name of compassion—so they don't get a bad rap. For any of them we can feel like a valid participant; join a group, have a practice, buy some books, get on mailing lists, hang out with like-minded people, accessorize. They don't conflict with our current conditions and can be easily integrated into our busy lives. A little meditation in the morning or evening, an hour of church on the occasional Sunday morning, sponsor a hungry kid, a little reading or discussion now and then, and our spiritual itch is adequately scratched. No one gets hurt or does anything crazy; certainly no one unplugs themselves from the great hive and wanders off on their own. Once in a while an overzealous kid might disappear into a Zen monastery, but they usually re-emerge a few years later, none the worse for wear, and probably write a book about their experiences so the time inside won't have been a total waste.

✧

"You know," Lisa continues, "I've read your books. I know where you're coming from, and I'm sorry to be in such a foul mood, but—"

"Really?"

"Really what?"

"Are you really sorry to be in a foul mood?"

She exhales loudly.

"I don't know. No, I guess not."

"Me neither. It's fine with me. Be in whatever mood you're in. You have enough to worry about without repressing your emotional state. You're in a semi-fuckular situation, why pretend you're not?"

"Semi-fuckular?" she laughs. "I guess that's a good word for it."

"Your life is ahead, not behind. You're on your own now."

"I have you," she says hesitantly.

"You only have yourself, but that's all you need."

She slumps back in her lounge chair. She looks profoundly weary. I speak words of comfort.

"You're an intelligent person who's been knocked senseless by this personal apocalypse. Take some time to get your heart and mind cleared out. You have to find your bearings and your balance. This is what it is; it's the same for everyone. Breathe. Walk. Sleep. Be easy on yourself. Give yourself some time, but not too much. Use the writing to get yourself sorted out. You should be busting through crusty old layers of crap like a berserker at this stage."

"That sounds relaxing," she says drily.

"Everything will be fine, better than you can imagine, but first you have work to do, hard work. It might take a while, but you'll get through it and the person you'll become will be unspeakably grateful to the person you are right now for going through this."

"No way to just skip this part?"

"Sure, that's what we've been talking about. The world is full of people and institutions that will answer yes to that exact question. You can try to back out of the whole thing by jumping into some other thing."

"I don't know if I can really go through this for the gratitude of some future me."

"Then make it about your kids. That got you this far. It sounds like you don't want to see them getting caught in the trap you just freed yourself from. Lead by example. Whatever it takes."

"Do I have a choice?"

"I don't think so."

"Me neither," she says. She lays the empty wine bottle on its side like a dead soldier and gets up and walks back up to the main house.

8. Utopia

IN CONTACT WITH THE FLUX of cosmic consciousness all religions known and named today will be melted down. The human soul will be revolutionized. Religion will absolutely dominate the race. It will not depend on tradition. It will not be believed and disbelieved. It will not be a part of life, belonging to certain hours, times, occasions. It will not be in sacred books nor in the mouths of priests. It will not dwell in churches and meetings and forms and days. Its life will not be in prayers, hymns nor discourses. It will not depend on special revelations, on the words of gods who came down to teach, nor on any bible or bibles. It will have no mission to save men from their sins or to secure them entrance to heaven. It will not teach a future immortality nor future glories, for immortality and all glory will exist in the here and now. The evidence of immortality will live in every heart as sight in every eye. Doubt of God and of eternal life will be as impossible as is now doubt of existence; the evidence of each will be the same. Religion will govern every minute of every day of all life. Churches, priests, forms, creeds, prayers, all agents, all intermediaries between the individual man and God will be permanently replaced by direct unmistakable intercourse. Sin will no longer exist nor will salvation be desired. Men will not worry about death or a future, about the kingdom of heaven, about what may come within and after the cessation of the life of the present body. Each soul will feel and know itself to be immortal, will feel and know that the entire universe with all its good and with all its beauty is for it and belongs to it forever. The world peopled by men and women possessing cosmic consciousness will be as far removed from the world of today as this is from the world as it was before the advent of self-consciousness.

—Excerpted from Cosmic Consciousness, Richard Maurice Bucke, M.D.

9. Dystopia

"**D**O YOU BEGIN TO SEE, then, what kind of world we are creating? It is the exact opposite of the stupid hedonistic Utopias that the old reformers imagined. A world of fear and treachery and torment, a world of trampling and being trampled upon, a world which will grow not less but more merciless as it refines itself. Progress in our world will be progress towards more pain. The old civilizations claimed that they were founded on love or justice. Ours is founded upon hatred. In our world there will be no emotions except fear, rage, triumph, and self-abasement. Everything else we shall destroy—everything... There will be no loyalty, except loyalty toward the Party. There will be no love, except the love of Big Brother. There will be no laughter, except the laugh of triumph over a defeated enemy. There will be no art, no literature, no science. When we are omnipotent we shall have no more need of science. There will be no distinction between beauty and ugliness. There will be no curiosity, no enjoyment of the process of life. All competing pleasures will be destroyed. But always—do not forget this, Winston—always there will be the intoxication of power, constantly increasing and constantly growing subtler. Always, at every moment, there will be the thrill of victory, the sensation of trampling on an enemy who is helpless. If you want a picture of the future, imagine a boot stamping on a human face — forever."

–O'Brien to Winston Smith. Excerpted from 1984, George Orwell.

10. Myopia

Courageous, untroubled, mocking and violent—that is
what Wisdom wants us to be. Wisdom is a woman, and
loves only a warrior.

–Friedrich Nietzsche

D R. KIM AND I ENTER the huge riding arena building a few
minutes late. We quietly take seats on a bench off to the side.
Thirty or forty people are seated on a big fold-away aluminum bleacher and
a woman I assume to be Brett is standing out in the sand facing them. She's
wearing jeans and a denim shirt. She's a rusty redhead, strong but not
stocky, mid-forties, outdoorsy and clean looking. At the moment, she also
looks like her patience is being tested. A man of a youthful sixty is
explaining that his spiritual mentor, shri someone-or-other, has instructed
him that it is every sentient being's duty to cherish the earth and work
toward the spiritual liberation of all sentient beings.

"Compassion for humanity is our reason for being," he explains. "Only
in this way does our time on earth have meaning and purpose. How could
I, for instance, possibly focus on my own spiritual liberation when so many
are still living in darkness?"

The man exudes an oily sincerity and I wonder if I'm in the wrong
place. His name, he tells us, is Stanley. He explains that he has been a long-
time spiritual seeker; forty some-odd years. He rattles off a list of names of
some pretty well known spiritual teachers and authors—American, English
and Indian—and refers to them as his beloved gurus.

"Much of the world is rotting from poverty, violence and disease," he
continues. "People everywhere live in hopelessness and despair. They don't
know there's a better way, that abundance, radiant well-being and transcendent joy are their natural birthright. They don't know that they are not
human beings having a spiritual experience, but spiritual beings having a

human experience. My guru teaches that it is the responsibility of those who have eyes to see to come to the aid of those less fortunate, because the spiritual ascension of the human race must include everyone; we can't leave anyone behind. We are our brother's keeper, we are the custodians of this garden-planet. We have an obligation as sentient beings to share a message of love and compassion with our fellow man. Until all sentient beings are able to see through spiritual eyes—"

"If you use the word spiritual again," says Brett in a strong but quiet voice, "I will whip you raw."

Oh good, I'm in the right place.

Stanley is taken up short by Brett's threat, but he smiles condescendingly and continues.

"Okay, sure, I've heard about your tough-love approach," he says with gentle disapproval, "but if you ever want to be standing before more than a handful of students and have the respect of the spiritual community, you'll have to adopt a more compassionate tone and broaden your spiritual outlook to encompass not just the radical fringe, but all your fellow beings. We're all on the same side, you know." He smiles and clasps his hands together. "We're all in this together."

Stanley is obviously a very intelligent guy, but I've never seen intelligence as a more-is-better type deal in this regard. He next launches into what is supposed to be a question, but feels more like a lecture. It starts off being about consciousness, which almost makes me tune out because there's only one thing to know about consciousness and talking about it pretty much means you don't know it. Then there's some stuff about an experience he had in meditation during which, if I understand correctly, he melted into his mantra, followed by some divine revelation, and then his mantra and his heart became one and were purified in a way that was somehow attributable to the supreme guru from which, he informs us, all other gurus descend, and by whose grace he was able to see beyond form into essence which, in turn, is love which, in turn, is God which, in turn, is supreme guru which, in turn, is Self, and so he came to truly understand that the knowledge of Brahman alone is real and the experience left his heart in a pristine, undiluted form for almost two weeks. I might not have all that exactly right. Stan ends it all with a question that has something to do with his search for happiness as it comes into confluence with mankind's quest for liberation.

"Okay Stanley," says Brett, "go ahead and take your seat."

"My teacher encourages open dialogue," says Stan, not sitting. "He says that the only bad idea is the one we don't express. In a world full of violence and contention, it would be a real travesty if those we turned to for spiritual guidance were unable to engage in a free-flow of ideas and rise above the petty tyrannies of anger and jealousy."

"Yeah," says Brett, "that'd be a helluva travesty." She turns to the group. "Now, for those of you who don't know, this ain't a debatin' society, and it sure as hell ain't a democracy. I ain't standin' out here tryin' to win your approval or sell you on my particular brand of bullshit. We ain't doin' no meditatin' or chantin', we ain't mergin' with our mantras or tryin' to cleanse our minds or purify our souls or get all happy or earn our eternal ree-ward, and we sure as hell ain't tryin' to save the world or rescue our fellow man. All we're tryin' to do here, the *only* goddamn thing, is figure out what the hell's going on. That's it. If you don't find that to be a worthwhile use of your time, or if you think you already know, then clear out and come back when you don't need to be dragged kickin' and screamin' every inch of the way."

She turns back to Stan.

"Stan, I gotta give you credit; I've heard every dipshit New Age cliché in the book, but I ain't never heard 'em all strung together like that before. What you need to do is give yourself a nice cranial enema and get all that forty years of shit outta your head. You're like a little boy talking about pirates and dinosaurs like you knew them all personally, except you're too old to be a little boy and that makes you hard to look at. I don't know what you been doin' since the nineteen-sixties, but it had nothin' to do with getting' your ass woke up. Musta been some totally unrelated enterprise. I've heard a lot of foolishness in my time and a lot of it sounded like that slop you were just spewin', but listen, I tell you this as a kindness; what you're talking about is nothing. Forty years of nothing. It means nothing. It goes nowhere. You are being lied to, you are the one doing the lying, and you are the lie."

I'm definitely in the right place.

Stanley begins to reply but she holds up her hand to silence him and addresses the woman at his side.

"Why'd you bring him here, Molly? He piss you off or something?"

Molly, an attractive woman in her fifties, doesn't reply. Brett walks toward her and looks at her hard.

"Oh, I know," says Brett with a laugh, "I get it. You two started datin', right? Figured you were both spiritual folk so it was a good fit. But then you couldn't hold your own against his bigass brain and his career discipleship and his line-up of beloved *goo-roos*, so you brought him here to let me deal with him, ain't that right you little chickenshit?"

She says it in a kind of affectionate way so neither Molly nor anyone else takes offense. In fact, except for a certain glassy-eyed rigidity that overtook whoever she addressed, no one ever seemed too offended by Brett's abrasive manner.

I was really starting to like her. Straight talk in plain English. I had never seen anyone like her before and I found her comforting. It's like thinking you're the only one of something, and then there's another one and it makes the world a different place; slightly less alien. Not like you're connected, but like maybe you could be.

Brett steps back a few paces to address the whole group.

"Whenever you have any sort of question like that, any sort of nonsense like that floatin' around in your head, your only goal should be to climb up outta the place where such a question seems to make sense. It's a short climb, I promise, just one little step up. All that smelly talk about experience, consciousness, mankind, happiness and *goo-roo* is just pure stinkin' denial and it don't belong here. If that's your thing, you're in the wrong place. We ain't here to indulge in that kind of playtime fantasy. Y'all pay good attention because what you heard is exactly the kind of fertilizer they're selling you out there. This gentleman, Stanley, is like the poster child for spiritual myopia. Picture him sittin' in the lotus position formin' upturned okay-signs with his hands, eyes closed, smilin' like a little bliss-bunny, and behind him this bigass dumptruck is burying him under a massive load of steamy manure. Y'all with me so far? And driving the truck, leaning out the window giving the camera a big okay sign and smilin' the way they do, is the beloved *goo-roo*. How's that for a New Age poster?"

I'm keeping an eye on Stanley in case he's gonna need tackling. He's tight-lipped but composed.

"I let Stanley ramble on a bit tonight because he's a prime example of someone who has managed, despite a good heart and a powerful mind, to keep himself totally in the dark through forty years of searching for the light. That's a helluva thing he's managed to do and it's an important thing for y'all to take a look at and try to understand because Stanley here is not the exception, he's the rule. Anywhere else they'd be lookin' at this guy like he was practically a guru himself."

She turns to Stan. "Written a book yet, Stanley?"

He's watching her with a half-smile, as if indulging her.

"I happen to be working on a book about my years with—"

"Of course you are. God bless you, I wish I could keep you in a jar." She turns back to the group. "What we see here with Stanley is a complete and total evasion; a *subterfuge*, as they say. There ain't no answer to the kinda question Stanley just tried to ask; the question don't even mean anything, it just sorta sounds like it does. That's the point. That's why it's a subterfuge. Y'all know what a *subterfuge* is?"

If anyone doesn't, they're not jumping up to announce it.

"Stanley, I don't know what the hell to tell you. If I could go back forty years and find you, I'd know what to say. I'd start by givin' you a sharp rap on the nose to get your attention, then I'd tell you what I tell these folks once a month. Stop being a dumbass. There ain't no law tellin' you to be a dumbass, you're doin' it voluntary, and my advice would be to give it up or forty years from now you're gonna have some crazy broad in your face tellin' you it's too late for you, that you had your chance and you blew it, which is what I'm tellin' you now. The Chinese have a saying: The best time to stop bein' a dumbass is forty years ago, and the second best time is now. Maybe a piano will fall on your head tomorrow and knock all that horseshit outta your head, but I don't see you havin' that kinda good luck."

He starts to speak and she cuts him off.

"Don't bother mincin' words with me, Stanley. You got your self-importance and your missionary ideals to make you feel like you're someone special doin' somethin' saintly, but both them things is a lie; you're just another scared kid hidin' from your own damn life. I can smell it like you been dipped in cheap perfume. You're scared to open your eyes so you dreamed up a world where you get to be Jesus savin' all the lepers and poor folk, and them all just kissin' your ass for bein' such a pal. Heaven'll be strikin' up the band when they see you comin'." She turns back the group. "Don't take it hard, none of you. That's what everybody does, includin' all your fancy *men-tors* and *goo-roos*, and the craziest thing about it is not seein' how damn crazy it is. Take five, everybody."

Stan and Molly leave the building briskly. Brett comes and sits down next to me. I guess I'm staring.

"What?" she asks.

"I think I'm in love," I reply.

"Shows you got good sense," she says. She offers a hand and we shake.

"Where are you from?" I ask. "Texas?"

"All over. Army brat."

"What about the accent?"

"Total bullshit. It's just a character that comes over me so I can talk to folks and not mess 'em up any worse than I found 'em. I ain't loud and I never cuss." She grins. "I'm shy."

"Quite a show you put on."

"Just clearin' the pipes. If you don't keep an eye on 'em they'll start bringing in their New Age buddies and the whole thing turns into a candle-lit hugfest, everyone singing Kumbaya and savin' the world. They bring me their ugly babies like I'm supposed to go all ga-ga and smooch 'em up."

"Ugly babies?"

"Their beliefs. All beliefs are like ugly babies, don'cha think? Everyone thinks theirs is the most beautiful in the world, but they all look and smell the same to me. I reckon it's our job to tell 'em their babies are ugly and to go throw 'em in the river. You ever make any sense of Buddhism?"

"No, ma'am."

"Me neither, just a lot of cheap perfume from what I can tell. I must be wrong, but I know I'm right."

"Very impressive teaching style."

"Thanks in part to you. Until I read your book I was a lot less clear out there. I knew what I knew but I couldn't find the words. The doc gave me your book and that's where I learned how to talk about all this. You have better success with men or women?"

"It's about even, I think, but women are more expressive. Men get to a point where they just go off by themselves and you don't see them for a year or two. How about you?"

"I'm battin' zero," she says, "but there's a few I'm watchin'. Give you a good feeling when someone makes it?"

I consider it for a moment.

"Not really."

She laughs and shakes her head.

"Damnedest thing, ain't it?" she says.

That was my first experience of Brett.

11. Big Mac Attack

I would rather be ashes than dust! I would rather that my spark should burn out in a brilliant blaze than it should be stifled by dry-rot. I would rather be a superb meteor, every atom of me in magnificent glow, than a sleepy and permanent planet. The proper function of man is to live, not to exist. I shall not waste my days in trying to prolong them. I shall use my time.

—*Jack London*

AFTER SHARING THE SMALL ESTATE for a few weeks with Lisa and Maggie, we develop comfortable routines that overlap once or twice a day while still affording plenty of space and privacy. They come down to the poolhouse at around eleven o'clock every morning for a swim and a glass of limonada and a half hour of lying in the sun on the loungers by the pool. It's very pleasant to have them around and doesn't interfere with my work.

A late lunch is my main meal of the day and I do the same thing every day. I lay out all the stuff I find in the fridge, starting with what I picked up at the stores and street markets that morning on my walk in town with Maya. I throw out whatever seems too old or unpopular and lay everything else out on the kitchenette's island counter. As the summer progresses and more people flow in and out through the course of the day, people will begin bringing in their own items picked up at the stores before visiting so the whole thing becomes quite a community venture. It's nice to have a no hassle, no cooking, easy cleanup way to eat without it being too boring. It's also a nice way to be a reasonably good host without having to really do much. I make a few trips to this buffet throughout the day and have a fish taco or something light in town on my nightly walk with Maya and visit to Frank, and that takes care of my eating needs and hosting duties.

I usually pick up a few items every day, something new or something to replace something we ran out of. Lisa got the hang of it from the beginning and started contributing to our stock. It's easy to get an idea of what's popular and what's not, but it's also nice to keep it interesting by introducing new things to see how they'll be received. Unpopular stuff naturally migrates to the back of the fridge or cabinets and gets thrown out once a week or so. Anyway, that's a big part of the daily routine down at the poolhouse where I work and where others come to visit or help or just to swim and eat and sunbathe.

After a few weeks of this comfortable ritual, Lisa pulls up a chair at the side of my table where she usually sits for a few minutes of conversation every day. Today she has an unusual request.

"Maggie wants to ask you if she can interview you, like Julie in the first book."

I push back from my work and study Lisa to see if I heard her correctly.

"Maggie read *Damnedest?*" I ask.

"She's read both of your books. More than once. She has the electronic versions on her laptop, so she read the extra material too. She says you hate yodeling, love death, and you think the universe is a big playful puppy. Is that right?"

"Uh, the puppy thing is," I reply. I look at her over the tops of my reading glasses. "Nothing about this sounds like a good idea, offhand."

"She read the books because," she hesitates and continues, "she overheard a fight between her father and me and she got the idea that you were to blame."

"For?"

"For, uh, well, the breakup of our home and family, I guess."

"I see," I say, but I really don't.

"I have to make a point," I tell her, "and, believe me, I'm very reluctant to say this, but the fact is that I cannot participate in, uh, human affairs. I'm sorry, I know how stupid that sounds, but that's really how it is. If you're suggesting that your daughter might benefit by spending time with me as part of some healing process or to get her back on the right track or something, you've got the wrong idea. Nobody benefits from me, not like that."

"No, that's not what I'm suggesting—"

"I have no framework, or even the memory of a framework, within which to conduct any but the most mundane interpersonal dialogue. I don't even know the words anymore, or why one thing might be better than another. I would exude wrongness—"

"I appreciate what you're—"

"I don't think you appreciate what a trainwreck—"

"That's not what I'm—"

"I'm completely useless regarding—"

"*Jed!*"

"Uh, yes?"

"May I continue without being interrupted?"

"Um," I have to think about that, "yes?"

"What if she stays away from personal matters? She could keep it clinical, impersonal."

"She could? I have no understanding. How possible or likely is that?"

"It's both, if she has adult guidance."

"You?"

"And her grandfather."

"Oh," I ponder, "it's a setup."

"It's been discussed."

"And you and Frank would be, what? Counseling her? Coaching her?"

"We could help her come up with good questions and understand your answers. Review her notes with her. I don't think it would be like we were trying to dissect you or anything."

I laugh at that.

"Dissecting is fine," I say. "There's nothing about sharp blades I don't like, it's the dull ones I find annoying. Regardless, I can't agree now. Bring her by and we can all talk and then we'll see."

She frowns.

"I don't see why it should be so complicated," she says.

"I don't see that it is," I reply.

✧

The reason I can't agree is because it's not there yet. This thing hasn't come into focus or alignment. I'm aware of it, I'll watch it, and if it becomes clear that it should happen, then we'll go ahead with it. This is how my agreement with the universe about the third book works. The only reason I'm here and in contact with these people is the third book. If it weren't for the third book there would be no question of being interrogated by a possibly angry or resentful young lady who is being coached by her in-crisis mom and somewhat lunatic grandfather. I wouldn't be meeting these people or answering any question more profound than debit or credit, paper or plastic.

This thing with the girl, Maggie, for instance. I have no personal interest in whether or not her project with me happens. It's not that I have the ability to care but for some reason I don't, it's that I don't have the ability. I have no framework within which one outcome might be better or worse than another. What I do have, though, is this arrangement with the universe. I'll write the book if it lays out that way; that's the deal. The universe knows exactly what I mean by that, and so do I. I mean just what we see happening in this situation with Maggie. The pieces have to fall into place, and they can't need me to force or finesse or finagle them. It's not really an agreement any more than inhaling constitutes an agreement to exhale. It's simply a recognition, an acknowledgement. I am part of a process. It works the way it works.

All I can say at this early stage is that it looks like the universe wants the third book because the pieces are falling unmistakably into place and they have been every step of the way. It's all coming together and I'm pretty sure the thing with Lisa's daughter will fall into place as well. It hasn't yet, though. It has not yet clicked into place, so we'll wait until it does or doesn't. Maybe it will and maybe it won't. I could mess it up by playing my part poorly. Saying yes to the girl before the yes became apparent to me would be incorrect and unpleasant. It would feel artificial, pushed, scared and egoic, i.e., not-right. There will be a time to say yes, and things will proceed perfectly, flawlessly, elegantly, if they are allowed to do so.

Lisa doesn't see why it should be so complicated because she doesn't see how simple it is. This isn't just the way I'm treating her and her daughter, this is the way I do everything. This is the way an integrated being maintains alignment and harmony with the universe, and how the effortless perfection that is plain to behold in every single aspect of non-egoic creation is enjoyed on the personal level as well. Through unconditional surrender I have mastered the universe. By releasing all control, I am in perfect control. Controlling nothing, I control everything. Only by taking control could I lose control.

I don't remember what it means to work, to toil, to do something unpleasant. I don't distinguish between work and non-work, weekday and weekend. I don't take holidays off or go on vacations. I probably spend, on average, four hours a day working, but I don't think of it as work any more than I think of walking the dog as play or shopping for lunch as a chore. The idea of doing something I don't feel like doing is almost absurd to me. If something needs doing, there will come a time when I feel like doing it. If that time doesn't come, it doesn't get done and didn't need doing. I have no schedules or appointments or set hours. I have no concept of duty, obligation, or responsibility. I have no affiliations or connections or ties.

For Lisa, though, that's what life was; schedules and obligations and responsibilities; an endless plate-spinning act. For her entire adult life that's all she's been doing, frantically keeping dozens of spinning plates balanced on sticks like an old Vaudeville routine, scurrying back and forth in a perpetual panic, terrified that one might fall and smash, adding more plates every year, performing this manic, macabre dance not for five minutes at a time, but every waking minute of every day for years on end with no end in sight, unless...

Unless she just stopped.

Which is what she finally did. She was stuck between two unthinkable things—keep spinning the plates and stop spinning the plates—but slowly, over three years, one of the unthinkable things became less unthinkable and she did it. She stopped. And all the plates came crashing down and made a terrible mess, and now here she is, trying to figure out what, if anything, survives such a calamitous betrayal. Was that plate-spinning act who she was? Or just something she did? It's two months later now and she still doesn't know.

Not everyone has it so bad, of course, and probably very few feel like they're drowning in their own lives. Some people have it much worse than Lisa did and some have it much better, but it's not quality of unconscious life that concerns us here, just unconsciousness, and that takes many forms. Manic plate-spinning is just one of them.

If I had to live one day from Lisa's old life, even a relatively easy day, or an easy day from her husband's life, for that matter, I would think myself accursed. Just getting together with buddies on Sunday afternoon to drink beer and watch a ballgame would be a hellish torment. The highpoint of Dennis and Lisa's year, the vacation, seems to me an unbearable hardship. If I had to spend five minutes on a cruise ship or in Las Vegas or anyplace with people in mouse costumes, I'd seek escape as from a burning house. That people subject themselves to such ordeals willingly, for pleasure and at considerable expense, is completely outside my comprehension.

As always, it's important to remember that it's not me personally we're talking about. These same things would be equally true for anyone in even a modestly developed state of Adulthood. Or maybe it's a facet of one-pointedness, of being a task-specific person, and anyone who is focused entirely on one thing to the exclusion of all others would find all off-task activities equally insipid. Or maybe it's both. Maybe anyone in a state of developing Adulthood will undergo a natural reduction in their interests from many to few and even to one as they come into alignment, as they clear the debris and uncover their true calling. Or maybe it's neither. Maybe I'm just becoming an old poop.

I look at people's lives and it never becomes less confounding to see the ways in which they squander the only true wealth they possess, despite not knowing when it will run out, only that it will, throwing minutes and hours and days away like hot coals. What else does it mean to be asleep than to dispose of our own lives so thoughtlessly? What could be a more definitive symptom of non-lucidity? Every minute we spend oblivious to the value of a minute is a minute of unconsciousness. This isn't some screwball scheme to latch onto the present moment in time, it's simply what it means to be awake.

Lisa has spent much of her life entangled in the thorny underbrush of her life. I don't think she's unique in this regard. I think most people are so bound up by their false beliefs, so tightly wrapped up in their fictitious personas, that they have no knowledge whatsoever of what life really is or how it really works, of what they themselves really are, or of their rightful place in creation. Few people have any comprehension of what heaven and hell really are; that they're rotting away in the latter never knowing that their birthright is the former. It may not seem like hell when we're in it, just regular life, but once we're out, as Lisa is just starting to discover, we see our previous condition as an insensible state of tormented writhing. Very few people seem to have even the slightest idea of what a living spirituality really is, what integration is, what wealth and power and beauty really are, the so-called experts least of all.

Is all that heaven and hell business overstating it? It feels like it is, but whenever I make an effort to challenge my perceptions in this regard I only manage to reaffirm and deepen them. Every once in a while, using libraries and bookstores and the internet, I seek out the best thinking, the most enlightened minds, the most lucid communicators of the loftiest subjects to find out what message they're putting out. At first I start feeling a bit more optimistic about the spiritual state of humanity, but then the puniness comes through, that horrid self-centricity which is the hardened steel and reinforced concrete of delusion, and I throw a grudging salute to Maya and remind myself not to look again.

✦

I emerge from my reverie. Lisa is staring at me expectantly. We are, I recall, discussing the idea of her daughter Maggie asking me some questions.

"If you want to know how I'd answer something," I tell her, "ask me something."

She thinks about it for a minute.

"Okay," she says through self-conscious laughter, "if you had to be an ingredient on a Big Mac, which one would you be? And why?"

I laugh too.

"That's your question?" I say. "Where'd you get a question like that?"

"A Human Resources manager asked me in an interview for an internship one summer."

"What did you answer?"

"Let's not make this about me."

I wait.

"It caught me off guard," she says, "which was probably the point. I said I'd be the special sauce because it's bold yet mysterious."

We both laugh at that.

"What's so mysterious about the special sauce?" I ask.

"Isn't it a secret recipe or something?"

"I don't know. I thought it was Thousand Island dressing."

"I don't know either. I'd never even ever eaten one; I just knew the ingredients from the commercials."

"Did you get the job?"

"Internship. Yes, I got it. So, how would you answer if Maggie asked? Which ingredient of a Big Mac would you be?"

"Whichever one had the power to terminate its own existence."

She stares at me, not sure if I'm joking.

"No, come on. What would you say if Maggie asked?"

"Whichever one had the power to terminate its own existence."

"Seriously?"

I take a few seconds to see if I have any other answer to the question, but I don't.

"Reckon so."

"But really, Jed, think about it. None of the ingredients of a Big Mac have the ability to kill themselves."

"Then I'd kill myself while I still could; before they came."

"Before *who* came?"

"Whoever was going to turn me into a powerless ingredient."

"You're not answering the spirit of the question."

"I think I am, though I doubt I'd get the job."

"Internship. Suicide wasn't one of the options."

"It wasn't stated, but it was there. It's always there."

"And that would be your answer to the question if Maggie asked it?"

"Well, I can't be sure, but it certainly sounds like something I'd say."

She stares at me for another long moment, then slumps.

"Oh nuts, it does, doesn't it?" She rubs her eyes. "Well, I can't argue with that. She's read your books. We're past the point of no return. Let's go ahead and try it."

✧

"Mr. McKenna, may I interview you for my summer composition project?"

"No."

"Why not?"

"I don't know."

"But why is the answer no?"

"Because it's not yes."

"Are you teasing me?"

"It sounds like I am, but I'm not. I'm treating you with respect. The answer is no because it's not yes."

"So if the answer were yes, it would be yes because it's not no?"

"No. If the answer were yes, it would be yes because yes was indicated."

"So now the answer no is indicated?"

"Only because yes is not indicated."

"Indicated how?"

"I don't know."

"But you know when something is indicated?"

"Yes."

"You can't just think about it and come up with an answer on your own?"

"Sure, and you could put on a blindfold and go through life using a stick to find your way, but why? You have eyes."

"I was thinking of asking my grandfather to help me with this."

I say nothing.

"Him and my mom could help me come up with good questions and understand your answers."

I say nothing.

"Do you think that might change your decision?"

"There's been no decision, just an observation."

"Could it change your observation?"

"Of course."

"Would it?"

"I don't know."

"But the answer could be different tomorrow?"

"Sure."

"Could it be different in ten seconds?"

"Sure."

Ten seconds later—

"Is it indicated now?"

"No."

"Can I ask you again tomorrow?"

"I don't know."

She looks at me for a few seconds.

"We've already started, haven't we?"

"So it seems."

"Then it must be indicated."

"Must be."

"May I ask what the indication is?"

"That we've already started."

She giggles merrily.

"Muchas gracias, señor."

"De nada, señorita."

⋄

"So, I guess I'll have some more talks with Maggie," I tell Lisa after Maggie has gone off to bed. "You should always be present, and I'd like a copy of her notes in case I want them for the book."

"Yes, fine, of course. Thank you for being so indulgent about all this, and balanced. I'm not feeling very balanced these days."

"It goes where it goes. You're aware, I'm sure, that if there's a custody battle, they'll make you out as a whacko cult broad and you'll never see your kids unsupervised again?"

"Yes," she says grimly, "but we're past the point of no return there too." She gestures to our surroundings. "We're already living in your compound."

12. This sentence is false.

For me, it is as though at every moment the actual world had
completely lost its actuality. As though there was nothing
there; as though there were no foundations for anything or as
though it escaped us. Only one thing, however, is vividly
present: the constant tearing of the veil of appearances; the
constant destruction of everything in construction. Nothing
holds together, everything falls apart.

—Eugène Ionesco

I'M WORKING, LISA IS FIDGETING. Doing nothing isn't easy for
someone who's managed to keep themselves manically occupied every
waking minute since they started walking and talking. The effort she's
applying to sitting quietly and not disturbing me is palpable; it fills the
space like a throbbing hum. Without moving or making any noise, her
energy is making my brain vibrate.

Or maybe it's just the meds.

It's mid-afternoon. We're on the pooldeck at my work table. Maya is
napping belly-up in one of the poolside loungers. Maggie spends after-
noons with friends at the public pool or in other activities. I've already had
a heck of a day and was just getting settled back into my comfort zone
when she sauntered along and seated herself with such a strained casualness
that the effort of not wincing makes me wince. I read the same sentence
five times before realizing there's no point. I maintain my working
demeanor for a few more minutes while I enjoy her discomfort. She holds
it in for a minute longer than I would have guessed she could.

"I could help you with your writing," she finally says, "or whatever."

I nod slightly and keep my eyes on the laptop screen.

"Not for payment or anything, just to be helpful," she adds.

I don't respond.

"I minored in English," she says a minute later. "I wanted to teach."

I nod absently.

"I'm very organized, and I'm a pretty good proofreader; lots of experience with legal documents and correspondence."

"Yeah, okay," I mutter, "we'll see."

"Oh, sure. Well, you know, whatever you think."

I observe her muted discomfort for another few minutes.

✧

"I know what it is to be suddenly disconnected," I could tell her. "I know what it's like at the beginning, when you're cast adrift, not a part of anything anymore, cut away from all the things that have always defined you. No home, no people, no place. Suddenly, everyone's a stranger. You've done unforgivable violence, committed a truly destructive act. You've lost everything through that destructive act, including much of yourself. I know the urge you're feeling to be a part of something again. I know how strong the urge is and how scary it is to be isolated and apart. This rebirth you've undergone is as reality-redefining as the physical birth process. The womb you've just expelled yourself from may have been toxic and suffocating, but it was also warm and safe and familiar, and now you're in a whole different world, blindingly bright and stark, and nothing looks or works like it did before. It's cold and lonely and everything is strange, and you can never go back."

That's what I could tell her, but I don't. She hasn't asked and it's not something I ever manage to say with appropriate solemnity. Personally, I liked the part where she is now; the severing of connections, breaking away from everyone and everything, smashing out of my old life. Yes, it was agonizing, but it was also ecstatic. I didn't have the problem Lisa has of being selective, of dumping some parts and keeping others; I was dumping the whole load. I wasn't saving myself for anything. I wasn't concerned with success because it never occurred to me that success was possible. I wasn't concerned with the rest of my life because it never occurred to me that I'd outlive my mania. I was just exhilarated and eager and experiencing my first taste of freedom. My subsequent life has just come as a pleasant afterthought. I never thought there'd be an after.

My initial break was the first time I felt clean and free and self-determinable, like my life was really mine, that something other than ignorance and lies was possible. There's no nice way to do it, as Lisa has learned. It's brutal and ugly and best done quickly. No one has any idea to what degree they are shaped by the people and conditions of their environment until they undertake to extricate themselves from it, and that's what Lisa is doing now; extricating herself. Not so different from having a baby, perhaps, but the person she's pushing into the world is herself.

✧

I print out a rough draft of a chapter about flow and manifestation and integration. I slide the pages over to Lisa.

"Okay, counselor, you're my new temp. What do you think?"

She receives them eagerly and spends a few minutes reading.

"I guess I should tell you," she says, "I'm not a New Age person. When you start talking about desire, intent, manifestation, flow and obstruction, I really might not be your best critic."

"Or maybe that's why you are," I say. "None of this is witchcraft or wizardry; it's just the way things work. Not just for me; for you, for everyone. You'll recognize it from your own life if you stop to think about it. There's no reason you can't comment on this material. Say whatever you want."

"Okay," she says, "how about an example of what you're talking about? About how these supposed powers work in your life. Something specific."

"Very good," I say. "The only power, though, is observation; seeing what is. So, the first thing that comes to mind is this morning when I was on the bike exploring the roads out around the western end of the lake. You know how the roads are, and you've seen the bike."

"That thing up by the gate? It runs?" She has a thought and laughs. "I just saw the most horrible lime green Ford Pinto parked up there. The whole roof was chopped off."

"The bike was a Triumph 650. I creamed it and had to buy the Pinto."

"Creamed it? What does that—?" For the first time she notices the cane leaning on the table next to me and leaps up.

"Oh Jed, Jesus! What happened? What did you do? Are you okay?"

She comes around the table to inspect me. She can see all the dressings on my left leg and the knee brace. She can see the dressings on my left arm but not the ones on the shoulder and scapula which are covered by my shirt.

"Oh my God," she says through her hands. "What happened? Are you okay?"

"Everything is fine, I promise." I point to the pitcher of limonada. "Could you please pour us some of that? It's been taunting me for the last hour. Then have a seat and I'll answer your questions."

"It looks bad," she says. "Seriously, are you okay?"

"I'm fine, thank you. A bunch of abrasions and a jammed up knee. Nothing serious. A little thirsty."

"But you couldn't cross the room to get a drink?" She pours the drinks and sits back down, her look of wide-eyed concern still in place.

"Everything's a bit seized up right now. The less I have to move, the better."

"This is from the motorcycle? You had an accident?"

"Trashed it, yeah. Some gringo in a rental cut me off, he was coming the other way and made his left turn across my lane right in front of me and I had to go off the road. Airborn out of the ditch for a few seconds and then *whammo!* Totaled it except maybe the engine."

"Oh my God, how fast were you going?"

"I don't know, sixty-five or seventy. Slower at impact."

"Were you wearing a helmet?"

"No."

Her hands are shaking. She's making a determined effort to stay calm.

"Oh, Lord. You didn't break anything? Didn't hit your head? No concussion?"

"A lot of abrasions, the knee hurts and I'm pretty sore all over. There was a lot of sliding and tumbling involved after me and the bike parted ways."

"Oh my God," she says again. "Then what? Did an ambulance come?"

"No one came, no one even pulled over. I chimed my bells pretty good on the gas tank, so that had my complete attention. It was a probably ten minutes before I was able to take stock of the rest."

"Chimed your—? Uh... *Oh!* Mother of Jesus, are you okay?"

"Fine, and that can be the last word on that. So, after awhile I made some calls, my cell phone was fine. I got some kids in a pickup to come out and trade the remains of the bike and a wad of pesos for that pretty little green Pinto with no roof. You're free to use it whenever you like. Keys are in it."

"I'll turn some heads in that. Have you seen a doctor?"

"I went to the clinic. I have to go back every day for the dressings, it's a little tricky. Just for a week or so. I'm a quick healer. Anyway, that's the answer to your question. You asked for an example of this integrated, co-creative relationship with the universe, and this accident is a very good example."

Such a good example, in fact, that I'm only now beginning to see it.

"I was thinking just the opposite," she says. "Obviously, you don't *want* to crash on your motorcycle. Obviously, you don't *want* to have all these injuries."

"No, that's true, that's where the surrender part comes in. Surrender is of the essence of this relationship I'm describing. You're right, my personal preference would be not to crash and get all banged up, but my preferences don't really factor in. I have one overarching preference, and that is whatever the universe prefers. I don't have to like it or understand it, though I usually do. This little accident I had is nothing; it's just the way the universe communicates, loud enough to be heard and no louder."

"And what would the message be?" she asks skeptically.

"In the very first instant of the accident, in the first second, I knew it wasn't a serious situation. I knew it immediately, faster than thought. Despite the fact that I was wickedly out of control and the next few seconds looked gravely unpleasant, I knew I wouldn't be killed or even badly injured."

"You don't call *that* badly injured?" she indicates my injuries.

"For crashing a motorcycle at seventy miles an hour? No, I call this a little tickle. Nothing broken. I didn't even scratch my head."

"It's nice that you can be so philosophical about it," she says.

"In the sense you mean, I'm philosophical about everything."

She takes her seat but remains very stiff.

"But how could you possibly know it wouldn't be serious?"

"Because it wouldn't make sense. This isn't a time for change. I knew it wasn't my time to die because the third book wasn't finished. I knew I wasn't going to be injured because there would be no point in that. Why would it happen? There's no reason for it. There are no lessons for me to learn, no karma to burn, no brownie points to earn. That's the long way of saying what I understood in that first second. Getting run off the road and knowing nothing serious was happening was practically in the same instant."

"You thought all that in an instant?"

"No, I *knew* it in an instant. I never bothered thinking it through or verbalizing it until now. It all sounds kinda dumb now, but it was perfectly clear at the time."

She looks perplexed. It's a topic that interests me and might be of practical value to her, so I try to do a better job of explaining.

"Thought is an unnecessary step. We can know things directly, instantly, without any need for thinking, at which the very best of us are comically inept. Why insist on converting knowledge out of its native format into bite-sized pieces our little brains can chew on? It's just another way we seek to bring the universe down to our size instead of expanding to our rightful dimensions."

"You're saying you don't *think*?"

"If something needs thinking about, then I talk it out or write it out, externalize it, but that only happens with regard to the books, which have to be written out anyway. I mean, I'd have to think about it, but I don't think I think about anything else."

She's giving me a very dubious look, which I kind of understand but mostly don't. I notice my mouth stays open when I'm not talking and wonder if that is a side effect of the pills.

"I know this is all pretty foreign to you," I say, "but it's just business as usual to me. This motorcycle thing is a somewhat dramatic example, but operating in the flow this way—moving with patterns, seeing the larger picture—this is how I function in all areas of my life. I'm pretty good at it, actually. Still learning, though, still figuring things out. I am only an egg."

She doesn't pick up on the reference. I wonder if the drugs are making my brain a bit wobblier than usual.

"But how?" she asks dubiously, "*really*. How could you have known all that?"

"Because everything works a certain way and I see how it works. There's no mystery. There's never a mistake, never a violation. These rules aren't meant to be broken. The dreamstate is very, uh, *orderly*. There is no randomness, no chaos. The idea of a serious accident, that I would get hit by a car and get hurt or die, I can't explain to you how impossible that would have been."

"Impossible?"

"No, not impossible. There's no right word. I have no lexicon for my way of being. It wouldn't make sense, it would be in violation. There's no better way to say it. It just wouldn't happen."

"But these things *do* happen," she protests. "People get hurt and die all the time. They die tragically, prematurely, in accidents, in fires, from violence and disease."

"Do they?"

"Of course they do."

"Wrongness is in the eye of the beholder."

"Huh? What does that mean?"

"Rabindranath Tagore said—"

"Rabindra who?"

"Rabindranath Tagore, mystic poet. He said we read the world wrong and say that it deceives us. That's true, but it's not necessarily true. We don't have to read the world wrong. I don't read it wrong, and it doesn't deceive me."

"Meaning?"

"We can read the world right. It's not that difficult. We can stop seeing randomness and chaos where there is order. We can stop seeing mystery where there are clearly defined patterns and inviolable laws. We can open our eyes and see where we are and how it works and how we work in it, with it. I know you don't see it yet, but it's certainly there to be seen, and you're certainly able. Nothing is hidden. I don't know how I came out of that accident okay, I'm not a great rider, but I knew that whatever was happening wasn't death or injury or even much of a nuisance because that would be not-right. That's how I knew. That's the point of the story. Things *don't* just happen. Everything makes sense once you see at the level of patterns; everything flows naturally from the thing before into the thing after. Nothing is ever just random or chaotic or happenstance. That would be, to me, utterly preposterous. It wouldn't even make for amusing fiction."

✧

What the unawake person sees in brief glimpses few and far between, the awake person sees at all times and in all things. To be asleep is to detect this ocean of being once in a while and to create superstitious explanations about invisible scorekeepers and stringpullers; of gods and karma, of luck and fate and destiny. Even with eyes closed, we are able to sense the motions and currents and majesty of this energetic ocean in which we abide. To be awake is to behold this ocean of being and not to imagine ourselves apart from it. There is nothing more mystical or spiritual than to see this ocean and to live in harmony with it. There is no other freedom than to cast off egoic restraints and live in accord with what is.

Lisa wants to know how I knew my motorcycle crash wouldn't be bad. If she and I sat on a beach and watched the waves roll in for an hour, I tell her, she'd probably have a pretty good idea of what the next wave was going to do and, just as importantly, what it wasn't going to do.

"It's not going to suddenly freeze or reverse its course or disappear," I say. "It's not going to turn into a band of mariachis and stroll up the beach to serenade us, it's not going to develop an egoic urge to express its individuality by spouting like a geyser."

"Obviously," says Lisa drily.

"Yes," I agree, "and the patterns in which we move are just as obvious once we learn to see them. We are always in them, a part of them, inseparable from them. It's all energy, consciousness. There is nothing else."

"You're waxing very poetic," she says.

"Stop this day and night with me and you shall possess the origin of all poems."

She sits and watches me for a few moments. I hold her gaze.

"I remember that," she says quietly. "That's by Walt Whitman. It's the first poem in your first book."

"Nisargadatta Maharaj said—"

"Nisarga who?"

"Indian sage. He said, 'In my world, nothing ever goes wrong.' That's an eyes-open statement. It's not his world that's different, it's him; his undistorted, unfiltered perspective. He has removed the artificial barrier of ego from the perceiver-perception-perceived union and so the three become one and perfection is the certain result."

"So this Indian guy was enlightened?"

"Yeah, but we're not talking about enlightened, we're talking about awake. You're waking up. You can stay where you are now, groggy and confused, as many people who make it this far do, or you can push on, continue what you've started. This stuff I'm telling you is like the coming attractions reel."

"So it's all just one big ocean, is what you're saying?"

"Here's another good one. Carl Sagan said if you want to make an apple pie from scratch, you must first create the universe."

"Meaning?"

"Say we're on that beach watching the waves roll in," I tell her. "You look out into the distance and see the first hints of a swell. As you watch, it comes toward you and grows and grows and finally, in its turn, it rolls and breaks and crashes and foams up onto the sand and gently recedes, making way for the next. You watch that and the appearance is that you've seen a complete wave from start to finish, from birth to death, but that's the smallest, most limited possible perspective to take. That's what we see when we chop everything into tiny little pieces, when we put up walls everywhere and slap labels on everything, as ego insists on doing. Beginnings and endings are not known to us, only patterns. That wave you isolated began where the universe began and ends where the universe ends.

As you sever attachments and stop squandering your emotional energy, your perspective broadens and you come to see larger and larger patterns at work, patterns within patterns, your own pattern swirling in among them, in no way separate or apart, in no way greater or lesser. You back away from that single wave and you see tides and thermal dynamics, back away further and you see global currents and lunar influences, back away further and you see planetary and solar and historical influences, and so on. Back away further, beyond your notions of time and space, and only now do you begin to see that wave, to know it, and to know, as a living reality, that the wave is you and you are the wave."

She sighs and looks at me in exasperation.

"Oneness and unity aren't profound feelings or spiritual beliefs or altered states of consciousness, they're just plain old consciousness; unadorned, uncorrupted, uncontaminated. We don't have to attend lectures or read books or kneel before altars and wise men, we need only cleanse our perceptual faculties, rid ourselves of all egoic befuddlement, see what is and stop seeing what's not. No teaching or teacher or path or practice required, just simple honesty."

"I'm not sure I'm getting it," she says.

"Well, you will, I think. Here's a little exercise. I can't write down the notes from this conversation because my brain is doing a weird pulsing, buzzing thing, so I'm gonna hit the head and go settle into one of those lounge chairs by the pool while you write out the notes from everything we've just talked about."

"Uh, I don't think I can," she says.

"You minored in English," I say as I struggle to my feet. "You wanted to be a teacher."

"But I don't really understand any of it," she protests.

"Understand it later, write it down now," I say as I begin my pathetic journey. "You asked for this. You think being an editorial assistant to a mighty spiritual personage is all candlelight and pretty life lessons? This is a place where heads come loose."

She grins like I'm kidding and gets to work.

13. All is Truth

O ME, man of slack faith so long!
Standing aloof—denying portions so long;
Only aware today of compact, all-diffused truth;
Discovering today there is no lie, or form of lie,
  and can be none, but grows as inevitably upon itself
  as the truth does upon itself,
Or as any law of the earth,
  or any natural production of the earth does.

(This is curious, and may not be realized immediately—
  But it must be realized;
I feel in myself that I represent falsehoods equally with the rest,
And that the universe does.)

Where has fail'd a perfect return, indifferent of lies or the truth?
Is it upon the ground, or in water or fire? or in the spirit of man?
  or in the meat and blood?

Meditating among liars, and retreating sternly into myself,
  I see that there are really no liars or lies after all,
And nothing fails its perfect return—
  And that what are called lies are perfect returns,
And that each thing exactly represents itself,
  and what has preceded it,
And that the truth includes all, and is compact,
  just as much as space is compact,
And that there is no flaw or vacuum in the amount of the truth—
  but that all is truth without exception;
And henceforth I will go celebrate anything I see or am,
And sing and laugh, and deny nothing.

                                        —Walt Whitman

14. In the Kingdom of the Blind

> The spiritual journey does not consist of arriving at a new destination where a person gains what he did not have, or becomes what he is not. It consists in the dissipation of one's own ignorance concerning oneself and life, and the gradual growth of that understanding which begins the spiritual awakening.
>
> —*Aldous Huxley*

IN THE KINGDOM OF THE BLIND, the one-eyed man is a boob. He is a butterfly among caterpillars, a vampire among humans, a one-eyed fool in a land of no-eyed wisemen. He is not superior, not powerful, just out of place; a stranger in a strange land. Why does he linger? What should he do? Speak? Teach? Play wise? What can the one-eyed say to the blind-since-birth? Why say anything? What does he want for them or from them? The blind know nothing of eyes. They know nothing of sight, and those who think they know, know wrong. Why speak at all? Why should the sighted add his voice to the din of unsighted who claim to see, and who, unfettered by truth, are free to tell a better tale? Why undertake so futile and thankless a mission? The sighted might start out with an attitude of patience toward the skepticism of the unsighted, remembering that he himself was once in such a blind and doubly-blind condition, but tolerance soon wears thin. Indulging ego's need to feel intelligent and discriminating is wearisome and only serves to unmask the folly of altruistic motives.

Or so I can imagine. I am not motivated by altruism or results, so seeing Maya maintain her stranglehold on a blacked-out humanity doesn't rub me wrong. I work for the universe, for the books, so whatever serves them serves me.

✧

"Okay then," says Lisa a few minutes later, settling into the lounger next to mine with her notepad and pen, "so why do you think it happened? What was the point of crashing your motorcycle? You said that you knew in the first instant that it wouldn't be bad. Was that the point, then?"

I shake my head to clear it. Doesn't work.

"Whenever I wonder why something happened," I tell her, "I think first about the books. Does it somehow serve the books? In this case, spilling the bike and getting a little busted up, the answer is definitely yes."

"It is?"

"It is, and you showed me that."

"I did?"

"You offered to help me with the book, so I handed you the rough draft of a chapter about how the integrated state actually works, which is what I've been working on for the last few days. You weren't satisfied with what I had written so far, so you asked for an example and there it was, ripped from today's headlines. The accident was the perfect way of saying what I was trying to say in that rough draft. I hadn't even really thought about it until you asked for an example. See how this kind of builds on itself?"

She shakes her head no. I shake my own head again. I'm only putting this together as I say it, so I need my brain to stop pulsing/humming. It doesn't stop.

"Not only does the accident serve the book," I say, "but the *way* the accident serves the book serves the book."

She looks even more puzzled. I circle back.

"When you read those pages," I say, "what did you think?"

"It was good," she says. "A little dry. I could tell it was a draft."

"Right, it was a work in progress. That's how I figure out what I want to say and if it's worth saying. The writing itself is my part in the process. I do my part and the universe does its part. Okay?"

"Okay," she says.

"So I gave you those pages and you asked for an example, which brought the bike accident to mind and made me realize that it was actually a much more suitable way of expressing this knowledge. Everything I was trying to say in that rough draft was summed up right there in that first instant of the accident."

"Then why did you think the accident happened before that?"

"I'm not a kid anymore and shouldn't be riding a busted-up old Triumph across Mexico. That came through loud and clear. I was going to take the bike to Puerto Vallarta next week, but I think those days are behind me."

"Thank God," she says, "though I'm not sure that Pinto's much better. So you thought the accident was just a warning for you to stop riding old motorcycles in Mexico?"

"I really hadn't processed it yet. I just got back here and sat down a few minutes before you showed up," I answer. "Anyway, you came and asked about helping and here we are."

"So in a way," she says, "the motorcycle accident was like a happy coincidence."

"Yes, and in that same way, my life is just one long string of happy coincidences. A coincidence is an unplanned alignment of events, things happening in a way that seems planned, even though it's just an accident. In my case, I don't see the accident part, just the planned part, the alignment, the coherence. Not just now and then, but all the time, more certain than sunrise. So yes, it's a happy coincidence from the eyes-closed perspective, but from the eyes-open perspective, this alignment is everywhere, all the time. It's like I live suspended in a network of invisible lines, and even though I can't see them, I know they're there, and I've learned how I fit in with them. They're always there, and should the day come when they're not, I'm content to fall."

We sit quietly for a while. She writes. I slip into a funky haze.

✧

The afternoon eases into early evening. Lisa works on her notes and asks questions. I hover in a buzzy, semi-awake state, happy to watch the pool and the distant views and to pet Maya and to rise and fall on this wave of slow-motion thumping that starts in my head and radiates outward. Now and then Lisa asks a question that initiates a fresh dialogue, followed by a pause as she takes more notes.

"Is this how it always works?" she asks. "The writing? I mean the way you worked on that chapter you showed me?"

"Pretty much," I say. "I work on writing something for awhile and I almost get it right, but not quite, but that's about as far as I can take it. Then something happens, the exact right thing at the exact right time, and the scales fall away and the whole thing just resolves into clarity. The last thread of the fabric is woven miraculously into place and only then do you see the whole tapestry as a single, unified whole and you grok in fullness. That was always my experience with Spiritual Autolysis, too. A lot of work goes into building this huge pile of brush, but not until that final, mysterious little spark comes from some unexpected direction and sets the whole thing ablaze have you really mastered it. In Spiritual Autolysis, that blaze reduces an entire mountain of ignorance to ash. In the book, it purifies and brings things into focus and you're left with some good material."

"And that's what happened here?"

"That's what *is* happening here. I did my bit, wrote those pages, worked on it to understand what I was trying to say and why, and that's as far as I got. Then you played your role and showed me what I hadn't seen for myself, that the bike accident provided the perfect way of saying what I was trying to say. The piece slipped perfectly into place and the puzzle was solved. Using your notes, I'll start over and in a few hours I'll have the finished work as it was meant to be."

"Okay," she says, "I can see all that, but how is it still happening?"

"Because the story isn't just that the accident and our discussions will replace that chapter. The way in which this whole process has unfolded reveals a larger dimension of the process, which in turn provides an important and necessary contribution to the book."

"You're losing me a little. The accident provides that?"

"The accident captures and consolidates the themes I was trying to express in that chapter I gave you."

"I got that," she says. "And I played a role in all this?"

"You still are. You're doing your part, I'm doing my part, the universe is doing its part, and now the book will have what it needs; a clear and lively illustration of my experience of direct-knowing and of what I mean when I talk about the co-creative process and the universe laying the books out for me. What was just pages of flat, lifeless explanation will now be dynamic and personal with a dangerous motorcycle accident, my injuries and your touching concern, my drug abuse, our dialogue and, of course, the star of the show, the process itself. The books always find their way like that. The exact right thing at the exact right time. Not just the books, of course, everything, but we're looking at the books now."

"But how do you learn your part? How do you know what to do and what not to do? How do you know how the whole thing works?"

I wonder about that for a moment.

"It's like balance, I suppose. If someone with an undeveloped balance mechanism asked you how you can stand up and maintain your balance without falling over, you couldn't tell them. It's just something that's perfectly natural to you; it developed in your early years without your conscious effort or participation. It's so simple and obvious to you that you can't understand why someone would ask about it, but to that person with no balance mechanism, it seems impossibly complex, maybe even miraculous or magical."

She taps the table with her pen in mild exasperation.

"And this is something you're used to?" she asks dubiously. "The way this whole thing is happening, with the accident and me and everything?"

"This is how everything works in my world. This is my experience of the dreamstate. Not just once in a while, but all the time. This is how integrated functioning is, elegant and smooth and easy, no rough edges, no gaps or sharp corners. It's always like this. I do my part and the universe does its part and everything just flows into an effortless confluence. This is how the books always work. This is what it means for the universe to lay them out for me. This is that process being illustrated. I play a role in the creation of the books, but I don't think of myself as their author, just a participant in the larger process."

"Still," she says, "you have to admit that many of mankind's greatest accomplishments would never have been possible without the drive and personal vision of men and women of very strong and forceful egoic constitutions. People who know what they want and get it without a lot of waiting and wishing and observing. We owe our civilization to them."

"Such as it is. If you still want to make that assertion in a few years, after you've had a good look around, I'd be grateful to be shown what you see and discuss it with you. For now, you can make note of the distinction between egoic demanding and the process of co-creative allowing."

"So now this is for me?"

"Of course it's for you. From your perspective, the whole universe is for you. Who else?"

✧

"Do you have other examples?" Lisa asks a bit later. "Besides the motorcycle accident?"

"I can give you endless examples," I say. "It's like me asking you for examples of when you thought about something. A motorcycle accident is a big, flashy example. Buying the house is a great example; the way the first house I tried to buy was a set-up paving the way for the San Miguel house is just gorgeous. Getting Maya is a great example, especially my part in the process; the patience and investigation and trust, the slow build, the effortless unfolding and perfect timing, the wonderful result. Writing the books is a great ongoing example of this co-creative process at work. Central to all these examples and countless others I could provide is the element of trust, of patience, of non-meddling. I have no ego making demands and insisting on ways and means, so events unfold in ways ego could never imagine or achieve."

"Those are all good examples," she remarks, jotting them down.

"But it's not these big blowout examples that I find most interesting. Those are secondary to the experience of the integrated state itself; the subtlety and elegance of it, the developing and refining of the senses, the entire state of living and being, of which whizbang examples are just a part. And one of the best parts of the whole thing, though it's lost to me now, is the mindblowing personal renaissance of being out of the segregated state."

"I'm not sure I follow," she says.

"The best part of being out of a dungeon is being out of a dungeon.

After that, the rest is just gravy. You'll know it for yourself soon enough, once you've settled a bit and can look back from a bit more distance and grasp what you've really done."

"I look forward to getting some distance from it," she says tiredly, "but I doubt I'll ever understand all this like you do."

"You can if you want, if you take an interest. I have a natural interest in the dreamstate and the workings of delusion and the creative process."

"How does this involve the creative process?" she asks.

"That's what the whole thing really is—life, I mean—a free-flowing, dynamic, creative process. Sometimes you hear creative-type people describing the way they step aside and allow the muse or inspiration to flow through them, or the way Michelangelo described seeing the statue in the rock, and then just chipping away everything that wasn't the statue; seeing the rightness and removing the not-rightness. It's like that, but in everything, not just artistic works. Your whole life becomes a creative process, a nuanced allowing, an imperceptible tendency toward rightness and away from not-rightness, as refined and subtle as your mechanism of balance."

She's quiet for a minute as she makes her notes.

"Aren't there books written about all this?" she asks.

I forget where we are. "All what?"

"Well, manifestation, I guess."

"Oh, yeah, there are a bunch of books, human and channeled, about manifestation of desires, the use of affirmation, wishcraft, laws of attraction, that sort of thing. The books I'm familiar with are all written for the segregated, ego-clad being, like how-to books for children, but children don't need books about how to act like adults, they need to *become* adults. The books promise ways of manifesting your desires, getting everything you want, but that's really the least of it, more like a pleasant side-effect."

In fact, I'm having a few pleasant side-effects as I speak. I notice that I still have pain, but that it doesn't hurt. Curious. I have almost no experience with medication, but it seems very pleasant so far.

"As you're probably starting to see for yourself by now," I tell Lisa, "being a rich, beautiful rockstar in the segregated state is nothing. Getting to the integrated state is everything. No matter who you are or what you want, spiritually, creatively, or anything else, job one is always the same; Human Adulthood. Nothing comes before that. There's no argument to be made in favor of Human Childhood except the arguments of fear and ego."

I close one eye and it's nice so I close the other.

✧

Lisa says something. I open one eye, then the other.

"What?" I ask.

"You said it's there for everyone," she says, "that even in the ego-bound state we can still participate, but I don't really see that. Where is that happening?"

It takes me a minute to parse her question.

"Everywhere," I say. "Everyone has some direct experience of what I'm talking about, where they sense that there's more to life than meets the eye, that there's something going on that they don't see. Maybe they have good instincts or intuition. Maybe they read their horoscopes in the paper, or play with tarot cards or read tea leaves or chicken gizzards. A lot of people detect higher powers at work in their lives; they experience periods of flow where everything goes just right, they see coincidence and suspect it's more than that, they acknowledge some behind-the-scenes agency at work and they call it synchronicity or serendipity or providence or God's hand."

Lisa is writing down the examples as I come up with them.

"I'm kind of out of touch with the human experience," I continue, "but I think most people see things they call miracles or divine intervention, guardian angels helping out, prayers answered, deities or discarnate entities participating in their lives. They see events unfolding just so, auspiciously or fortuitously or whatever; the certain accident they miraculously avoided, the money that came at just the right time, how just the right person came into their life. God working in mysterious ways, that sort of thing. Do you not think so?"

"I don't know what I think," she says heavily. "It's all so much. How does someone even get started with all this?"

"Manifestation is the visible part of the integration iceberg; the gross level of integration that even the most eyes-tight-shut person can some-times detect. When people begin, *if* they begin, they begin by manifesting small, simple things; good parking spaces and luck with green lights, for example. It works and they think it's pretty nifty, but most people never go much further with it. They hit a roadblock when their bank accounts don't grow or their waistlines don't shrink and they dismiss the whole thing as, literally, wishful thinking. They don't engage the process or allow it to engage them. The tipping point comes, *if* it comes, with the realization that little successes like parking spots and traffic lights aren't the excep-tion, they're the rule, and when they don't come as requested, it just means you didn't understand the rule. But you can."

She sighs and makes notes.

"Some people go further with it," I say. "They read some books, learn to see the process, understand it, own it. They merge into the process, and, to some degree, learn to put these forces to work in their lives. That's nice, but they're still cheating themselves, like working in the mailroom of a company and swiping office supplies, never realizing that they own the company. Something like that."

"I'm not sure I understand this at all," she moans as she writes.

"Understanding it conceptually doesn't matter much." I look at the cool blue water of the pool in front of us. "You learn to swim by jumping into the water and swimming, not by sitting in a classroom studying aqua-dynamic theory. Practical application is what matters, and you're already in the pool, so to speak. The rest takes care of itself through natural processes of experimentation and observation and play, just like you developed your balance as a toddler. You weren't born with a finely-tuned balance mecha-nism; it developed over time as you got up and started using it."

A pain shoots up from my left knee and I make an unmanly chirp.

"Are you okay?" she asks, getting up. "Can I get you anything?"

"I'm fine, thanks," I say, and for the most part it's true. My body is happy. All the hurt areas feel pretty happy, and the unhurt areas all seem happy too. Nice pills. They're not making me groggy and my brain seems to work. I've sometimes thought that, after the books are done, it might be interesting to get addicted to something to see what that's like, but I probably won't. I have a lot of dumb ideas about things to do after the books. Probably I'll just find some way to keep writing.

Lisa sets fresh drinks on the table between us. She settles back into her lounger.

"Where were we?" she asks.

"You're the one with the notes."

"Okay," she says, consulting them. "How would all this apply to someone in my situation? Where would someone like me actually begin?"

"Your thoughts and emotions determine your dreamstate reality. That's where you start. From there it's just a matter of simplifying the equation and eventually seeing that your thoughts and emotions *are* your dream-state. It's all just consciousness, *you* are just consciousness. There is nothing else. Once that goes from thought-level concept to full-immersion aware-ness, you naturally merge with the currents instead of being tossed about by them."

She groans as she writes. I can see this is very challenging material for her. It's not so long ago that she would have scorned such talk.

"Okay," she says, "I'd agree that probably everyone has some experience like what you're describing, or some religious or mystical explanation for things like that. I always just thought of it as serendipity, I guess."

"So you never prayed for anything?"

"Prayed? Well, yes, I've prayed. I prayed for my babies to be healthy and whole. I prayed to pass the bar. Probably a few other things. And I guess those prayers were answered. Is that your point?"

"Not really. From your perspective, your prayers were answered, or, at least, events transpired as you prayed they would. I assume you don't really believe your children were healthy and you passed the bar because you prayed, do you?"

She shrugs. "Couldn't hurt," she says with a smile.

"Exactly," I say, "that's probably how most people see it. They pray only when it's most important. They make deals. No atheists in foxholes, as they say. But then, when the crisis is over, so is their urgent pleading with the unseen whatever to which they had addressed themselves."

"The unseen whatever?"

"God, higher self, angels, Jesus, Allah, Buddha, totems, ancestors, whatever. I might also say that even if your babies hadn't been healthy and you hadn't passed the bar, your prayers would still have been answered."

She seems displeased by that.

"That doesn't make any sense," she says tersely.

"Not from the segregated perspective, but from the integrated perspective it's just obvious. There's no alternative. We think miracles happen and prayers are answered only when it's something good; when it's in line with our hopes and desires which, in Human Children, are always fear-based. We don't acknowledge the same forces equally at work when the results are not in line with our hopes and desires. We're very selective in our perceptions. Good luck, bad luck, it's all the same; the ebb and flow of tides, it just gets interpreted differently."

She writes but doesn't comment. I try a different approach.

"An ego-clad, fear-based being might use prayer or divination or manifestation to get the things they want; health, love, career, money, family, vanity, the usual suspects. Once freed from egoic constraints, however, all such fear-driven wanting disappears and desire becomes very organic and non-specific. My prayer, if I were to utter one, might be for whatever's best, or that I should proceed without error, something like that."

She writes. I look at my toes and wiggle them. I get a little skeezed out if I think about toes for too long, so I'm glad when she interrupts with another question.

"You didn't pray to get your grandfather's house?" she asks. "Or the first one you tried to buy?"

"No. I expressed intent through desire and action, but I never prayed in the sense you mean, like wanting something and asking for it. Even that is symptomatic of the distrustful, segregated mindset. The Integrated State is seamless; it's without all these artificial boundaries and distinctions, such as one entity asking for something and another granting it. I want what's best and I trust the universe, not my little brain, to be the judge of what's best and how best to make it happen. If I had locked my sights on that first house, decided I wanted it and became insistent, I would have derailed the process, but I was open and observant and sensitive and came away with a much better result than I could have imagined or orchestrated."

"You might not be so calm and cool about it if it was your child you were worried about instead of a house."

"If I was claiming to be very strong in my beliefs, you'd be correct, but this isn't how I believe things work, it's how I *see* they work. When your eyes are open, you see everything and belief becomes irrelevant and forgotten. You have trouble with that because you don't know your eyes are closed; you think they're open, and you naturally assume that you and I are in the same condition."

"Believe me," she says, "I know we're not."

"You *believe* we're not in the same condition, but you don't *see* it. You're very close, though, you'll see soon enough. My point is that what people see in these occasional glimpses, by all these various names and explanations, is this ocean of being working in tireless, errorless perfection. That's what the dreamstate is, that's what we are, that's what consciousness is. You are nothing but consciousness, everything that tells you more than that is like a built-up crust of hard-packed emotional energy that has formed around you like a shell. All true growth and development is first and foremost a process of chopping away this crust. Ego sends us searching in the direction of learning, of becoming more and adding on to ourselves, but everything we claim to seek lies in the opposite direction; of unlearning, of letting go, of reducing. We think the goal is to become someone, but the universe can only be ours when we become no one."

She groans again.

15. Manifest Destiny

> I ask you only to stop imagining that you were born,
> have parents, are a body, will die and so on. Just try,
> make a beginning — it is not as hard as you think.
>
> –*Nisargadatta Maharaj*

THE SETTING SUN TURNS THE lake a fiery orange and streaks the mountains with vertical sidecast shadows. Lisa sets out a few simple food items, but the meds make everything taste hinky so I don't eat. We relax and let the conversation wander pleasantly off-track for awhile. Eventually, she veers us back into it.

"You're saying you can have anything you want?" she asks as she reads through her recent notes. "Is that right? Like everything is governed by some kind of magical energy and if you can tap into it—"

"Yes and no," I interrupt. "It's not so much that someone well established in the Integrated State can have what they want, but that their wants and needs are in natural harmony with their dreamstate circumstances. In other words, it's not that I can have anything I want, like I wiggle my nose and it appears, it's also that I wouldn't want anything I couldn't have. I can't manifest a pile of money or a speedboat or a bowl of fishhead soup because I have no authentic desire for those things. The difference between authentic and inauthentic desire is central to all this, but most people are completely cut off from their authentic desires."

"Cut off by what?"

"Ego is always the bad guy. Compare your own desires from a few years ago to your desires now. What kind of things did you want? To be a partner in a law firm? To drive a Lexus? To have more money? A bigger house? A tighter butt?"

"That sounds familiar," she says sheepishly.

"And where are those desires now?"

"I don't know. Just gone, I guess."

"Naturally, just gone. That's the eliminative process at work. You didn't have to struggle with each and every little bit of egoic material, you just struggled to take a difficult step and, in moving forward, you left a huge mass of coagulated debris behind. Now you're starting to discover your authentic desires, and they don't have anything to do with getting more stuff or increasing your status or improving your image. Your authentic desires won't have anything to do with projecting an imagined self into the world, with grooming the reflection you cast in the eyes of others. All forms of adornment and ostentation will lose their appeal and even become distasteful, and a roofless old Ford Pinto will start looking much more comfortable than a shiny new Lexus."

There's another pleasant lull before she looks to see if I have more. I return to her question about getting everything I want.

"Something like manifestation of authentic desires is a little hard to explain because the Integrated State is outside the conceptual framework of the Segregated State. Am I bending to fit the universe or is it bending to fit me? The question doesn't survive translation. The distinction between me and not-me has no meaning. The constraints of time and space and causality and duality have no counterparts in the Integrated State." My knee sends up a sharp message. "Speaking of getting what I want, can you hand me my pills?"

She gets the bottle out of my bag and reads the label.

"Oh Lord," she says, seeing what the meds are. "This is strong stuff, people get addicted to this. Are you not telling me something?"

"Did I tell you the part about handing them to me?"

She reads the warnings on the bottle. She starts passing them over to me, then pulls back.

"So, you want these pills?" she asks.

"Was I speaking in tongues?"

She mulls it over.

"Is your desire authentic?" she asks with a sly grin.

"Very," I assure her.

"So why don't you manifest them?"

"I did," I reply, "I manifested a busted-up Ford Pinto so I could manifest my busted-up ass over to the pharmacy where I manifested a method of payment, then they manifested a bottle of pills which you just manifested from the bag. Whole lotta manifestin' goin' on."

She scowls.

"That doesn't sound very mystical."

"I didn't say it was. Maybe you have some screwy notions."

She mulls some more, still holding my pills.

"But you can't manifest the pills these last few feet?"

"Can't I?"

She shakes the bottle at me.

"I can withhold them," she says.

"Can you?"

This is a playful exchange. She's exploring ideas, and I'm trying to help her see what's there to be seen.

"But," she says, "if I don't give them to you, what then?"

"What then what?"

I like this therapeutic technique of turning every question back on the questioner. I should've thought of it years ago—a lazy man's Socratic method.

"Well, then you're in pain and you're not getting what you want."

"Yes?"

"But that contradicts what you're saying."

"Does it?"

"Doesn't it?"

"Not really. There's no rule that says I can't be in pain, or that I have to get whatever I want, or that we can't sit here and explore these ideas this way. Something so bizarrely unlikely as those pills not making it these last few feet wouldn't happen without a clear reason, though; and certainly not just whimsically or randomly. Anyway, we're not in a situation like that. You're not going to do what you're saying."

"But I *could*," she says.

"Could you?"

She mulls some more and hands the bottle to me.

"Like I said," I say, pausing to swallow some pills, "it's not voodoo or mysticism or special powers. Those are segregated ways of explaining phenomenon that are perfectly normal and natural from the integrated perspective."

"Oh boy," she moans, "what have I gotten myself into?"

I shrug.

"Your life," I say.

✧

Speaking with Lisa is an interesting experience at this stage. I can see her vacillating between intellect and heart, between how she thinks she should be and how she wants to be and, perhaps, wants *not* to be. She's used to projecting a whole troupe of complex characters—woman, mother, wife, boss, attorney, friend, etc—all strong and confident and well-grounded, and she's not used to this new role where she's weak and ignorant and helpless as an infant. No one is used to it, and the more rigidly fixed we were in our previous life, the more difficult our transition to our new life will be.

This conversation we're having right now isn't really intended to teach her anything. I don't expect her to break her addiction to thought and logic overnight. I'm just trying to help her stretch out and soften up, give her a chance to adjust to her new environment, maybe show her some pretty new ideas she can play with. Like any newborn, she has muscles she's never used, ranges of motion she has yet to explore, and senses that she will need to develop. Not surprisingly, the most amazing discovery of someone newly liberated from a lifetime of suffocating bondage is the absence of suffocating bondage. She has recently emerged from a three-year journey through the birth canal, completing her death/rebirth transition from womb to world, and the freedom she's just beginning to discover can be a very scary thing.

✧

"Are you familiar with the eighty-twenty rule?" I ask her.

"Twenty percent of the effort accomplishes eighty percent of the work?"

"And vice versa. Well that's the deal here, too. Eighty percent of this transition you're in can be accomplished with a relatively small amount of effort. All you have to do is get past the idea that you're a human being on planet Earth. Flush that belief out of your system and a huge mass of backed-up mental and emotional sewage automatically gets flushed out with it."

"Oh," she laughs, "just like that, huh? Just get over my peculiar little notion that I'm a human being on planet Earth?"

"Well, I didn't say it was nothing. It takes some honest effort, and it takes some time to process the ramifications. Why, does that seem like a big thing?"

"Are you kidding?" she asks.

"It *is* a big thing?"

She's giving me a funny look.

"I can't tell if you're kidding," she says.

"Okay," I say, "I guess it sounds like a big thing, but it's really just one simple tweak in your thinking. Once you make this adjustment, you'll be far ahead of most of the respected experts in the field of human development and spirituality, totally off their maps, and you'll have taken an enormous step forward in your own process."

I'm still getting the funny look.

"Once I realize that I'm not a human being on planet Earth?" she asks.

"I take it you think you are."

"Uh, yeah, kinda."

"Well yes, of course you do," I say, "I'm just suggesting you take another look at it. Think about it. No offense, but most people don't really think. They think they think, but they'll really go to any lengths to avoid it, and if they can't avoid it, they quickly discover that it's not something they've done before."

The funny look is looking less funny.

"Now you're telling me I don't know how to think, but that I shouldn't be offended?"

"Yeah, is that weird too?"

She pauses to select her words.

"Are you completely out of touch?" she asks.

"Define 'completely.'"

She takes a deep breath and lets it out.

"You know, Jed," she says, "until recently, a scowl from the girl at the coffee shop could throw off my whole morning. I'd put on makeup and brush my hair to go out to the mailbox. I'm trying to think in terms of small steps here."

"So revisiting the assumption that you're a human being living on planet Earth would be, like, a really big step?"

She takes another pause.

"Can I ask you something?"

"Sure."

"How long has it been since you were, you know, normal?"

"You mean, like, a regular person?" I ask.

"Yes."

"I don't know," I say. "Twenty some-odd years, I guess. If ever."

"Jed, I wouldn't presume to—"

"Presume away."

"Well, you say that you're sort of fading out of existence, right? Getting more and more out of touch?"

"Something like that."

"Is it possible that your memory of what it's like to be a normal person is no longer very clear?"

"Thou presumest rightly," I agree, "but I'm still not sure this is as big a deal as you're making out. Let's use the movie *The Matrix* to map this out. My outside-the-matrix character is telling your inside-the-matrix character what the deal is; that you're living a fictional life as a fictional being in a fictional universe. I'm not saying you should break out of the matrix, just that you can have an unimaginably better experience of your existence within it if you understand the wholly fictitious nature of it. Most people, of course, have no idea, or have only a conceptual grasp."

"But *The Matrix* is just a movie," she says.

"And this is just the dreamstate," I reply. "The movie *The Matrix* is solipsism, the cogito, Plato's cave, brain-in-a-vat theory and a great popcorn flick all rolled into one. It's the death knell of philosophy and science and religion. Nothing is what you think it is, nor is it not. That's the dreamstate."

"This sounds familiar," she says. "Are there any spiritual or religious groups who believe they're not human beings on Earth?"

"Sure," I say, "they're called cults and we tend to ignore them until they start racking up a body count. I'm not encouraging you to believe you're *not* a human on Earth, only to question your belief that you are."

"The difference is—"

"Belief. It's about belief. All beliefs serve as self-limitations and they're all false."

"But if I'm not a human being on planet Earth, what am I?"

"You're asking me?"

"Uh, yes."

"Well, to me, you're a minor character in my dramatic dreamscape. A semi-coherent energetic pattern making a brief appearance on the stage of my awareness. A bit player whose timely appearance meshes precisely with current themes."

"Aww," she grins, "I bet you say that to all the girls."

I laugh. She chews on her bottom lip as she stares at me.

"This isn't the pills talking?"

"I don't know. Sounds like me."

"Yeah."

We sit quietly for a few minutes. I can feel her agitation.

"You should watch *The Matrix* again," I suggest. "Lots of useful stuff there. Remember when Neo was unplugged from the matrix? He asks why his eyes hurt, and Morpheus answers—"

Lisa provides the line.

"—because you've never used them before."

"Yes," I say. "Welcome to the desert of the real."

She laughs uncomfortably.

"In the movie," I continue, "Neo is rejecting one layer of delusion in exchange for another, just as the inhabitants of Plato's cave are trading the illusion of the shadows on the wall for the broader illusion of the cave itself.

In *The Matrix*, when someone is freed, they move into the broader cavelike reality of underground ships and caverns and Zion and, as the movie portrays, it can seem like a very bad bargain. Someone might wish to re-enter a state of comfortable delusion rather than undergo the rigors and hardships of cave life. They might want to crawl back into the womb."

"You can't do that," she says quietly.

"No, I don't think so," I say, "Are you okay?"

"Yes, please continue. This is interesting."

"You sure?"

"I'm starting to understand some things better," she says. "I'm starting to kind of see myself in this metaphor."

"Good, otherwise it's just a movie."

"That's what I thought it was," she says.

"It's a tool," I say, "a map on which we can plot our journey, or one leg of it. If the Neo character were really trying to awaken *from* the dreamstate, he wouldn't have accepted the subterranean world of Morpheus and Zion and freedom-fighter drama so easily. He'd have recognized it as merely another layer of delusion and kept going."

"Further," she says.

"Exactly, always further. Layers on top of layers, turtles on top of turtles. Neo never found out how deep the rabbit hole goes, he just went down one level, and having escaped from the matrix, he is now more firmly in the grasp of delusion than ever. He knows the matrix is an artificial reality, but he thinks he's out of it, so he's much more effectively impris-oned than before. He misinterprets his new state as freedom, but it is only a more convincing illusion of freedom."

"And how does this apply to me?"

"This is your situation."

She checks her notes.

"Now I'm more firmly in the grip of delusion than ever? Meaning?"

"Meaning you've spent your discontent. You fired your rockets and here you are."

She frowns.

"This isn't negative," I say, "this is good. You may not be happy and well-adjusted yet, but you're definitely in the right place. You got out of the place where you didn't want to be, where you'd rather die than stay, and now you're awaking within the dreamstate."

"But not from it?"

"No, your discontent wasn't of that nature. You're like Neo."

"And you're like Morpheus?"

I laugh.

"Only in the tourguide sense," I say. "I'm showing you around a bit, explaining where you are and how things work. You have some groovy new abilities you can play with and learn about and get good at."

"I still can't imagine not believing I'm a human being on—"

"No one can ever imagine the next step until they've taken it. Every barrier seems impassable until the time comes when all other choices have dissolved and it's forward or perish. Could you have imagined a year ago what you've accomplished now?"

She laughs at the idea.

"No," she says.

"You take one step, which is always an act of destruction, then you pause, rest, recuperate, reflect, maybe even think you're done, and then the next step starts to appear and the option of not taking it starts to disappear. You've been through this once, so I assume you recognize what I'm saying."

She nods slightly, head bowed to her notes.

"So now I'm describing the next step, and it's a doozie, almost of the same transformational magnitude as the one you've taken, but much less difficult. It's only natural that it looks impossible to you, but gradually, the impossibility will be in *not* taking this step."

She seems discouraged.

"No one traipses merrily along through this journey, Lisa. There is no bravery here, and no one takes a step out of desire. You go forward when you can't stay where you are. That's the process. That's how you got this far and that's how you'll keep going, if you do."

She writes, head down, quiet.

16. Actor Without a Role

It is not that you must be free from fear. The moment you try
to free yourself from fear, you create a resistance against fear.
Resistance in any form doesn't end fear. What is needed rather
than running away or controlling or suppressing or any other
resistance is understanding fear; that means watch it; learn
about it; come directly into contact with it.

–J. Krishnamurti

A WEEK OR TWO LATER I am on the mend and off the meds. I'm
back to my routine of dog walking and strolling through town and
visiting Frank in the evening for a nightcap. I spend most of my time at
my work table, and Lisa spends several hours a day helping me and has
replaced one of the local retirees who had been assisting me but who was
made uncomfortable by the material and stopped coming.

"Can I ask you about Brett?" Lisa asks.

"What would you like to know?"

"I don't know, where'd she live? Where was the farm?"

"Virginia, in the Shenandoah Valley. I liked going down there because
it's beautiful driving, especially at night. Put on some good music, take
your time, see where you are. Like a magic carpet ride. *Very* pleasant."

"What did she look like?"

"Redhead. Shoulder-length hair always tied back. Sturdy, strong, not
heavy, naturally pretty. She usually wore jeans, a denim shirt not tucked in
and cowboy boots." I look at Lisa over the tops of my reading glasses.
"Why?"

"Just wondering. How old was she?"

"Like you, maybe a few years older. Forty?"

She's silent for a few minutes. I go back to my work.

"And she had a horse farm?" Lisa asks.

"Brett?"

"Yes."

"I suppose that's what it was. She had horses and dogs and cats, lots of land, a lake, a barn, the big indoor riding arena."

"Did she have people living there? Like students on the premises?"

"Uh, no, she kept all that confined to these monthly Sunday meetings. Doubled up with a Saturday meeting a few times when I was there, but that was an exception. Other than when the people were there, the students, I don't think she had a thought for anything spiritual. It wasn't part of her life. She wasn't writing a book, didn't give talks or interviews, didn't travel, she just had the group that came on those Sundays. Dr. Kim seemed to be the one who made everything happen, not Brett. I think she just put up with it."

"Family?"

"A daughter and a granddaughter that I know of. Our biographies were never really exchanged."

After another long pause she asks another question.

"Did she seem happy?"

✧

It occurs to me that Lisa might be looking at Brett as a role model, like someone she can look up to from her new and shifting vantage. She wonders if she can look to Brett to get an idea of where she herself is heading, or should be heading. I have no confidence in my ability to judge what's going on inside people, but it seems both clear and understandable that Lisa would want to spot a familiar face on the distant shore and that she might be forming an image of Brett in her mind to fill that need. Whether that's good or bad I don't know, but I do know that Lisa is not in the process of becoming what Brett became. Brett was awake *from* the dreamstate, which means she had moved from self to no-self, like dying without dropping the body. Lisa is awakening into Human Adulthood, which is the move from segregated to integrated self. It's huge, but it's about transition with*in* the dreamstate, not transitioning *out* of it. Brett made the same transition to adulthood but, as with me, it was just the first leg of a longer journey.

In her proof-reading of book notes, Lisa has developed an affinity for anything related to Brett, so I print off a few pages she hasn't seen and pass them over to her, hoping that she'll understand the subject matter and see how it applies to her panicky desire to grab onto someone or something.

✧

"Is this like satsang?" asks one girl, a newcomer.

"I ain't exactly sure what a satsang is," replies Brett, and a general discussion opens up with most everyone relating their satsang experiences. There are upward of forty people in the bleachers tonight, all of whom seem to have an opinion to express or an experience to share on the subject of satsang. Brett lets them go on for several minutes about tranquility, deep awareness, shared silence, shakti, and how evolved and elevated and enlightened various teachers were or weren't before she steps back in.

"Okay, okay, everyone settle down now. I think I got the idea, and to answer the original question, no, this ain't that. Makes me sad to hear y'all talk like that, about profound experiences and highly evolved teachers and whatnot. Seems like we can't make half an inch of progress around here. Let me say it again; I got no feelin' for all this silence, peace and tranquility business, and ain't nobody is special. Just like Mr. McKenna told ya, we're all here together in a leaky boat on a shoreless sea. Ain't no better or worse among us. No one's higher or lower, ahead or behind; we're all in the same damn boat with the same damn view. The storm is ragin' and the clock is tickin'. We don't know where we are—or who, what, why, when or how for that matter—and anyone says otherwise is talkin' out their ass. This boat is full of ass-talkers. They like to make it seem like we're all in this boat together, but the fact you gotta learn is that we are each of us alone. Black sky and black water all around and the closest thing to solid land is this little ship which, by the way, is leaking like a rusty bucket. It might go down in fifty years or five minutes, no way of knowin' when, but it will go down and that's a fact."

That shuts them up.

"This sure isn't like any satsang I've ever been to," whispers a gaunt man up front, and there's some restrained laughter. Brett laughs too.

"Y'all are in this trance," continues Brett, "and you come here askin' me to help snap you out of it. I can't help you, though. You gotta get to where you want it enough to do it yourselves, but that ain't easy cuz you got yourselves lulled into this damn complacency which sucks all the urgency out of your plight. It's like a coping mechanism. Y'all know what a *coping mechanism* is? It's like a tranquilizer. We keep ourselves strung out on tranquilizers all the time, but if you come here you're sayin' you want to kick that habit. We're all in the hands of a loving God, that's one kind of tranquilizer we like to swallow. Means you can just sit back and pass the time. Be nice and say you're sorry when you done wrong and your lovin' God won't cook your ass. Reincarnation is another pill that goes down easy. We're coming back again and again so we got all the time in the world. We're subject to a bunch of karma-dharma dipsy-doodle and we just gotta be good little sheep; no pressure, no urgency, nothing to do but lay low and ride it out. Or maybe we're all divine beings of light and all we gotta do is sparkle and shine and live a pretty life, play nice and not kick up a fuss."

She kicks up a spray of sand.

"Y'all startin' to see a theme emergin' here? Be nice, be quiet, be good, don't ask questions, don't use your minds, don't make a ruckus—sound familiar? That's what all this satsang talk sounds like to me, like you start feelin' a little agitated so you need a fix, got to get some more tranquility, like that's the purpose of these teachers and gurus you keep talkin' about, they keep you mellow, keep you doped up so you don't gotta face your situation. Sounds like the exact opposite of wakin' up to me."

Some heads nod, some shake, no one speaks. Most of them know what happens if they try to assert their beliefs as facts, or mistake the popularity of a belief for the probability of it being true. Brett lights into that kind of flabby talk like a mad mama bear.

Now she takes it up a notch.

"But here we are on this storm-toss'd ship, and if someone starts tellin' me everything's all glorious and divine so I should just sit down and shut up, be cool, be mellow, close my eyes and clear my mind, I'm *gonna* kick up some fuss. I'm gonna ask that person to make some serious sense, and

I'm gonna wanna see some evidence. I ain't got no time for ass-talkers with all their dainty ideas about heavenly booty. I don't wanna hear a lot of fancy sermons and poems and clever guesswork, I want some facts. Anyone sayin' they know somethin' is sayin' they got the most precious commodity to be found on such a ship, they got some *knowledge*, and if they say they got it, I'm gonna wanna see it, and if they can't produce it, I'm gonna take that hard and I'm gonna wanna chuck 'em outta my damn boat, maybe do some keel-haulin'. Y'all know what *keel-haulin'* is? It means death to the ass-talkers. They ever tell you that in your little singsang circle-jerks?"

Nervous laughter ripples through the bleachers.

"But they ain't got no knowledge," she continues, "that's what I learned in my life, that's what I know that y'all don't. There ain't no knowledge to be had. All they got is tranquilizers, which is all most folks want anyway. This little ship we're talkin' about is full of every kind of crafty drug pusher sellin' every kind of painkiller you can imagine, and business is always good because we're all a bunch of strung out junkies lookin' for our next fix. Y'all hear me in the back row? We gotta stay doped up. We're all just lookin' for a pill we can swallow, something that'll take the edge off, dull the senses, and make everything look all soft and rosy all the time. Once you're hooked, it's damn tough to kick. Self-deceit is the hardest habit to break cuz it tells us we ain't self-deceived."

She pauses and drinks.

"So how do we break this habit," asks the girl who started this with her satsang question.

"Easy," Brett answers. "You just gotta do two things. First, you gotta know you're hooked. I don't mean know it like you know it now, like an idea you heard someone say. I mean you gotta know it complete, like in every fiber of your being, like every thought is darkened by it, like every sight and taste and smell is poisoned by it. You gotta know it like a fiery pain. Y'all know what *pain* is?"

No one is laughing now.

"Then, once you get to that point," she says as she uses the heel of her boot to draw a deep line in the sand between herself and the bleachers, "the next thing you do is draw a line, just like Mr. McKenna keeps tellin' you.

That's how it's gotta happen. You draw a line. You make a stand. You say, that's it, I've had enough. This is as far as I go till this shit starts makin' some sense. And you mean it with your whole life and being. You put it all on that line. Until you do that, you ain't done nothin'. You're just goin' along to get along."

✧

Lisa sets down the pages and rubs her temples and sits quietly for a few minutes before speaking.

"Is that right? About crossing the line?"

I don't answer her question immediately. People around me get used to my silences. The answer will be along shortly and I may or may not share it. It's not the correct answer that eludes me, but the handling of it, though it's not up to me to act as arbiter of what's good and bad for others. I patiently observe. I act when I see what to do, and I don't when I don't.

The situation here is that Brett was a zero-tolerance anti-bullshit hardliner and Lisa is transitioning into Human Adulthood. The misconception lies with Lisa who has started to identify with Brett, to look at her as a beacon of light in the darkness. Understandable, but probably not wise.

After a few minutes during which my mind wanders completely away from Lisa's question, I look over to see her patiently watching me and I remember her question about crossing Brett's line in the sand. I don't struggle to concoct a reply. Often, the right answer is full disclosure. Just lay it all out where it can be seen and let people do what they want with it. Lisa is drowning. She's trying to grab onto something and she sees Brett. Who am I to withhold? Let her have whatever she wants. That's the answer.

✧

Usually, when we think of someone drawing a line, making their stand, we think they're committing themselves to an all-or-nothing battle; here and now, on this spot, live or die. That's the kind of ultimatum Brett was describing. She made it sound like a fight, like put up yer dukes, but it's really not. It's the end of fighting, the end of a lifelong struggle. Drawing this line doesn't mean battlestations, red alert, defcon one and all that. It's not that kind of battle. It means we have to lower our shields, not raise them. An objective observer might look at the vast majority of spiritual seekers today and classify them as spiritually self-lobotomized. They set out to find life and discover truth, and wind up sitting in a dark room repeating a meaningless syllable, eyes closed, brain silenced, convinced that they're actually making a great journey. That's how easily and effectively we are undone, and it's because the enemy is within, running the show, redeploying all of our mental and emotional resources against us. Instead of adopting a warlike posture, we must, counter-intuitively, lower our shields and defenses. This seems confusing until we understand that we are both the protagonist and the antagonist in this conflict, both attacker and defender. This is the paradoxical nature of the struggle. We can't win by fighting. The very thing that fights, that resists, is the thing we seek to overthrow. Only by vanquishing ego can we prevail. Only in surrender can we find victory. This is the part so few get, and fewer get beyond. This is the part where everything starts sounding all sagely or zenny or Orwellian, but that can't be helped. If you want to say that all religions and spiritual teachings share a core truth, it can only be this: Surrender is victory.

And that's what I tell Lisa. She's quiet for a long moment.

"Does this apply to me?" she asks.

"You spent three painful years fighting against the process. Only when you stopped fighting did you start winning. You may not see it clearly yet—"

"I'm starting to. I really am. This is all so new."

"What you've gone through was a big deal, like a dam bursting. Such an event requires a long, slow build-up as a hardened and reinforced structure slowly succumbs to forces that must eventually prevail. The release, when it finally comes, is going to be violent and tumultuous and destructive, but the dam created an unnatural imbalance and it had to give way sooner or later. After the dam bursts, the built-up pressures are expended, the waters settle, equilibrium is restored and everything returns to its natural, harmonious, balanced state. Maybe you feel bad about the villages and crops that got decimated or the man-made lake that got drained, but whatever relied on the imbalance provided by this unnatural obstruction was always in peril; doomed from the start."

"Then why don't we see it happening more often?"

"These dams are very strong and generally outlive their builders. Most people manage to keep energetically reinforcing this artificial obstruction their entire lives and to die before it gives way. You didn't."

"So I drew this line? I did that?"

"Of course. At the level of awakening within the dreamstate, you've been through this process. You thought of it as a psychotic break when your son said he wanted to be like your husband and you snapped and grabbed Maggie and left. That was the long-awaited dam burst. The end of one thing and the beginning of another."

"It seems like a total mental breakdown. It's hard to think of that as some sort of spiritual victory."

"It's not *some* sort, it's the *only* sort."

"Hard to believe."

"That's because the waters haven't settled yet. You're still seeing the cataclysm, the fall-out, the collateral damage. When everything settles, when *you* settle, you'll see this new landscape and reckon it an earthly paradise compared to what it was."

"It all seems so cruel."

"I know it looks that way, but when you look at the larger forces at work, what seems cruel is revealed as the natural order of things, as balance being restored. People want desperately not to go through what you've gone through. Everyone wants to maintain their state of radical imbalance, all their energy and lifeforce held to one side of this artificial barrier, rather than undergo this personal apocalypse. Most people manage to hold the waters back their entire lives, but you didn't, so now you get a different kind of life."

"Lucky me," she mumbles.

"Lucky you," I agree.

✧

"Brett was fond of pointing out that there are no levels of advancement in this regard. Death and rebirth is a very specific event, not one that is gradual over many years. She said that there are no beginner, intermediate or advanced levels, and she was right. It all comes back to surrender, which follows naturally from seeing what is, rather than faith or belief which are how we muddle along when we don't see. That's a message that bears a lot of repeating, or so it seemed to Brett. And to me. You get a lot of people approaching spirituality like they know something, like they're pretty far along, and they don't realize that there is no such thing as pretty far along. You've either crossed the line or you haven't. You're either in the process or you're not. Knowledge, understanding, scholarship, experience, none of it means anything."

"She sounds like a very strong woman."

"Brett?"

"Yes."

I consider.

"No?" she asks.

"It misses the mark," I say. "The world is full of strong women. You're a strong woman, your mother was a strong woman. If you call someone like Brett strong or weak, start applying attributes, you've already missed the one thing worth knowing about her. When you get past the surface of Brett to the part that was worth knowing about, there's nothing there. That's what all this is about. The rest is costume."

"And that's true of you too?"

"It's true of everyone."

✧

Lisa has no precedent for what's happening to her and, more importantly, she has no precedent for becoming something for which she has no precedent. Never before, in all her many personal and professional accomplishments, has she been in a situation where she couldn't see what she was doing by looking at thousands or millions of others who had done it before her. I'm only figuring it out now, as I watch her, but that's what I'm coming up with and I'm reasonably sure I'm right. She's starting to sense the broader dimensions of her aloneness.

Lisa has no idea where her life is going. It must be far more traumatic and unnerving than she's letting on, as if she woke up in the middle of the night and ran away from her tribe into self-exile, and now it's the next morning and she's wandering around in the wilderness, lost, alone for the first time, with no way to know what direction is best or how fast to go. I'm only picking up on it now as she tries to build up an image of Brett and I ask myself why she has this interest in a woman she never knew and never would. Lisa doesn't know who to be now that she can no longer be who she was. She's an actor without a character to play. She doesn't know how to dress, how to eat, how to act, what to say, what to do. She doesn't even know what her motivation is.

Good for her.

17. A Literate Ignoramus

The books we need are the kind that act upon us like a misfortune, that make us suffer like the death of someone we love more than ourselves, that make us feel as though we were on the verge of suicide, or lost in a forest remote from all human habitation — a book should serve as an axe for the frozen sea within us.

—Franz Kafka

I WISH I COULD HAVE met her," says Lisa, putting some Brett pages down, "though I guess she wasn't the sympathetic type."

"She was very different when she wasn't in front of her group," I say, "less fiery, less accent, nicer; definitely preferred animals to people. Whether she would have gone hard or easy on you I don't know."

"Why would she have gone hard on me?"

"For your own good. T'were best done quickly, like pulling a tooth. Brett might have felt the kindest thing would be to take a lash to you, keep you from dawdling and making things harder than they have to be."

"Am I dawdling? I seem to be lying around a lot. It feels like I should be doing something. Doing more."

"There's a natural pacing to things. If you get too scared or too smart and start messing around, you'll probably just foul yourself up. You've released the tiller, don't panic and try to grab it back. Take it easy on yourself, all is well."

She sighs.

"I don't know what to do next. I feel like, I don't know, like I have to be *doing* something."

"Your old relationship to time has been destroyed. You should take some time to think about that, to think about time, your time. How you spend your days and weeks and years, what they are to you and what you want from them."

"That's totally outside my way of thinking," she says. "My whole life has been a madhouse of things needing to get done right away. I can't remember ever thinking any other way."

"You're off the clock now. The race is over. When the next thing needs doing, you'll know it. This stuff is governed by a perfect intelligence. No thinking or meddling or second guessing required. Just relax into the process, trust it, don't struggle against it. That's what it's all about."

"That's what you were saying to Maggie, wasn't it, about not choosing to wear a blindfold and walk with a stick?"

"Sounds like."

"And that's how you live your life?"

"Seems like."

She sits watching me. She hasn't fully closed her mouth.

"But really, though. I mean, *really*?"

"Really."

She's staring at me as if suspended somewhere above this conversation, unable to come down on either side. She thinks that life as she has always known it is normal and natural. It may be the former but it's far from the latter. From my perspective, I feel comfortable saying that we human beings have no idea of what we truly are or of what we are truly capable. None whatsoever.

She's still staring at me.

"Say what you want," I tell her.

Her mouth is still open and now her head has taken on a slight wobble.

"It can't be, though" she manages, her mind in conflict with itself.

I give her a nudge.

"You were some kind of control freak or something?" I ask.

That's all it takes.

"No," she says defensively, "not a control freak, exactly. Maybe by your rather laid-back standards but, I mean, we had a very complicated and demanding life. There wasn't a lot of room for, you know, carelessness. Everyone had to do their part or the whole thing would... meals, laundry, bills, shopping, school, work, social commitments, schedules, chores, my

God... errands, sports, getting everyone where they have to be on time, a million things, at home, at work, at school, everywhere, everyday, no days off... it all has to get done, you know, and I'm the one who had to make sure it did. Does that make me a control freak? I had to be very organized and I was. I had to keep everyone on task, you know, there's so much to do and there's no room for screw-ups or everything else gets messed up. I don't think that's being a control freak, I was just running a normal, busy household."

"So then, no? Not a control freak?"

She takes a breath.

"I don't think control freak is an appropriate designation. I did what I had to do, that's all. I was good at it. I was proud to do it well."

"May I make an observation?"

"Yes, okay."

"You might get offended."

"I'll try not to."

"Okay, it's a very common thing, but of the utmost importance. You don't know how to breathe."

"Oh," she says, nodding vigorously, "yes, I know. My trainer told me the same thing. I'm trying to—"

"Stop, please. It's not that you're not doing it right, it's that you don't know how to do it at all. Your body doesn't know how. I've been watching you. You yawn like it's illegal, you sneeze like a kitten, your voice is nasal and puny, you're never really relaxed. Learning to breathe is a big deal, it might take you a year to break bad habits and learn good ones. It's critical to everything, and it's not easy. You really have to put your attention on it; learn about it, develop the muscles, make it a habit. You have to retrain your mind and body. It's not a simple thing."

"Oh my God," she says in exaggerated despair, "as if I don't have enough to worry about, now I don't know how to breathe!"

"This comes before everything. If you don't breathe well, nothing else is going to work right; the mental, physical, and emotional stuff all relies on full, healthy breathing. Here, hold your hand out."

I hold mine up next to hers. Mine is mannequin steady. Hers is wet-kitten trembling.

"Do you have trouble falling asleep at night? Lay there fretting about stuff you know shouldn't be bothering you so much?"

"No," she says. "Maybe."

I wait.

"Yes."

"That's because your body and mind are oxygen deprived and that puts you in a panicky state. Practice proper breathing when you go to bed and you won't have that anymore. I don't want to lecture you, but nothing is going to work right if you don't breathe properly. You really should learn about this and why it's important and how to do it. Make it a top priority. This is the best advice I have to give."

I sit back and take a slow, deep breath and release it.

"Breathing and wakefulness go together. It's cleansing, refreshing, centering, all that. For me, breathing consciously evokes the warm feeling of gratitude for what I have mixed with the recognition that, with every breath I take, it's all passing away. This isn't mystical or enlightened, it's not a path or a destination, it's just basic awareness."

I can see she's getting offended and trying to hold her tongue, her musculature is tightening and her breathing is becoming hitched.

"Yes," she says tersely, "you talk about breathing in your books."

"Try to observe your current state," I suggest. "This is the kind of thing I'm talking about. You have no shock absorption. Every little bump in the road feels like a boulder. Your hackles go up and your fight or flight response gets triggered by things that should blow over you like a breeze. Do you ever take naps or baths?"

"I'm not really the kind of person who can just—"

"That's old thinking and it needs to be re-evaluated in light of your changed circumstances. You wanted to know what to do next? This is clearly it. You have to retrain your body and mind and emotions. You're becoming a new person and things like breathing and naps and bubble baths and long walks and tickle-fights with your daughter should no longer be viewed as non-productive activities. They are no longer non-essential, they are now *of* the essence. This isn't a tidy, compartmentalized little process you're going through. You are being completely reconceived and you have to be receptive to the process in all things and at all levels. The degree to which you resist or ignore or neglect or otherwise thwart the process is the degree to which it will cause suffering."

Still, I can tell by her body language and facial expressions that she's not receiving this well.

"You're probably going to resist this breathing thing and blow it off in a day or two, so I'll do you a favor and force you into doing it."

Her eyes widen at the challenge, but she doesn't say anything.

"Maggie doesn't know how to breathe either. Scared, mousy little upper-chest breathing, just like you. You've gone to all this trouble to keep her from making the same mistakes you made, so here's a wonderful place to focus your efforts. You have to learn yourself so you can teach her. So there you go, now you'll be doing it for your daughter."

⊹

An hour later I'm napping on one of the recliners by the pool and Lisa is doing some research on the laptop. Maggie has joined us, I learn, when I open my eyes and find her staring at me.

"Are you awake?" she asks.

"C'est mon métier," I witticize groggily.

"I have a question," she says.

"Okay."

"You know how Jolene has her experience in church? In the first book, where she sees everyone as cows, and that changes her whole, like, outlook?"

"Um, yeah," I reply, and make a mental note to give the first two books a quick read-through before finalizing the third.

"What was your thing like that?"

I know she doesn't think of it this way, and her mom is only half listening, but precocious little Maggie just asked me about my first time.

"Well," I tell her, "there was this guy named Mortimer—"

⊹

Sometime in my late teens, I picked up *How to Read a Book* by Mortimer J. Adler, and it was, quite unexpectedly, one of those wonderfully devastating books that tear down walls to reveal new and previously unsuspected vistas. I had read hundreds of books by that time, including a lot of the heavy stuff, not necessarily for classes, but just because I fancied myself a reader. I read a lot and I enjoyed it enough to keep doing it, but then here comes this book by Adler and in the first ten or fifteen pages I found out that I'd never really read anything.

Bam!

I didn't know how to read.

It was an epiphany, a thunderbolt, a mini-enlightenment; my first big one since Santa-gate. Not only was I not appreciating literature anywhere close to the level it merited, but far worse, I was effectively inoculating myself against it. I was penetrating books only to the degree necessary to cross them off my must-read list. I returned to many of the books I had read and thought of as friends, only to confirm what Adler said; these books were almost complete strangers to me. I knew them as intimately as if I'd merely read brief synopses of them years ago. I was, as Adler put it, a literate ignoramus; I had read widely, but not well.

Looking back on it now, I mark *How to Read a Book* as my first book and have since gone back to reread many books correctly. I also realized that I was reading for a lot of wrong reasons and became much more selective and self-serving in my reading choices. I began owning the process instead of being owned by it, making determinations as to what was good or bad by my own lights instead of by the weight of common opinion.

It was quite a bewildering experience to have the rug yanked out from under me like that, but it was also a thrilling discovery. That's the death/rebirth experience right there. Yes, a guy named Mortimer popped my epiphany cherry. After that, it was just a matter of scale.

Rather than being hurt or angry to have my ego balloon popped, I was exhilarated to find out that what I thought was solid and real could be so easily reduced to vapor. He was calling me a blockhead, an ignoramus, and sophomoric, which some might find offensive, I suppose, but it was true. He was absolutely right. Mortimer Adler was the first guy to call me on my bullshit and I'm still grateful to him for it. Sad to say, but yes, I enjoyed having my nose rubbed in my own shit, and yes, I think it's a pre-requisite for any form of growth in life. Man is a self-fertilizing animal. We rise up out of our own shit, or not at all.

Adler wasn't enlightened. He didn't have robes or carry flowers, but when it comes to real teachers, I think of thoughtful guys like Adler, guys who smash people's glass houses, not the guys who help erect and preserve them. Jesus never did as much for me, or any priest, or even any of the teachers I had known and trusted. What the hell was going on with them? Adler's book came out in the nineteen-forties. Why wasn't his book handed to me on the first day of my education, before any other book? Why did they let me waste those thousands of hours misreading books, plowing through them like they were nothing more than notches on my library card? Were there other areas of my life where I was so misinformed and mistaken? Why were all my teachers and professors giving me good grades? What the hell was wrong with them? That's another wonderful lesson I took from Adler's book: Those who you're most likely to trust for what you need to know may not know it themselves. You're on your own.

Think for yourself, or not at all.

✧

The Adler book taught me many lessons that would take root and develop and become the most important in my life.

Because what I had learned about my own reading ability was as true or truer for virtually everyone else, it taught me that everyone could be confidently, convincingly, and completely wrong. Suddenly, I was looking at everyone in a much different and harsher light. Adler showed me that teachers and writers and experts could not only be wrong, but could be the very agents by which wrongness is perpetuated in the world. Unwitting double-agents, you might say, but for whom? Slovenly and lemming-like habits of thought, I incorrectly assumed.

This was a very important lesson in universal doubt and distrust which I went on to further refine and appreciate, and which I now hold to be the fundamental guiding principle of an honest life: Guilty until proven innocent. False until proven true. Every belief is wrong until proven right. No man, teaching, religion, system of thought, doctrine, ideology, or creed is sacred unless it's indestructible. If something is worth understanding, it's worth self-verifying. If it's not worth self-verifying, it's trivia and may be safely disregarded.

Impartial distrust, combined with an understanding of the word further, is all that is needed to awaken from the dreamstate. Honesty and perseverance must invariably lead to the truth-realized state. Where else? And how else to get there? Add Spiritual Autolysis and white-hot intent, and you'll be the one writing the books in a few years.

The Adler experience taught me that wrong-knowing, rather than not-knowing, might be the truer and far more insidious form of ignorance; that what we consider our strengths can be the devious hiding places of our most debilitating weaknesses.

It taught me that what we do see is nothing and what we don't see is everything. It taught me that where I thought things ended might be where they were just beginning; that there was a world beyond the world I saw, a me beyond the me I knew. And, likely as not, more beyond those.

It taught me that finding out you're wrong was much better than finding out you're right. That disillusionment and disenchantment were the better part of the process of growth and learning. It taught me that the pain and embarrassment of discovering our own folly and falsity was the price of moving beyond it—no pain, no gain—and that the blows that my self-image had to endure were blows it *should* endure and perhaps there was something of the flagellant in me, and should be.

It taught me the startling truth that a kid not yet in his twenties could see beyond what the experts saw, and could leave them all behind. That's big and important. All the recognized experts can be just as wrong as those who recognize them as such, and it's possible, even easy, to move beyond them all. Simply by taking one small step, I had effectively moved into a new and much less populated realm of understanding. If you understood what I said about *Moby-Dick* in *Incorrect*, you see a perfect example of this exact thing. I wasn't the first guy to make sense of that book because I could out-think all the great thinkers who'd read it and delivered their high-blown and nonsensical pronouncements upon it, it was simply that I was able to see it from the more elevated perspective at which it resolved into clarity and made perfect sense. It's not about knowledge or scholarship or intelligence, it's about clear-seeing.

Although I was surprised and disillusioned to discover that so much of the well-read world, educators and educated alike, functioned at such a shallow and easily transcended level, I overcame the temptation to place the blame for my ignorance anywhere but on myself. The shutters that had been closed against the light were mine to open or not. I was influenced, but not constrained. The chains that bind us in Plato's cave are strong, but they are not locked. If we don't set them aside and stand up and make a start, we have no one to blame but ourselves.

It taught me that, having taken one step, there might be more steps to take. And having understood that the cause of my ignorance was within, I was open to the idea that there were more such blindspots within. I was no longer one of those die-cast people, just as Jolene was no longer one of those cows. Now I was something else, and I could continue to develop along those lines.

It taught me that there were two kinds of understanding; understanding for success and understanding for life. Understanding for success meant following the herd. Understanding for life meant following reason and facts and your own head and heart, wherever they may lead. Understanding for life was an entirely different pursuit, and one I much preferred. It showed me that these two paths diverged and that, as Frost said, taking the one less traveled could make all the difference, and I say now that it did.

In short, Mortimer J. Adler introduced me to Maya. He showed me how to see her, and to see her is to destroy her.

That sounds like a lot to learn from one simple insight, but that's the nature of insight, and of the process of unbecoming. It's like the pin that pops a balloon, or the spark that triggers an explosion, or the breeze that topples a house of cards, or the crack that bursts the dam. That's the momentous difference a single click of our mental dials can make. When's the last time you completely revolutionized yourself? When's the last time you became fresh and wide-eyed and new?

✧

These books I write carry the same message as Adler's book, only on a different scale. We can't escape the fact that, in these books, I'm calling all believers delusional and all beliefs untrue. If I'm wrong in this, then I'm just another ass-talker, as Brett would say, but if I'm right, then it's a pretty damning indictment of all belief systems and everyone who subscribes to them. Says Adler:

> I have said some things about the school system which are
> libelous unless they are true. But if true they constitute a grave
> indictment of the educators who have violated a public trust.

He goes on to say of schools what I say of all teachers and teachings:

> If the schools were doing their job, this book would not
> be necessary.

And on experiencing great teachings at second or third hand:

> They may be all right if all you want is some kind of information,
> but not if it is enlightenment you seek. There is no royal road.
> The path of true learning is strewn with rocks, not roses. Anyone
> who insists upon taking the easier way ends up in a fool's para-
> dise—a bookful blockhead, ignorantly read, a sophomore all his
> life.

After that, it's just a matter of scale.

18. Spiritual Dissonance

If the eye never sleeps, all dreams will naturally cease. If the mind makes no discriminations, the ten thousand things are as they are, of single essence. To understand the mystery of this One-essence is to be released from all entanglements. When all things are seen equally the timeless Self-essence is reached. No comparisons or analogies are possible in this causeless, relationless state.

—Sosan

How is it possible that so few are able to find the only thing that can never be lost? How do we actually accomplish the miraculous feat of seeing what's not and not seeing what is? By what specific mechanism does delusion maintain its hold over those who seek to free themselves of it?

When it comes to determining what makes it into the books, one thing I consider is what I would have liked to read about back when I was trying to get all this stuff figured out for myself. One question that always weighed on me was, what's the big mystery? Why should it be so hard to find answers to such simple questions? What's true? What's going on here? What's the point?

Who am I?

People generally seem content to believe that the universe is a mystery and the meaning of life is unknowable and to leave it at that, but someone who wants answers to the larger questions cannot be so easily dissuaded. Obviously, it seems to be a mystery, but why? What is the nature of this mysteriousness? Is it the nature of the universe to be mysterious? Is it the nature of meaning to be unknowable? Are we drugged or bound or hexed? Is there some agent or agency in charge of keeping us in the dark? Who or what is withholding or hiding reality from us? Why should something so simple be so difficult?

What I discovered was that our ignorance isn't compulsory, it's voluntary, even self-inflicted. Nothing is hidden or withheld, truth is not inherently mysterious, and there is no conspiracy to keep us ignorant. There is, however, an actual process, a mechanism of delusion, which is at work inside each of us. The name I use for this mechanism of delusion, borrowed from Hinduism, is Maya. Maya, it should be remembered, is not an actual arch-deity thwarting us from on high. Maya is inside us, a part of us, and in complete control of us. Maya is the fear that permeates us so fully that we don't know it's there. Maya is the organizing principle of emotional energy in the fear-based, segregated state, and Maya *is* inherently mysterious.

✧

It's late afternoon and things are winding down on the pooldeck. It's been a busy day with more people coming and going than usual, but now it's down to Lisa and Maggie and me. I'm at my big table, Maggie is working on some project at the raised island in the kitchenette, and Lisa is by the pool soaking in the mellowing rays.

This estate we're on is not what I was looking for when I came to Mexico. I wanted something cozier; more like Frank's house, but not in town. This place is ridiculous in many respects—too big, too fancy, too high-tech, too ostentatious, too expensive—but it's also perfect. I am very happy in this poolhouse and often sleep here instead of in the casita. It's a lovely place to live and work, quiet and private with magnificent views, but I could have found those qualities elsewhere. What I like most about this place, and what I wouldn't have found in a house more like Frank's, is having Lisa and Maggie on the grounds. If they were staying in their own place, or with Frank, I would see very little of them, but here they are, and they both, in different ways and to different degrees, play important roles in the creation and content of this book. I don't have to chase them down or make phone calls and appointments to talk with them, which would be in violation of my agreement with the universe, and which is exactly the kind of thing I wouldn't do. They're right here, close, available, accessible. This is another good example of the book being laid out for me, and of my part in recognizing patterns and moving with them, like renting this totally inappropriate property when my rational mind had me looking for something very different, like inviting virtual strangers to come live here, like the unexpected windfall that arrived, perfectly timed to cover the higher rent, like everything that has brought me to this place and put me in touch with these people and others who are so integral to the process and content of the third book. And like much more than I have space to share here.

✧

Maggie finishes whatever she was doing and comes over to take a seat at my table. She sits quietly for a few minutes before asking what I'm working on.

"Cognitive Dissonance," I answer.

"I don't know what that is," she says.

"Neither do I," I say, "I'm trying to figure it out."

"What is it?"

I read from my notes:

"Cognitive Dissonance is a term used in psychology to describe the discomfort we feel when our thoughts and beliefs come into conflict with each other."

She scowls at me.

"Give a for instance," she says.

"Okay, say for instance that I'm opposed to the slaughter of innocent animals, but I also like to eat meat. See what I mean?"

"So you're doing something that goes against what you believe?"

"Right, which is okay as long as I'm not very aware of it, like if it stays in the shadowy outskirts of my awareness. If it doesn't bother me, it's not a problem. What's an itch if it doesn't itch?"

"If it doesn't itch," she says logically, "then it's not an itch"

"Then what is it?"

"Nothing?"

"Right."

"But then, if it *does* itch—?"

"Right, if it does itch, then it becomes a problem, and I'll have to do something about it."

"Like scratch it?"

"That's one possibility. What's another?"

"You could ignore it."

"You could try. What else?"

"I don't know, put something on it?"

"Right," I tell her, "or maybe just remove the cause, as in pulling a splinter or flicking off a bug."

"Yeah," she says.

Other answers I would have accepted include painkillers, as in drugs or alcohol; amputation, as in cutting off the afflicted area; and suicide, as in jumping out a window. But those are a bit above Maggie's paygrade.

"So what do you do," she asks, "if you eat meat but don't want the animals hurt?"

"That doesn't seem like the right question. I might have gone my whole life eating meat and not wanting to see animals hurt."

"So that's not the problem," she works it, "the problem is—"

I wait.

"—that it started to itch?"

"That sounds right, doesn't it? It's not a problem until it starts to itch. If circumstances force me to become acutely aware of this dissonance in my cognitions, my thoughts, then it will cause me discomfort, and that discomfort will require relief. The most obvious way for me to relieve my discomfort would be to stop eating meat. But beliefs are much easier to change than behavior, and I really don't want to stop eating meat, so I'd probably just change my views on the slaughter of innocent animals, and keep eating them."

"Like how would you change your views?"

"Maybe by deciding that if they weren't raised for food, they would never have had life at all. Then, instead of being responsible for the killing of animals, I'd be responsible for giving them life. Problem solved."

"But is that really true?"

"I don't think it has to be true," I reply, "it just has to stop the itch."

✧

I don't want to be limited to a textbook definition of Cognitive Dissonance, so we'll rechristen it Spiritual Dissonance and define it afresh. Spiritual Dissonance is what occurs where our inner world meets our outer world; where what we think is true butts up against what appears to be true; where internal belief collides with external reality. It's the discomfort that occurs where self and not-self come into contact.

Ego is like the thin sheath of atmosphere between the earth of self and the infinite space of not-self, holding one in and the other out. We live out our lives in this narrow band, never digging too far down or testing our upper limits. This is where our emotional energy is spent, pumped into this gap between two incompatible surfaces, keeping them from grinding against each other and jolting us out of our slumber.

That grinding, when it does occur, is Spiritual Dissonance.

Spiritual Dissonance is the mental/emotional counterpart of negative physical drives like hunger and pain. We experience physical discontent because we are hungry, so we eat. We experience physical pain because our finger is in a flame, so we pull it out. Similarly, when we experience the discomfort of Spiritual Dissonance, we seek relief, though it's not likely to be as simple and direct as pulling a finger out of a flame.

Spiritual Dissonance is a necessary and vital function of the human condition. It's how we operate. It can, like anything, go haywire, but for most of the people most of the time, it's nothing more than the meeting of two slightly imperfect surfaces; the outermost inner and the innermost outer.

A common example of Spiritual Dissonance would be; If God loves us, why does He allow so much suffering? The certainty of God's love is the internal belief. The obviousness of human suffering is the external reality. Is God unable to end suffering? No, we must answer, because He can do whatever He wants. Therefore, He must allow or even cause suffering. But how can that be if He loves us? Something somewhere has to give or, preferably, we avoid asking the question in the first place.

An ad hoc hypothesis is one way of dealing with messy problems such as this. We come up with a new belief to stuff into the gap between two existing beliefs, like plugging a chink in the wall of our prison cell where a discomforting light is getting through and disturbing our repose. Such a hypothesis in this situation might be, "Because God loves us, He gave us free will and we use it to create our own suffering." This is like a belief patch; we discover a bug in our belief programming, so we install a belief patch and all is well. The walls that enclose us are made of belief, so a belief patch is likely to blend in well and last as long as the wall does, if we don't tamper with it.

Another way we can respond to this problem is to recuse ourselves from such weighty deliberations altogether. "The Lord works in mysterious ways," we can say, and be happily done with it. Similarly, we might relieve our discomfort by deferring to specialists. "It's the job of the clergy to grapple with such imponderable issues," we might tell ourselves, "it's for the shepherds to worry about such things, not the flock."

Or, we might redouble our emotional investment in God and simply dismiss logical inconsistencies with haughty contempt or mocking disdain. Or, we might go the other way and dismiss God altogether, citing conundrums such as this to bolster our case. Or, best and most common, we can go the ignorance-is-bliss route. We can ignore the question altogether, or deny it, or simply stay occupied and distracted so this question and countless others like it can never gain a foothold in our awareness.

Or any number of other scenarios. The main thing is to stop the discomfort, like removing the battery from a blaring smoke detector so we can go back to sleep.

Meanwhile, somewhere, a fire burns.

✧

Lisa overheard Maggie and me talking about Spiritual Dissonance and has joined the conversation.

"It's at the egoic wall, the imaginary line where self ends and not-self begins, that Spiritual Dissonance occurs," I explain to both Maggie and Lisa, trying at the same time to get it figured out for myself. "The egoic wall has no independent reality. When we stop pumping energy into it, it starts dissolving. That's what ego is, a self-segregated state, and that's the use to which we put our emotional energy. The egoic shell in which we dwell is of our own making, like a force field that requires a constant source of emotional energy"

Maggie yawns and goes back to her project at the raised table in the kitchenette. Lisa looks confused.

"And what about our mental energy?" she asks. "What about our intelligence?"

"Intelligence is subordinate to emotion," I say. "*Way* subordinate. Even our greatest thinkers seldom do more than justify and rationalize their beliefs. That's why I try to impress upon people that real thinking is not what they think. Real thinking is invariably destructive and pain-causing. It leads to reduction in the buffer zone between these rough surfaces, resulting in abrasion and meltdown. Like an engine running hot without oil, friction is going to build and it's going to result in catastrophic failure. Normally, we are sensitive to even the slightest level of abrasion and make micro-adjustments as necessary, but it's possible to override that autonomic process. We can think our way out of the false self instead of believing ourselves into it."

"You're talking about what, exactly?" she asks.

"You withdrew your investment of emotional energy from that buffer zone and it started grating and getting more and more heated and raw and eventually the machine broke, and here you are."

She looks perplexed.

"And *how* did I get here?"

"You stopped pouring your life energy into defining yourself as a separate entity and allowed yourself to become undefined. Now, all that energy that you wasted on creating and maintaining your segregated egoic identity can be turned to new and much more interesting purposes. A whole different way of being, of knowing, of perceiving. A whole different way of wanting and getting, of doing and not doing, of interacting with the universe."

She shakes her head in exasperation.

"But it's not magic? You're not saying that?"

"Or, as I think, it's *all* magic. The dreamstate is a magical place and we are part of it. We *are* it. We are not the lowly squatters or trespassers or uninvited guests we commonly assume ourselves to be."

"I don't know," says Lisa, shaking her head. "I feel like I'm in a movie and I don't know what kind it is; like if it's sci-fi or fantasy or just regular drama. These things you're saying, it doesn't sound like my world. I don't recognize it as reality. It sounds wonderful, but it doesn't sound *real*. It sounds made-up, like something for children."

"Which brings us back to Spiritual Dissonance."

"Oh, because my beliefs are coming into conflict with reality. Well, I agree with the conflict part."

"You've probably never been exposed to the idea that thought shapes reality, that thoughts are things and things are just thoughts. A lot of smart people are struggling to understand that there's a mind/body connection. It gets even harder to comprehend a mind/*everything* connection, or to go even further and see that there's really no mind/everything *dis*connection in the first place. If you were confronted with this sort of thinking in the life you left behind, you might have simply scoffed at the gullibility of some people and forgotten about it immediately."

She nods vigorously in agreement.

"But everything is different now. Your internal and external situations have dramatically changed."

"You're talking about miracles, right? Isn't that what you're saying?"

"I'm saying it's *all* a miracle. We're not innocent bystanders or helpless victims; we are members of the universe, shapers of our dreamstate reality. The transition to Human Adulthood is our birth into this reality. It's not just the next stage of what we are now, it's a whole different relationship to our surroundings, our environment, our universe; a truly integrated, co-creative relationship. We do ourselves a terrible disservice by trying to be positive and upbeat and cheerful about our circumstances. What we are now, as we understand ourselves to be, even by the most optimistic reckoning, bears no resemblance to what we really are. This whole thing is really much cooler than anyone has imagined. Compared to our potential, we're still just little monkeys, and nasty little monkeys at that."

✧

The most devoutly religious and spiritual people—those who reset their coordinates and retask their lives to pursue spiritual growth or reshape themselves to conform to religious ideals—would seem to be the most likely candidates for the type of spiritual rebirth I'm describing, but they are invariably the ones most effectively shielded against it. Even the most committed spiritual aspirants are seldom more than amateurs and hobbyists, as dedicated to their spiritual practices and ideals as others might be to their model trains or needlework. The most sincere seekers are the most desperate to stay lost; that's the real dynamic at work in the spiritual quest. They're not seeking truth or answers; they're seeking relief from Spiritual Dissonance. Providing this relief is the lifeblood of the religious and spiritual marketplace. It has nothing to do with truth or awakening. In fact, just the opposite. In the final analysis, stripped of all its holy pretensions, the entire spiritual marketplace is really nothing more than an existential quick-lube shop, and while there may be an endless variety in packaging, there is really only one product.

Spiritual Consonance is what all seekers seek; an end to discomfort, not delusion. But the consonance they seek can only be found in deeper unconsciousness, which requires the reduction of dissonance. There is such a thing as true Spiritual Consonance, an integrated, natural and exceedingly desirable state, but acting tranquil and serene has never gotten anyone there and never will.

How is it possible that so few are able to find the only thing that can never be lost? It's not easy. It takes everything we have, but it's the one thing at which mankind truly excels. We're not as brave or courageous as we like to believe, we're not as intellectually well-endowed as vanity tells us, and by our own moral reckoning we are the least of all creatures, but there is this one thing we all do remarkably well, and only when you get clear of it can you look back and see what a miracle of consciousness engineering self-delusion really is.

19. The Ministry of Awakening

Crimestop means the faculty of stopping short, as though by instinct, at the threshold of any dangerous thought. It includes the power of not grasping analogies, of failing to perceive logical errors, of misunderstanding the simplest arguments if they are inimical to Ingsoc, and of being bored or repelled by any train of thought which is capable of leading in a heretical direction. Crimestop, in short, means protective stupidity.

—George Orwell, 1984

B OB IS A SPIRITUAL DILETTANTE, someone whose spiritual pretensions are nothing more than a well-practiced sleight-of-mind, himself deceiver and deceived. Bob and I have been acquainted for almost a week at this point, and he knows that I see him as a dilettante and that I value his insights for just that reason. In fact, as we sit together in gliders on the flat roof of the guesthouse, he has just finished reading a draft of the preceding Spiritual Dissonance chapter.

"You might want to think about this," says Bob, looking at me over the tops of the pages he's holding. "These amateurs and hobbyists, as you call them, are your audience."

"My audience?"

"Well, your *intended* audience," he clarifies. "It might not be wise to alienate them like this."

"If I have an intended audience," I reply, "it's people who know they're stuck and want to get unstuck, not people who don't know they're stuck and just want to pass the time and pass judgment."

He sighs in exasperation. We've been having more or less this same conversation for several days.

"And what do you suppose is the difference?"

"The former would receive criticism with gratitude, and the latter as a personal attack. Awakening is a process of breakthroughs, and break-throughs don't come from incense and candlelight and inner peace. You look at spiritual aspirants as those most likely to achieve awakening, but Maya has them so bamboozled that those who seem the most advanced are simply the ones who are burrowing downward the fastest."

"But, Jed, honestly, you can't say things like that—"

"Sure I can. This isn't my pet theory, this is what I see, and if I see it, then it's there for anyone to see. All they have to do is look. I can say that, can't I? Open your eyes? Be honest. Take a look?"

He's getting more exasperated. He's fun to exasperate. He's a few years older than me, maybe fifty, well-groomed, well-dressed, well-spoken, well-rounded and well-, well, well-everything. He's warm, genuine, engaging, informed and charming. He's written a book and it's that, through some chain of acquaintances, which has brought him to me. He's staying at the nicest hotel in the area and driving a rented Land Rover.

"You're making this all seem too cut-and-dried," he insists, not for the first time, "like there are only two sides to the issue, but that's a very dangerous oversimplification. When you talk about spiritual aspirants, you're actually talking about millions of people around the world, *billions* of people, following many different disciplines and paths, many of these paths ancient and highly revered. You can't just throw all this spiritual and cultural diversity into one box and slap a label on it and declare victory over human delusion. It's not that simple."

That's why I like having Bob around. He says things like that.

"It's *exactly* that simple," I reply, not for the first time. "Waking up from the dreamstate is a very straightforward business. It doesn't take decades. It doesn't look like tranquility or like a calm, peaceful mind. It doesn't look like saving others or saving the world or even saving yourself. It doesn't look like a thriving marketplace where merit is determined by popular appeal or commercial success. Waking up looks like a massive mental and emotional breakdown because that's exactly what it is, the granddaddy of all breakdowns. That's the only way it works. I know there are thousands of books out there that say otherwise, and I can tell you that they were all written by Maya. Once you understand what Maya really is, once you see her for yourself, that becomes perfectly obvious. You'd see it like you see the sky."

He waves my own pages at me.

"But you can't level these broad condemnations—"

"Why not?" I ask. "Am I wrong? Is there some purpose of spirituality other than to awaken from delusion? Is there some guiding principle other than truth? Am I wrong in thinking that Maya has thoroughly captured the hearts and minds of those who would seek to escape her? Are they not completely indoctrinated, enslaved by orthodoxy? Are they not sitting with their eyes closed, trying to quiet their minds and stop their thoughts? Are they not promoting peace and tranquility and silence as spiritual ideals? Are they not practicing a heart-centric, emotion-based spirituality? Do they not possess strong convictions and deeply held beliefs that bind them more securely than chains?"

"Yes," he says with a heavy sigh, "you might be wrong."

It's taken awhile to strongarm him into saying that.

"Exactly," I agree, "I *am* wrong. There *is* some other purpose to spirituality. It's not about truth or awakening from delusion. It's about the exact opposite of that."

"What?"

"I'm agreeing with you," I say.

"It sounds like a very backhanded agreement," he says. "I think that the issues here are more complex than you—"

"The only complex issue is staying benighted in a sunlit world. We have taken the simplest of all possible things and complicated it beyond comprehension. We have dreamed up these ridiculous spiritual ideals to which we can perpetually aspire but never attain. We have bought darkness in the name of light, lies in the name of truth, and ignorance in the name of knowledge. We have convinced ourselves that what could not be closer is most distant, that what is for all is only for the few, and that the one thing you cannot *not* attain is hopelessly beyond reach. That's the perfect recipe for a long and happy failure. In other words, that's the work of Maya, without whom there is no dreamstate in which to debate and write books, or from which to escape. Wouldn't anyone whose eyes were open and who saw this surreal situation clearly want to make some effort to describe what they were looking at?"

"Well, that all might depend on how you define—"

"I'm defining the dreamstate as the state in which a person sees what's not and doesn't see what is; eyes closed, imagining reality instead of eyes open, observing it. With eyes closed, one is forced to live in an imagined, constantly conjured faux-reality."

"The dreamstate," he says.

"The non-lucid dreamstate," I say. "I inhabit the same dreamstate as you, but I am lucid within it. Those who are non-lucid within it live behind closed eyes in an imagined world, an imagined reality. This imagined belief structure has no inherent stability and requires constant emotional reinforcement. This is most pronounced and visible with fundamentalism in any belief system—their belief structures are the least stable and require the most emotional reinforcement—but it's true of everyone who's not awake."

"News to me," he says a bit sourly.

"No it's not," I reply, "Practically everyone who talks about awakening and enlightenment is really talking about some degree of simply opening their eyes—nothing at all to do with truth-realization. This is what all the mystical teachers and poets are really talking about. They've gotten a glimpse of the integrated state, a taste of lucidity, and it's like the most extraordinary thing to them. Really, though, it should be the most ordinary thing. It's only extraordinary because we are so cut off from it."

"You're dismissing the entire spectrum of spiritual motivations and aspirations," he says. "You're reducing this entire debate—"

"Yes," I agree, "I'm dismissing spiritual aspirations *within* the sleeping dreamstate; quality of life issues like happiness, peace, health, prosperity, and so on. And salvation and life everlasting to take it a small step further. Greed, vanity, ego, all arising from fear. Yes, I categorically dismiss all of that. It is the muck and mire in which mankind wallows, and from which sincere aspirants must extricate themselves."

Bob shakes his head as if I'm just not getting it, but I do get it. I understand his presence here, with me, at this time. I understood it within a few minutes of first meeting him. I know why he's here, from my perspective anyway. I'm speaking a bit forcefully to Bob not because I want to penetrate his defenses, but because I want to observe them. It's Bob's impenetrability that I am being shown, that is being put on display for my benefit, for the benefit of the book. Bob will probably be the last spiritual, New Age type person I will ever spend time with. I still have Brett's eulogy in Virginia to deal with, but I won't have this kind of opportunity there. This is my last chance to see Maya up close and personal, to see how deftly she blocks and parries and deflects and absorbs every attempt to get past or through her, to try this and that angle, this and that point of entry, and find all attempts effortlessly thwarted, to see how easily she does something so seemingly impossible. Bob knows all this; I shared it with him as soon as I saw it myself. He's not offended and doesn't feel I'm being patronizing or condescending. For his part, he won't get from me what he came for—something to do with his book, but which is not mine to give—but I'm sure he'll get what he was meant to.

"I've met hundreds, maybe *thousands* of spiritual people, Jed, from all walks and disciplines, at all levels of development from novice to famous masters, and I have to say I think you're grossly mischaracterizing who these people are and what it is they're doing—"

"Abiding Non-Dual Awareness, Human Adulthood and Altered States," I say. "That's all we have to work with. It's one of those or it's just sitting at the bottom of a hole passing the time, waiting to die. I say all this in complete non-judgment. You seem to think I'm trying to offend spiritual people, like I'm a mean guy saying mean things, but my only real interest is in trying to bring some common sense and clarity to the most muddled and elusive topic in the history of man. What actual people do with their actual lives is outside my small sphere of interest. To the best of my knowledge, spiritually-inclined people, from all walks and disciplines, at all stages, are really doing nothing more than maintaining or deepening their entrenchment, and maybe piddling around with mildly altered states. Now, maybe there's something I don't know, and if there is I would be truly grateful to hear it, but what I *do* know is that very few spiritual people are divesting themselves of their egoic bonds and undergoing the death/rebirth process necessary to make the transition into Human Adulthood, and virtually no one is actually awakening from delusion. These subjects aren't even a part of the spiritual lexicon. Just to discuss these topics, I've had to devise a makeshift terminology; Truth-Realization, First Step, the Dreamstate and the Awakened State, Human Childhood and Human Adulthood; Integrated and Segregated States. These concepts are of the essence of human development, and yet we don't even have words for them."

To his credit, Bob doesn't launch an immediate counter-assault. This is something we've discussed, the idea that I'm not trying to win his heart or convince his mind, that I'm just trying to say what I see and that it's all friendly and cordial and even, as far as I'm concerned, academic.

✧

I point to the book on the table between us.

"Have you read *1984*?"

"Back in high school, as I recall."

"I've been having a wonderful time with it. Orwell's original title was *The Last Man In Europe,* but the publishers asked him to change it. He went with *1984*, of course. I think he should have just shortened it to *The Last Man*. Do you remember Newspeak?"

"Yeah," he says, "they were cutting back the language. They kept coming out with new versions of the dictionary with less and less words."

"Doubleplusgood," I say. "Do you remember why?"

"The reason for Newspeak? Uh, no, I don't think I knew there was a specific reason, besides general control and oppression."

"They were eliminating concepts," I say. "They weren't just taking away people's freedom, they were taking away the *idea* of freedom. Eventually, the very thought of freedom would be unthinkable because there would be no word for it."

He looks puzzled.

"So, you're saying, what? That we're moving toward some form of spiritual totalitarianism?"

"Not at all. If that were the case, we'd see it coming like a black cloud rolling across the earth. What I'm saying is that it's already here. The reign of Big Brother is so firmly established that no alternative exists in the minds of men. The very concept of freedom has been so thoroughly abolished, is so absent from our collective worldview, that it is, literally, unthinkable. There is no possibility of human development in practice because it doesn't exist in theory. There's no such thing as a radical or revolutionary anymore. There is no insurgency, no rebellion. There may be a few isolated pockets of plotters, but nothing even likely to arouse Maya's notice. There is no interest in freedom; it's all been channeled safely into non-threatening, ego-gratifying avenues; career and family, religion and spirituality, hobbies and addictions. Freedom has been effectively wiped out of existence. The idea no longer exists. The game is over."

"That seems rather bleak."

"It's 1984 for mankind now, and probably will be forever. The real message we can take from Orwell's book has nothing to do with anything so trivial as political oppression or the erosion of privacy rights, it has to do with the reduction of man's perceptual faculties to a narrow field of vision, like blinders on a beast of burden, rendering us unaware of alternatives, knowing nothing other than slow, pointless plodding toward our own burial ground. *1984* isn't a future possibility, it's a present fact."

I pick up the book and read a paragraph from the appendix:

> The purpose of Newspeak was not only to provide a medium of expression for the world-view and mental habits proper to the devotees of Ingsoc, but to make all other modes of thought impossible. It was intended that when Newspeak had been adopted once and for all and Oldspeak forgotten, a heretical thought—that is, a thought diverging from the principles of Ingsoc—should be literally unthinkable, at least so far as thought is dependent on words.

"We're living in the Dark Ages, Bob. You don't see it, but I do. You think I'm saying something bad, but I'm delivering the best possible news. We can stop putting a positive spin on our circumstances and actually change them, radically improve them, far better than anything depicted in our fairy tales and mythologies and medieval superstitions."

Bob is looking at me like I'm the bad guy. I sigh.

"You seem to think that I'm opposed to human spirituality, Bob, like I'm saying it's not a very effective path to freedom."

"Isn't that what you *are* saying?"

"No, I'm saying it's unrelated; spirituality is a state-sanctioned enterprise. None of those things, not Buddhism or Sufism or any New Age stuff or Hinduism or Kabbalah or anything else, pose any threat to the status quo. Their practice does not result in progress. I'm not saying they're bad at it, as you seem to think, but that it's outside their scope and charter. Religion and spirituality as they have always been known are of no practical value whatsoever. The individual who wants to explore life and their relationship to their universe must harden their heart, sharpen their mind, and strike out on their own. And what they'll find when they get clear of this whole mess is that humans may have come down from the trees, but we have yet to take our first step."

"Well, evolution can take thousands of years—"

"I don't think so, Bob, not this kind. My experience is that this kind of evolution isn't of the species but of the individual. I'm not talking about what people can do together, but what one person can do alone; a serious person who is willing to make a fresh start and play the game as it is, not as they've been told it is or as they might wish it is. To strike out and test the limits of what it means to be a conscious being in a conscious universe *is* within the scope of the individual. Any group of two or more people are necessarily externalized and immobilized by their very togetherness, but a single individual can go and keep going."

"I'm certainly all for the individual," says Bob sportingly, "but you can't deny the contributions of those who came before. It is the great teachers and texts, dating from antiquity to modern science, from which we receive our understanding and to which we owe a debt of—"

"Science is just another belief system, and a fundamentalist belief system at that. No understanding means anything unless it translates into action; change, actual progress. Otherwise, it's just another evasive tactic. It's because we accept our meager illumination as full sunlight that we don't possess the explosive and self-destructive levels of discontent necessary to make a break. Not until we begin hacking away at our mental and emotional entanglements can we swim up and break the surface into the full light of wakefulness. And not until we do that can we understand in what a cold and miserable darkness mankind dwells. That's personal revolution, spiritual warfare. That's the only point there is to this whole business, and it doesn't look at all bleak to me."

✧

Over the course of many hours together it becomes clear that Bob views me as some sort of party-pooper, like I'm being a drag for not putting on a funny hat and singing along with the world community of spiritual merry-makers, like I'm a grouchy pessimist who sees only the dark side of things and has no hope for humanity. The truth is that I am probably the most optimistic, pro-human person there is. Mine is a realistic, pragmatic optimism; an optimism based on common sense and direct experience and easily verifiable results, not on religious fairytales and mystical superpowers and New Age marketing hype. If I seem negative, it's because I know something of our potential. If I seem disrespectful of our great thinkers and spiritual leaders, it's because I see them not as liberators, but as unwitting co-conspirators in a crime against humanity; a crime of subjugation and spiritual castration.

✧

Everyone should be familiar with terms like those I've been forced to invent and many others. Books like *Damnedest* and *Incorrect* and *Warfare* shouldn't be revolutionary or revelatory, they should be completely unnecessary because everyone should be talking and writing about these subjects. Human development and potential should completely saturate our thinking to the exclusion of all the diversionary fluff with which we stuff our heads. These topics should be as familiar to people as their mother tongue. Human Adulthood should be as primary in education as Mortimer Adler's three R's: reading, writing and reckoning. Everyone should be making the transition to Human Adulthood in their early teens and it should be a celebrated life event, not the personal holocaust it is when it occurs belatedly. Truth-Realization would hardly be everyone's chief concern, but there's no reason for people who have an honest relationship with life not to know what it is.

There should be no reason for a Jed McKenna. None of what I have to say should need saying, much less come as a surprise. The real issue here isn't that I'm so far ahead, but that humanity is so far behind. We can keep telling ourselves how wonderful we are, how brave and spirited, but that's a part of the pathology of our sleep disorder. We can keep sniffing around in outer space and on ocean bottoms and in laboratories in order to maintain our conviction that we're courageous explorers of the unknown, but that's symptomatic of the same pathology. Any and every outward pursuit is treated as noble and important because we're all in the same club and those are the rules; even warring and embittered factions within the club are in full agreement on this point. How can it be that we're essentially the same now as we were at the most distant reaches of recorded history? Why does our outer environment change while our inner landscape stays the same? Because that's the first rule of this club:

Always Outward. Never Inward.

So it follows as a matter of certainty that anyone who espouses any teaching or doctrine or philosophy is necessarily a member of the club. Any spiritual teacher who allows students to ask questions and gives them answers is a member of the Outward Only club; an unwitting—and thereby all the more insidious—agent of ignorance. The world is full of respected and beloved spiritual and religious teachers. People ask them questions and they provide answers; question and answer, question and answer, on and on, talk and more talk, more like spiritual therapy than spiritual warfare, but all questions, no matter how sincere or heart-felt, are really the same question, *Outward?*, and all answers, no matter how profound or wise, are really the same answer, *Yes.* The subtext of every question is, *Am I making progress by asking questions and trying to understand the answers?* And the subtext of every answer is, *Yes, you are going somewhere while sitting here talking or reading. This is progress. Be at peace. You are progressing and well-progressed.* That's the obvious lie we want to hear and those who tell it most convincingly are the most respected and revered and sought after.

A shining example of this is the much-beloved Ramana Maharshi. His core teaching, if you ask Bob or any of Ramana's many fans, is, "Ask yourself, Who am I?"

So what's the problems with that?

There is none. In fact, it's perfect; a complete spiritual teaching in five words. So perfect, in fact, that anyone who actually does it will actually awaken. *Ask yourself, Who am I?* If you do it, you will become enlightened. There is no possible alternative. The only way self-inquiry can fail to work is if you fail to do it. That's a pretty important point so I'll say it again: The only way self-inquiry—*Ask yourself, Who am I?*—can fail to result in enlightenment is if you fail to do it.

"So," I ask Bob, whose book is dedicated to Ramana, "why aren't Ramana's many thousands of adoring students and devotees awake? That seems like a pretty fair question, doesn't it?"

"I don't think it's fair to assume—" he begins.

"No need to be defensive," I say, "I'm agreeing with Ramana. I'm saying self-inquiry is the bomb. I'm completely on board."

"But you're also saying... what are you saying?"

"That Ramana's failure to produce awakened beings was nearly total."

"Oh, well, that's hardly—"

"When, on the face of it, his *success* rate should be total. Shouldn't it?"

"I don't know, I suppose—"

"So what are we missing? Why isn't this adding up? What aren't we understanding about this?"

I glance over at Bob as he chews on the problem. He is visibly agitated; experiencing a degree of Spiritual Dissonance, it's safe to assume. He's sure Ramana was a great man, a great teacher, a saint, a sage, whatever he thinks all that means. That's the inner belief. But even after trying to quibble about Ramana's success rate for fifteen deleted paragraphs, he has to agree that it's abysmal at best. That's the outer reality. Eventually, he can no longer help but see the obvious.

"They're not doing it?" he says, making it a question.

"Who's not doing what?"

"Followers of Ramana; they're not doing the self-inquiry practice."

"Yes," I agree, "if we stated the situation correctly—self-inquiry leads to awakening and Ramana's followers don't awaken—then that's the only conclusion we can come to. So then, if that's his teaching, then why don't his students practice it?"

"I just don't think—" he starts and stops, then starts again. "I don't agree that, I mean, I've done it myself, you know. I've practiced self-inquiry—"

"The sincere practice of self-inquiry would require a year or two of excruciatingly intense processing to go all the way through," I say, cutting off his attempt to scurry out a back door. "It's not like a question to be answered or an epiphany to be realized or a thought to be pondered, it's more like a mountain of ignorance that has to be pulverized into particulate, stone by stone. Do you understand that?"

He sees that door slam shut.

"Yeah, okay. Yes."

"So you didn't actually do it?"

He sits quietly for awhile.

"Well, I thought I did, I suppose. I kind of thought I was doing it, by following Ramana's teachings, by reading and trying to understand the dialogues and the books written about him, I guess I thought the whole thing was this sort of process of self-inquiry. I thought that if you were into Ramana Maharshi, that's what it meant, that you were doing self-inquiry just by learning what he taught."

The inner twelve year-old is thus revealed. Here's this intelligent, accomplished, distinguished-looking guy seeing his fabrications dismantled, like a kid caught cheating by the teacher.

"As opposed to a specific process?" I ask.

"No, there was kind of a process too. I did this thing where I'd go into a sort of introspective mode, well, once in a while. Like, I'd ask myself, who is experiencing this? Who is having this conversation with Jed right now? Who is out sunning himself on this beautiful day?"

I'm not too surprised to hear about Bob's weak and ineffectual method of self-inquiry; witnessing in its mildest and least disruptive form. I don't assume that if I had this conversation with a random sampling of a thousand Ramana devotees that I'd get these same responses, but I do assume none of them would be awake. And though I don't think that many would claim to be awake, I do think that most or all would claim to be making real progress in that direction.

Looking at Ramana Maharshi and self-inquiry affords us a very clear view of this phenomenon, but now that we know what we're looking for, we can increase our altitude and broaden our perspective and take a random sampling of all spiritual seekers. Why isn't anyone going anywhere? Because they've convinced themselves that they *are* going somewhere. Why? Because their spiritual masters and advisors tell them they are. Why are their spiritual masters and advisors telling them they're going somewhere?

To get the gig.

We pick our teachers. We get what we wish for. We want cozy, uninterrupted slumber and the dream of spiritual progress, and that's what we get. If all Ramana had ever said was, *Ask yourself, Who am I?*, if that had been his answer to every single question put to him, then he'd have been the perfect teacher with the perfect teaching, but no one would have ever heard of him and we wouldn't be discussing him now. We know about him because of all the thousands of questions people asked him and all the thousands of answers he gave, but every single one of those questions was the exact same question: *Outward?* And every single answer he ever gave was the exact same answer:

Yes!

Self-inquiry was not Ramana's core teaching. That's Maya's shell game and we're the suckers lining up, eager to get fleeced. But as every swindler and conman knows, you can't cheat an honest man. Ramana's true core teaching, if you care to pull back the curtain and look, was *Outward*. In real progress, there are no questions or answers, there is no knowledge or teaching, there is only going and not going.

Inward.

✧

The book *1984* takes place in the country of Oceania where the motto, (which Thomas Pynchon perceptively called "the koans of an aberrant form of Zen") is "War is Peace, Freedom is Slavery, Ignorance is Strength." Oceania is governed by four ministries, the names of which "exhibit a sort of impudence in their deliberate reversal of the facts." The Ministry of Love is where all the torture and brainwashing are done. The Ministry of Peace wages a never-ending war. The Ministry of Plenty is in charge of restricting the supply of food and goods. The Ministry of Truth is in charge of lies and propaganda. In keeping with that impudent naming practice, we can look to our own Ministry of Awakening, the spiritual marketplace, where we find all the sages and teachers and philosophers and scholars hard at work doing exactly what our own Big Brother, Maya, wants them to be doing:

Making sure everyone stays sound asleep.

20. Ordinary Super-Powers

Prayer is not an old woman's idle amusement. Properly understood and applied, it is the most potent instrument of action.

—Mahatma Gandhi

IN THIS BOOK, I'M PUTTING a lot of emphasis on the daily reality of the person who is awake within the dreamstate; the Lucid Dreamer who is able—not as a random event but as a matter of course—to shape his living reality in ways and to a degree that might be considered by the Non-Lucid Dreamer as the stuff of fantasy fiction. That's certainly how it looks from the respectable point of view, but we have no time for respectability here. If I needed anyone else's respect, I realized long ago, I wouldn't have my own. If we want to get anywhere or understand anything, respectability has to be discarded like the refuge of fear it is.

When we are looking at the influence of unseen forces in daily affairs—in the acquisition of a house or a dog, in the rightness of a motorcycle accident, in the writing of a book, in the way the ball bounces or the cookie crumbles—the overarching significance is not that these unseen forces are miraculous powers of the few, but the natural and rightful abilities of all. They are commonly dabbled with and dimly perceived and called by many names from the eyes-closed, segregated perspective, but they can only be truly possessed and developed from the eyes-open, integrated perspective.

When, after I scrambled to come up with the buying price, the house I was trying to buy in Ajijic fell through, I was not dismayed or disappointed. I knew exactly what was going on, even though I had absolutely no idea. Then, when the other house, my lifelong ideal house, became available shortly thereafter, I wasn't shocked or amazed, I was pleased and grateful. When Maya, the dog, appeared, I wasn't falling all over myself in a panic to acquire her. I recognized her immediately because I had been moving toward her for months. It never occurred to me that she wouldn't become mine. I wasn't at all surprised to learn that her current owners were trying to find a new home for her.

I can go on with stories like these, and on and on. I could write pages every evening about the patterns that had been visible in various stages of unfolding only that day; of waves just becoming visible as distant swells, of waves building and cresting, of waves crashing and washing up the shoreline and receding back into the ocean. From these patterns I know what will happen and, just as importantly, what won't. I didn't know the first house deal would fall through, but I knew it was part of a larger process that was yet to be fully revealed, and I never suspected that bad luck had befallen me, or that the universe was acting in some malevolent or random fashion. When my grand uncle's house came into the picture, and me in the highly unlikely position to act on it, I wasn't flabbergasted or stunned, I was like a kid who claps in delight when a magician, after a suspenseful buildup, makes a pony appear.

The best lessons come from all the small, everyday stories, stories of smooth, effortless functioning, of doing less and accomplishing more, of ease and contentment and unwavering, never-misplaced trust. When something seems to go wrong, it's invariably part of a larger right. I eat when hungry, sleep when tired, walk when I feel like walking, zone out or work or nap or read when I feel like it. I am neither lazy nor industrious. I never do anything I don't feel like doing and nothing ever goes undone. When I think of something I'd rather be doing, I do it. If I were to develop an authentic desire to, say, climb Mount Everest, then the wherewithal to do so would appear in a timely and effortless fashion. If I were to develop an *in*authentic desire to climb Everest, then I would quickly recognize it as such and let it fall away.

If this were just about me, if I were somehow special, it wouldn't be worth mentioning, but it's not about me, it's about everyone. It's about who and what we are here in the dreamstate. It's about how things really work, or how they *can* work if we open our eyes and look and participate.

✧

I'm in the sand at Brett's. A woman in the front row named Karen raises her hand.

"You said in your second book that if we don't have the desire to move into Human Adulthood, we should pray for it. Can you talk more about prayer? How to do it? How it works?"

Others chime in. It's a popular topic.

"Sure, we can talk about prayer if you like," I say. "Prayer is a real thing and it really works, but the *word* prayer is kind of weak and misleading. It's a segregated, eyes-closed term for an integrated, eyes-open process. It's a child's way of explaining adult things, like saying that babies are delivered by a stork. That's charming and amusing until you want to grow up and start having kids, then you're going to need a better idea of how things really work. Or like a child saying airplanes are held up by fairy powder. It's a cute explanation, but if you want to get a plane to stay up, you're going to need a more realistic understanding of aerodynamics."

"Okay," Karen says, "but it's not pure science, is it? You still have to be deserving somehow, don't you?"

"Yes," I say, "in the same way that a plane has to be deserving of staying in the air. If it obeys the rules, it's deserving. If it doesn't obey the rules, it falls down. Instant karma. We can participate in shaping our reality to a far greater degree than a word like prayer would suggest, but we have to understand the basic principles and reshape ourselves to them."

Everyone is attentive now. This is starting to sound like the fountain of youth, Santa's lap and a winning lottery ticket all rolled into one. They see that Brett has an idyllic, stress-free lifestyle, away from the world and surrounded by beauty and tranquility and the animals she loves. They know from the books and some talk on the subject that I live comfortably, that I don't struggle or put up with much unpleasantness. They can see that we live well but not ostentatiously; simple, comfortable, unornamented and unadorned, yet lacking nothing. They think we know something about quality of life and about shaping our environment, and we do. They hope that this knowledge is something they can use in their own lives to make profound improvements, and it is.

"Do you know what I'm talking about?" I ask them rhetorically. "It's not just manifestation; it's good and bad luck, it's being in and out of the flow, it's about things going your way or going against you. It's not fickle or random, it's a process of visible patterns, and we can see them and learn to move with them. If you can detect the outlines of this, feel your relationship to it, see how it works when it does and why it doesn't when it doesn't, then you can start the process of reverse-engineering it, dissecting it, observing it to better understand how it works and put it to work more and better in your own life. And by doing that, you will be dismantling your own ego structure because ego is always the thing that gets in the way, that tries to steer us across or against the natural currents of being. Am I starting to sound like a hippie?"

They laugh.

"Luck is like prayer," I tell them, "insofar as it's an eyes-closed explanation of things that can be seen and understood with eyes open, like storks and fairy powder. Fate is another example. These terms are like the superstitions of primitive people to explain things they barely see and don't understand."

"Hey, wait a minute," says a young guy named Logan in a tone of mock indignation. "Did you just call us primitives?"

That gets a laugh.

"Actually, yes," I say, and they quiet down. "I mean, how would you define primitive people? People who are not highly developed. People with beliefs we would probably consider unsophisticated, maybe even comical. People who live in conditions we would consider sub-standard. People who make up far-fetched stories to explain processes they don't understand. People who could elevate themselves out of these conditions, but don't. Would everyone agree with that?"

No one says they wouldn't.

"Then yes, someone established in the Integrated State would certainly apply the term spiritual primitive to anyone in the Segregated State, and with far more justification, I would think, than we might apply the word primitive to anyone we'd see in the pages of *National Geographic*."

A weighty hush descends over the group.

"How exactly are we supposed to take that?" asks Logan.

"Everything I say should be taken as an invitation," I reply, "an invitation to participate in your own life, to take personal responsibility for your own development instead of abdicating it to churches or clergy or gurus. You should take it as wonderful news. Yes, compared to your potential, you are developmentally stunted and spiritually primitive, but you don't *have* to be. In the sense that you are a primitive, your evolution is within your control. I was in this state, Brett was in this state, and we saw that it was highly undesirable and clawed our way out of it. It can be done. Whether we set our sights on spiritual growth or enlightenment or truth-realization or adulthood, it all starts out the same way. I mean, that's what you're here for, isn't it? To grow? To explore? To change?"

That was a better question than I understood at the time.

✧

"What about things like astrology and numerology and tarot," someone asks, "and all the other methods of insight and divination? How does all that factor in?"

"Good question," I say. "All these various methods that aid us in knowing what to do and when to do it are rendered unnecessary and obsolete as soon as we open our eyes and see our environment and how to operate in it. This urge to gain some measure of control stems directly from the eyes-closed, fear-based perspective. It's a symptom of the Segregated State, of operating from a place of fear and distrust, of keeping a death-grip on the tiller and feeling that your mind, your little brain, is in charge, of feeling that you are an unwanted guest in a hostile world and you need to arm yourself in order to survive and thrive. Once we move into the Integrated State and get our bearings, all such urges are forgotten. Methods of divination might make very good sense in the Segregated State, but it makes a lot more sense to find your way into the Integrated State where you'd have no further use for such methods. I move in alignment with clearly visible forces and energies, so all other methods and forms of navigation, whether star charts or stock charts or weather charts or anything else, are of no more use to me than a seeing eye dog. I have no need to avail myself of navigational aids for the visually impaired. I can see for myself.

You can too. That's the point of all of this."

✧

We take a break during which several people come up to me to voice their views in support of astrology and tarot and other such things, but they're all children's toys and when we grow up we leave them behind and I can't think of anything more to say about them. After twenty minutes we all get situated and enjoy a few minutes of open dialogue. Karen complains half-jokingly that she's always prayed for a certain car but never got it, which provides an adequate segue back into our main theme.

"If you think of this process of manifestation as a way of getting what you want," I say, "then you're already off-track. The way it really works is more of a seamless unfolding. It's not something you can improve, only impede. The only way you can make it work better is to remove ego from the equation. As soon as you start imposing your beliefs on the process, it necessarily begins to degrade. Even to impose your beliefs about time and space on the process, or your beliefs about causality and duality, is to diminish it. As soon as you start asserting your beliefs, you start closing it down to your level instead of opening yourself up. And since, furthermore, this process is really about conscious being, about who and what and where we are, developing a progressively deeper understanding of the process is synonymous with actual progress and growth. Same thing, okay?"

Lots of unconvincing nods. Brett weighs in.

"I hope y'all are listenin'," she hollers from her seat. "This ain't no New Age gimmick or some late night infomercial where bikini models are washing a Ferrari in front of a mansion that could all be yours for three easy payments."

She stands and walks out front with me.

"We're livin' in a corrupt world," she tells them in her most forceful tone. "There ain't but one malevolent force in the universe, and we are it. It ain't that we're bad people, it's that we ain't fully formed, and what you get then is an abomination. Y'all know what an *abomination* is? It's like what them Chinese princesses do to their feet, keepin' 'em all bound up so they stay tiny instead of growin' to their rightful size. Them feet is an abomination, but the *cause* of them feet is this corruption I'm talkin' about. Priests who molest children is an abomination. Politicians and corporations violatin' the people's trust is an abomination. Every single one of us, even if we never done a wrong thing, is an abomination as much as the worst folks you can name. You could make a list of human abominations that'd wrap from here to the moon and back, but I reckon there ain't really but one corruption at the heart of all abomination and that's ego. There might be millions of symptoms; there ain't but one cause."

She pauses to let that set in and continues her color commentary.

"Now, I know what y'all are sittin' here thinkin'. You think Mr. McKenna is gonna let you in on some big secret, and then you're gonna be livin' on Easy Street cuz you'll have some special knowledge that gives you special powers, and in a way that's right, but not in the way that gets you a sports car or makes you a bikini model. He's talkin' about the same thing we always talk about here, the only thing there is *worth* talkin' about; nasty, disgusting, repulsive, slimly ego. Y'all are gonna wanna put all this magic to work in your own lives and that's fine, I reckon you can do that in some small way, but if you're gonna play with this shiny new toy, you should try puttin' it to some good use. Use it to get yourselves shook loose of all those layers of armor and baggage and filth you're dragging everywhere and callin' by your own name. Get your ass naked. Peel off all that crap so you can live your life direct instead of piecin' it together based on rumor and speculation like you do now. Desire it, pray for it, manifest it, ask the Tooth Fairy for it, but use these things Mr. McKenna's tellin' you about to get your ass woke up, so when your life is over you can look back and say you were in it and didn't just sleep through it like your doin' now."

Brett resumes her seat.

✧

I resume where I'd left off.

"What we're talking about when we say manifestation is the true creative process wherein authentic desires become reality. Once you understand the desire part, then the becoming part takes care of itself."

"When you say reality—?" asks a thirty-ish guy named Sean.

"I mean consensual, dualistic reality. This is the dreamstate we're talking about, not truth."

"They're mutually exclusive?"

"Well, yeah," I say, "since truth exists and untruth doesn't."

"Oh," he says, "okay."

"This isn't truth stuff anyway, this is rightful inheritance stuff. This is about understanding your place in things. We're talking about the fact that the universe you find yourself in is yours to do with as you please. If you think of it in terms of a dream, then what we're talking about is like lucid dreaming, shaping the dream to your will, as opposed to non-lucid dreaming, being shaped by events and environment and so forth."

"This seems like a mixed message," says an older guy, "on the one hand, you talk about releasing the tiller, and now you seem to be saying we should grab the tiller and take control of our lives."

"Good point," I say. "It's about taking control of your life and that means one thing; releasing it. Unconditional surrender. That's something to be done consciously and with clear intent. Nothing comes before the transition to adulthood and no one moves forward without it. The mixed message comes from the paradoxical nature of losing your life to find it."

"This is all so confusing," says Karen, who got this conversation rolling with her initial question about prayer. "It would be so nice if you could just press a button or take a pill and all this stuff just makes sense."

Everyone laughs in commiseration.

"Regardless of how complex and daunting all this may seem," I respond, "I assure you, there's only one thing to worry about; making the transition to Human Adulthood. That's where life begins. Nothing else means anything. There is no secondary objective or consolation prize. No amount of knowledge or understanding or spiritual experience could be of any value if you're still stuck in the Segregated State. That should be simple enough; you have one goal, to move from the Segregated State to the Integrated State, die to the flesh and be born of the spirit. That's the button you have to press."

Silence while I take a drink.

"But how do we really do that?" asks Karen. "I mean, *really*."

Everyone speaks up now in support of this question. They want to make something happen in their lives, at least, that's the role they're playing. One of these thirty might actually do something in the next decade, but probably not. They don't understand the nature of their captivity or the fact that they're happy in it, so their chances of moving beyond the talk stage are very slim.

"You have to open your eyes," I reply, "that's the answer. Look at life honestly, see it clearly, and everything else follows naturally from that. Everything follows automatically from clear seeing."

They stare at me in silence for a few moments.

"Like, how are we not being honest?" the younger guy, Logan, asks with a welcome edge of attitude. I consider his question as I pace. There are many answers, but the most obvious is probably the most revealing.

"By coming here," I say. "What we're all doing by coming here to these meetings is essentially dishonest. We tell ourselves that we're here as part of our process of spiritual growth, or because we want to understand new ideas, or we want to make some positive changes in our lives, but is that true? People don't really want to change, and those who do don't go to meetings or listen to people talk about change or read books or whatever. They take action. They take up arms. they make something happen. They don't simply move from one part of the herd to another."

I could be much harsher about the self-deception these folks are practicing by coming here, but I really don't want to be harsh at all. I never want to get impassioned or confrontational, but when the subject is the Integrated State, the urge is there; the urge to shake people awake, to slap them out of their stupor, to rub their nose in their own goofy beliefs. It seems like it would work, but I know it wouldn't. Logan speaks up and saves me from myself.

"I disagree with that," he says excitedly, "I think what we're doing by coming here is pretty cool. It's like we know we're stuck in this bad situation you and Brett talk about, like we're unconscious or imprisoned or whatever, and we come here to meet, like a band of secret plotters! We come here because we want to kick some ass!"

Logan's youthful enthusiasm is infectious. Everyone laughs, a few clap.

Even Brett is smiling.

"That's a nice thing to believe," I say after everyone is quiet again, "sometimes I almost believe it myself, but the reality is very different. Realistically speaking, what we're really doing here is no more radical than thumbing through a magazine or going to the mall."

This elicits a response of murmured disapproval.

"This is not a secret meeting and we are not revolutionaries plotting the overthrow of an evil dictator. This is a toothless conspiracy, like a prison Escape Club. It's listed in the prison directory after the Drama Club and before the Glee Club. This event, us coming together here and discussing these subjects, is a sanctioned event, fully approved by the very regime we plot against. All the books and magazines and events of the Escape Club are prison-sponsored. 'Wherever two or more are gathered together,' says Maya, 'I am in your midst.' There are no secret gatherings, there is no plotting, there are no overthrows. The only escape possible is one person, on their own, alone, slipping off by themselves, into the black."

"Into the black?" asks Logan.

"You have to go into that darkness you've spent your life avoiding and denying. You have to get to the place where you'd rather go into that blackness than continue avoiding it. Coming here is just another way of maintaining plausible denial. I agree it's not fair, it's way too much. You should have done it when you were twelve, but how could you have known? But now your situation is much worse, and that's what it takes."

"I'm sorry," say Logan, "I just don't see it."

"Yeah," I say, nodding, "that's my point."

"Oh," he says.

"Think of the tremendous explosive force of a space shuttle launching off the pad, the amount of raw energy it takes to escape from the earth's gravitational pull. What would that sort of explosive force look like in your life? What would it take to ignite it? What could fuel such a powerful event? Not love. Not serenity or compassion. Not pretty stories about the life everlasting or a heavenly abode."

I pause for a quick metaphor switch.

"In the prison of Human Childhood, we are not really alive. Until you understand that, until you see it for yourself, there is no way you can muster the mental resolve and emotional intensity necessary to change your circumstances. We like to believe it's about becoming more spiritual and more compassionate, but that's just what they tell the prisoners to keep them cheerfully and harmlessly engaged. There is only one possible objective, you must die to be reborn, and to do that I recommend you use Spiritual Autolysis to begin the process of thinking clearly and freeing your thoughts from emotion-dense clouds of self-limiting beliefs. Use Spiritual Autolysis as a mental approach and prayer as an emotional approach. Pray for intent. Pray for authentic desire. Pray to be able to pray better."

"Or?" asks Logan.

I shrug.

"Or this," I say raising my hands to indicate life as they presently know it, but *this* doesn't seem so bad to them, so real change is real unlikely.

✧

Our eyes are wide open and we see reality with perfect clarity. This is so obvious that it's beyond any possible doubt. It's also untrue. Our vision is so obscured by the mental and emotional flotsam and jetsam of selfhood that what we call stark reality is really just a soft glow seen through tightly shut eyelids, just enough light getting through to illuminate the internal dreamscape. It is owing entirely to our belief that our eyes are open that the spiritual quest is doomed from the start, and that so many who think they're well along or finished have never really begun. No matter how unwavering we are in our commitment or how steadfast in our determination, no matter how much knowledge we amass or wisdom we attain, no matter what hardships we endure or what sacrifices we make, no matter what scriptures we adhere to or what deities we appease, it's all just a desperate ploy to keep ourselves from doing the one thing that could make a difference: taking personal responsibility, thinking for ourselves. At the point where we begin our search, we have already overshot the objective, and every step takes us further away.

In the search for truth, God, meaning, supra-consciousness, divine union, bliss, salvation, or whatever other spiritual tail we might chase, self is never itself subjected to critical scrutiny. We simply accept that we are as we think we are and that reality is as we think it is and go from there. We accept these facts as established and certain and proceed from that point onward. Thus, the primary error from which all others arise has already been committed and is safe from detection and correction. All our discernment and discrimination and intelligence is turned outward from self, not inward against it. To put it in terms of the cinematic retelling of Plato's cave allegory, *The Matrix*, what growth or development is possible if we never discover that we're living in a glass coffin and "reality" is being piped in like elevator music?

21. The Power of Prayer

Of the terrible doubt of appearances,
Of the uncertainty after all—that we may be deluded,
That maybe reliance and hope are but speculations after all,
That maybe identity beyond the grave is a beautiful fable only,
Maybe the things I perceive—the animals, plants, men, hills,
    shining and flowing waters,
The skies of day and night—colors, densities, forms—
Maybe these are, (as doubtless they are,) only apparitions,
    and the real something has yet to be known;
(How often they dart out of themselves,
    as if to confound me and mock me!
How often I think neither I know, nor any man knows,
    aught of them.)

—Walt Whitman

PRAYER DESERVES A CLOSER LOOK. Prayer is where the rubber meets the road. It's the thing that, regardless of other things, all these people in this horse arena have experimented with. They've all prayed heartfelt prayers, and they've all reflected on the efficacy of prayer. They all have some sort of deep, personal experience of prayer. They have nothing in the way of knowledge, and might assume there's none to be had, but there is. Everything that works, works a certain way, and prayer works.

The thing they don't know is that prayer isn't about changing the rules, but coming into alignment with them. It's not about wishing things were otherwise, but merging with the way things are. It's not about the once-in-a-lifetime miracle, but the every-breath miraculous. Living with eyes closed, we lack not just vision, but perspective. We don't understand our relationship to our environment or anything in our environment. We think things are ours that are not ours, that things last that don't last, that things are true that are not true. We flex our fingers and we think: "Of course my hand works. It's my hand. It does what I tell it to." But layers and layers of wrong-knowing are harbored in even this seemingly simple observation.

"I'd like to spend a few minutes taking a closer look at what's wrong with the word prayer," I continue. "Not what's wrong with the actual process, but what's wrong with the way we understand it, as typified by the word prayer. Maybe we can demystify it a bit, clear away the mystical mist and see it as a natural and dependable process. Okay?"

Seems to be.

"For one thing, the word prayer has the feeling of one entity making a request of another; as if a little guy is asking a big guy for something, like a peasant begging a king for a crust of bread. This common assumption—that we're weak and helpless children in Big Daddy's house—infects many people's thinking and is very symptomatic of Human Childhood. Okay?"

Lots of unsure okays.

"Okay. Another misleading thing about the word prayer is the connotation that you may or may not get what you're asking for. This ties in with worthiness, like you'll only get what you pray for if you deserve it, like Big Daddy has to be pleased with you before rewarding you, as if there's a judging agent or agency to whom one's prayer is really a plea or a plea bargain. This is what's behind sacrifices and tithing and all the other things we do to try to get into Big Daddy's good graces."

I see recognition in their faces.

"I would also say that prayer is an underperforming proposition," I continue, "meaning that when prayers *do* seem to be answered, the answer probably won't measure up to what was prayed for. Contrast this to eyes-open manifestation which will, as a rule, exceed our highest hopes and expectations."

That gets a muffled response of nods and grins, as if they're all familiar with the ask-and-ye-shall-receive routine where you really, really ask and only sorta-kinda-maybe receive.

"Another thing about prayer is that it seems like a last resort, like conventional methods have failed, so we're turning in desperation to prayer.

Like with a pimple on prom night, maybe we try diet changes and skin cleansers and make-up first, and when all else fails, we turn to prayer."

"Ask," jokes Jeff, "and the good Lord shall provide."

"Very good," I say, "and that raises another problem with the word prayer. It's inextricably tied in with all our religious baggage. All you want is a pimple to disappear before prom night, and now there's Jesus, the son of God, who died a crappy death for your crappy sins, who you haven't spoken to in years, and now you're gonna call him up to bitch about a zit."

They laugh.

"Unlike prayer, manifestation is a first and only resort. Once we understand what it really is and how it really works, it naturally becomes our sole mode of operating in the world; not just in getting what we want, but in knowing how to want and what to want; in knowing what to do and why to do it. Instead of a desperate plea for something we want, manifestation becomes our way of moving through life, of interfacing with the universe."

I pace in the sand and let the words come.

"Which brings us to the most important difference between prayer and manifestation; prayer is specific. You want something so you ask for it; a zit to disappear, good news from the doctor, your child to have ten fingers and toes. But manifestation isn't specific. It's not just about getting what you want, it's about everything you do and how you do it and who you are and how you move through the world. It's about shaping the dreamstate and moving within it in this seamless confluence of self and not-self. It's the erasing of the line between dreamer and dream. You're not just manifesting a car or new shoes, you're manifesting yourself, and all the rest follows naturally and effortlessly from that. You can see why prayer is a pretty skimpy little concept next to that."

"Is manifestation anything like synchronicity?" asks Karen.

"Sort of," I say, "but synchronicity is another ambiguous term, like prayer, that we use to describe a phenomenon we dimly perceive and don't understand. I think Dr. Jung coined the term synchronicity. The commonly cited example is that Jung was discussing scarab beetles with a patient in a New York highrise when a very unlikely beetle appeared outside his window. That's actually a good example for our purposes because it shows how starkly brazen synchronicity has to be before we are able to detect it. We might think of synchronicity as this kind of outlandish coincidence, but if our eyes were open, we'd see that synchronicity is not a rare occurrence at all; it's the basic organizing principle of energy. If you need an Egyptian beetle to tap on your Manhattan window to teach you about synchronicity, then the real lesson isn't that you've seen something very unusual, but that you're too blind to see what's very normal."

"But how is it possible for everyone to be as blind as you're saying?" asks Jeff, who is sitting with Karen.

"For that very reason," I reply, "because it's everyone."

"And how would we actually go about opening our eyes?" asks Jan, a fifty-ish female with close-cropped gray hair who has made several remarks on this and previous evenings which seemed more intended to convey her skepticism than to get answers. "It *is* a metaphor, I take it."

"Maybe," I say. "Or maybe that's the real seeing and what we do with our physical eyes is the metaphor. We begin seeing clearly by first seeing that we are asleep; locked in the constricting coils of our own emotional energy. Once we truly understand that we are asleep within the dreamstate, then we can begin in earnest to awaken ourselves, which is done by hacking away at these constricting coils. This is the transition that, in a healthy society, we would all undergo naturally and with relative ease in our early teens. In the world as we know it though, very few ever make the transition, and of those who do, far fewer manage to continue developing beyond it to any significant degree. There's always a spiritual inertia at work, resisting motion or change. It's built-in, way deep. That's why a word like *further* is so important."

"But you have?" Jan asks. "You've continued developing beyond the transition to adulthood?"

"I have, yes. I would probably be the equivalent of a young adult. Well, young adult with an asterisk, I suppose, due to the enlightenment thing."

"So you'd be a young adult?" Jan asks defensively. "And the rest of us are what, just children?"

"Not really children," I say. "More like unborn, yet to emerge from the womb. Life begins when we are born of the spirit. There's no possibility of development prior to this emergence. When I say I'd probably be like a young adult, I mean a young adult in a world where we developed in a healthy, normal manner; where life was a continuous journey of growth and expansion and understanding, where a thirty-five year-old was a significantly more developed being than a thirty-three year-old, not just more solidified. Such a world wouldn't even have words like luck or prayer or manifestation or synchronicity. Those words are appropriate in an eyes-closed world where our best thinking is quasi-mystical guesswork based on flimsy evidence like bugs on windows, but not for an eyes-opened world where everything is visible and plain to behold."

✧

Jan has been making skeptical but non-productive comments throughout the evening. Nothing of any particular merit, just doubtful remarks made in dubious tones, as if she's too smart to be buying what I'm selling. Her brand of snootiness is a type of spiritual shielding that is not unusual in these forums. From her perspective, I'm the used car salesman trying to sell her a lemon. I'm the sleazy politician trying to swindle her out of her precious vote. I'm the greedy corporation dispensing sugar-coated cancer. I'm the proselytizing TV preacher trying to wrangle her into the fold. I'm the smooth-talking guy on the next barstool trying to turn her heart against her head. We are surrounded by this buyer-seller dynamic in all areas of our lives, and spirituality is no different.

To someone like Jan, I'm just one of many suitors vying for her spiritual heart and, she may well assume, her purse. She thinks she has something I want, and she's right, though she doesn't know what it is and wouldn't be reluctant to provide it if she did. I don't want her heart or mind or money. I don't want to save her or enlighten her. I don't want her to believe in the spiritually elevated character I'm portraying so I can believe in it too. All I want is thoughtful dialogue, insightful feedback, challenging conversation, but she can't give me that because she's too wrapped up in her defensive role of discerning spiritual consumer to come out and play.

✧

We take a fifteen minute break during which Brett and I go for a walk and talk about small things. When we return everyone is already back in their seats and quiet. I look at Brett and she scoots me back out in front.

"So how would manifestation deal with a pimple on prom night?" asks Brad, getting a laugh.

"That's a good question," I say, "but it's not an apples-and-oranges comparison because, at the heart of this conversation, we're not talking about two methods, prayer and manifestation, we're talking about two paradigms, segregated and integrated."

"Okay," says Brad, "so how would you personally deal with a zit on prom night?"

His question gets a lot of crowd approval. I look over and see Brett grinning at me. I grin back.

"To start with," I reply, "instead of making it wrong, I'd know without question that it was right and wonder why. So right away, there's a divergence away from segregated wrongness toward integrated rightness. I might spend a minute wondering if I'd committed an error of some sort, if I had lapsed into unconsciousness, resulting in this untimely blemish, but that's just habit and I wouldn't find any such error. Then I'd spend another moment wondering if there was anything to be understood—clearly understood, not make-believe or guesswork—from this curious pimple. I doubt I'd see anything at this stage, but it's always good to check. I would remain alert, however, since the appearance of this pimple in these circumstances would strike me as so unlikely as to certainly have ulterior, though as yet unseen, workings."

"You wouldn't try to heal it or hide it?" asks Brad.

"I probably would, sure. If I was in a situation where I wanted to look my best, I wouldn't be any happier to have a zit than anyone else would. I wouldn't pretend I was okay with it; I'm not in the habit of trying to act other than as I'm inclined. I play my role faithfully, whether or not I understand every detail, and in these circumstances my character would wish to heal or hide the blemish."

"What did you mean by unseen workings?" asks Karen.

"I'm not new to all this. I've been doing this for a long time, prior to my awakening, even, and it's a built-in function of my waking consciousness now, not something I have to stop and think about and perform. In this scenario, where I'm going to a special event, a prom, which entails dressing up, personal grooming, planning and special arrangements, the appearance of a pimple would be about as subtle, as they say, as a fart in a bathysphere. I may not understand the purpose of it right away, but something this unlikely would not remain a mystery for long. An explanation would surely be forthcoming."

"Forthcoming like how?"

"I can't stretch this scenario out that far. Within a few hours, certainly within a few days, what seemed like a minor nuisance would be revealed as a perfect piece in a larger, elegant whole. It would all make perfect sense."

"But sometimes a zit is just a zit," says Brad philosophically.

"Maybe in your world," I say, "not in mine. That would be like if a walrus crawled in here right now and you asked me about it and I said sometimes a walrus is just a walrus."

"Well," says Brad, "if a walrus crawled in here right now, I think there'd be some sort of rational explanation for it."

"That's exactly what I'm saying," I agree, "we'd be sure there was some explanation, even though we had no idea what it might be yet, and even if we never found out for sure. Saying a walrus is just a walrus would be a totally unacceptable way of explaining such a bizarre event. Likewise, I wouldn't dismiss this zit we're talking about as just a bizarre event, or assume it wasn't understandable just because I had yet to understand it. That sort of insistence and distrust is wholly segregated and egoistic. Even if I never understood in fullness, I could never make the assumption that it had been—how do I even say it?—a random event? Chaotic? An element of disorder? There is no disorder. Nothing is random or chaotic, only fully perceived or not. This isn't what I believe, as you must assume; this is what I see."

"You wouldn't pray or manifest for the zit to disappear?"

"No, that would be making it wrong, which wouldn't even occur to me. I may not like having a zit, and I may try to hide it or heal it, but I wouldn't think of it as wrong."

They don't look like they believe me.

"In this prom scenario," I say, "my wishes would already be in place. At some earlier point, I would have spent a few seconds expressing the desire that the evening went well—that everything happened for the best, whatever that might be—and I would have released that desire. I would have let it go and forgotten about it. There would be no panicky revising of my desires based on the appearance of a pimple. That sort of fearful distrust could not occur in me. None of this is vague to me, it's all very specific and constant. If the universe wants me to have this pimple, then obviously that's what I want too. I may not like it or understand it at the time, but I know it's part of something I don't fully see yet, and I know that the reasoning will become clear soon enough. Something this peculiar wouldn't remain a mystery for long."

Now they're quiet. I can see the next question coming before anyone thinks to ask it.

"Let's not leave this at the trivial level of a facial blemish," I say. "If I get trapped in a burning car tonight, I would still not think to ascribe wrongness to the situation. Being trapped in a burning car and having a pimple on prom night are only different in scale. I may not like burning to death, and I may not understand it at the time and I would certainly fight against it, but I wouldn't assume that the universe had made an error, or that me being trapped in a burning car was somehow *not* the way it was supposed to be."

"So you'd be okay with it?" asks Brad.

"I don't understand what it would mean *not* to be okay with what is. I can't process that. It doesn't translate into anything I can make sense of. It has no counterpart in my paradigm. Being in a burning car would cause me to feel a profound degree of discontent which I would seek to remedy, probably by escaping from the car and extinguishing the flames, but I wouldn't think of it as somehow other than right."

They don't look like they believe me.

"The thing I'm not explaining well," I tell them, "is that this is not a different system of belief, it's a different paradigm of being. It's not something you can plug in to your worldview. My surrender to the perfect and unerring will of the universe—which I do not perceive as a thing apart from myself—is absolute. This is not like a belief that can bend or break under pressure. No crisis of faith is possible because there is no faith involved. This is a different state of being I'm talking about; as distinctly different as awake and asleep, as adulthood and childhood, as sanity and insanity. We approach spirituality under the false assumption that we need more knowledge or deeper understanding or stronger beliefs or special experiences, but it's none of those things; it's an entirely different state of being. I have seen this relationship work with unerring perfection for more than two decades. I am not an outside observer of it, I am a co-creative partner with it. It's not a relationship between two entities; it's a new and different *type* of entity. This is what it means to be in a different paradigm. This is what it means to say that my reality is different from your reality. And as long as you're all staring at me like I'm a headcase anyway, I might as well put the cherry on top: If I get a pimple on prom night or find myself trapped in a burning car, my response is never fear or anger or disappointment or doubt, my response is always the same. It's thank you. It's *always* thank you."

They don't look like they believe me.

22. The Best of All Possible Worlds

> "Do you believe," said Candide, "that men have always
> massacred each other as they do today, that they have always
> been liars, cheats, traitors, ingrates, brigands, idiots, thieves,
> scoundrels, gluttons, drunkards, misers, envious, ambitious,
> bloody-minded, calumniators, debauchees, fanatics,
> hypocrites, and fools?"
>
> "Do you believe," said Martin, "that hawks have always eaten
> pigeons when they have found them?"
>
> "Yes, without doubt," said Candide.
>
> "Well, then," said Martin, "if hawks have always had the
> same character why should you imagine that men may have
> changed theirs?"
>
> *–Voltaire, Candide*

THERE ARE TWO LITERARY OBSERVATIONS that would be fun and illuminating to make at this point. The first is *Candide*, which was Voltaire's satiric response to the optimistic assertion by Gottfried Leibniz that "All is for the best in this, the best of all possible worlds." This assertion actually comes as a solution in the pseudo-philosophical line of inquiry called Theodicy, which seeks to ease our Spiritual Dissonance by reconciling our inner belief in God's love with the outer reality of suffering and evil.

Theodicy is not a valid philosophical inquiry because it presupposes an omnipotent, omniscient, beneficent God, and seeks to reconcile evil within those preset terms. In this same sense, all philosophy is pseudo-philosophy and all science is pseudo-science because, as a precondition of their very existence, they accept the make-believe reality of the dreamstate as *real* reality, and erect their systems of knowledge on that baseless basis.

Candide, like Buddha, was raised in privileged isolation, shielded from the ugliness of the world, and, like Buddha, goes out and discovers it for himself in a way that is devastating to his cultivated worldview. Both Candide and Buddha then undergo suffering and hardship owing to wrong-thinking, and both eventually end up finding their respective middle ways.

Candide is raised to believe that everything is part of God's plan and that, whether we see it or not, everything is for the best. To interpret any horror or evil or suffering as anything other than for the best is simply to display an ignorance of the fact that God has a grand design which we are not fit to judge. The main theme of *Candide* is the satirization of this absolute optimism by taking it out of the theory of the classroom and subjecting it to the practical rigors of a gruesomely un-best world. The story subjects its characters to every natural and man-made horror and every sort of suffering to put this optimism to the test, and their philosophy fails miserably. In the end, even Dr. Pangloss, the optimistic philosopher, admits that, though he still maintains that all is for the best, he doesn't believe it.

In the words of the yet-untested Dr. Pangloss, professor of meta-physico-theologico-cosmolo-nigology:

"It is demonstrable," said he, "that things cannot be otherwise than as they are; for all being created for an end, all is necessarily for the best end. Observe, that the nose has been formed to bear spectacles—thus we have spectacles. Legs are visibly designed for stockings—and we have stockings. Stones were made to be hewn, and to construct castles—therefore my lord has a magnificent castle; for the greatest baron in the province ought to be the best lodged. Pigs were made to be eaten—therefore we eat pork all the year round. Consequently they who assert that all is well have said a foolish thing, they should have said all is for the best."

Overlooking the intellectual whorishness of it, and despite the faultiness of the reasoning by which the result was arrived at, the philosophy of Candide's instructor, Dr. Pangloss, is ultimately and knowably correct. If we algebraically reduce the equation by canceling out equal and opposite judgments—taking good from one side and evil from the other, for instance—we are left with an egoless and spiritually palate-cleansing observation: Whatever happens must be the best thing that *could* happen, because it is the thing that *does* happen. Ultimately, the only criteria we have by which to determine what is best is what occurs.

Or, as Alexander Pope succinctly put it: Whatever is, is right.

The ocean cannot violate the idea of an ocean. If there is conflict between idea and actual, then the idea is in error. The ocean can't be in error because what it *does* is what it *is*. The tsunami that wipes out villages isn't good or bad, or right or wrong, it simply is.

The destination isn't where we're going, it's where we are. This is the clear and natural egoless perspective. Where is the part of the ocean that feels bad about the tsunami that wipes out entire villages? Where is the thinking part of the ocean where actions are interpreted and future behaviors adapted or modified accordingly? Where is the planning and scheduling done? Where does it store its memories and knowledge and opinions and beliefs? Where is the feeling part where the ocean senses its own majesty and power and beauty? Where does it feel pride and shame? Where does it fear the time when it will no longer be? Where does the ocean keep its hopes and ambitions? Its regrets and misgivings? Which part conspires against one human enterprise and in favor of another? How does the ocean judge? How does it know right from wrong?

Finding no answers to these questions, are we to assume that the ocean is an inanimate, lifeless thing with no intelligence? Obviously not. The ocean is a living, vital, dynamic system of pure intelligence. It performs an operation of incalculable complexity every second of every day, around the world, from one end of earth time to the other, with never the slightest deviation from perfection. This pure intelligence is found everywhere from galaxies to sub-atomic particles, and everywhere beyond and in-between. Every insect, every person, every thought, every breeze, every planetary body, every dustmote and doorknob, every drop of dew and speck of time. "I believe a leaf of grass is no less than the journeywork of the stars," wrote Whitman. "I discovered the secret of the sea in meditation upon the dewdrop," wrote Gibran. The ocean is just one infinitesimal part of an infinite system in which we too are infinitesimal parts, yet no part is greater or lesser. No part is apart; every part contains the totality. The ocean is a single thing; to be a part of the ocean is to be the ocean. *Tat tvam asi*: That thou art.

This, too, is the egoless perspective of the Integrated State.

The universe is pure intelligence; absolute, unerring, perfect. So what's the difference between the ocean and the stars and the subatomic world and you?

Ego.

Ego-clad beings alone are capable of imperfection. We alone, in our segregated condition, are capable of all the things the universe isn't; error, folly, emotionality, stupidity, appreciation, love, hate, exploration, awe, self-importance, meaning, art, genocide, and a very long list of other qualities including, most importantly for our purposes, aspiration. We can aspire beyond ourselves, beyond segregated selfhood; we can transcend our own natures. We can aspire to divest ourselves of our self-limiting programming and merge back into the integrated condition from which ego artificially segregates us.

Ultimately, of course, an ego-bound humanity is a subsystem, just like the ocean and the stars and the grass, and what looks like error from within is perfection from without. We are perfect in our imperfection; flawed by design.

When we divest ourselves of our egoic insistence on judging actions, intentions, thoughts and feelings as right or wrong, good or bad, positive or negative, we see that the only criteria by which anything might be judged is by whether or not it occurs. The heretic is correct in committing his heresy, if he does, and the angry mob is correct in burning him to death, if they do. There is no right or wrong or good or evil, only is and isn't.

Whatever is, is right.

All is for the best in this, the best of all possible worlds.

✧

The other literary observation to make here is *1984,* where the difference between a belief and a paradigm is highlighted by protagonist Winston Smith's axiom: "Freedom is the freedom to say that two plus two make four. If that is granted, all else follows."

What Winston learns later, during the course of his de/reprogramming in the Ministry of Love, is that what can be granted can also be *un*granted, and that two plus two actually equals five, or three, or whatever the party says it equals. Making that minor adjustment to Winston's belief-set, however, is not enough for his benefactors/malefactors. Even his last shred of selfhood, that truest truth in his heart of hearts, which he is most certain can never be taken from him—his love for Julia—can, as he will learn in Room 101, be stripped away in a minute or two, just like any other belief.

Thus is Winston Smith's Buddha killed.

With the exception of the subjective I Am, all knowledge is just belief, and all beliefs are just costume jewelry that can be torn off and tossed in the gutter like the cheap egoic adornments they are. We don't have beliefs, they have us.

Two plus two makes four is exactly as true as two plus two makes five. The truest truth we keep in our heart of hearts is no more true than the truths we tell children and traffic cops. Two plus two makes whatever we say it makes. This is what O'Brien, Winston Smith's savior/persecutor, refers to as collective solipsism—or its opposite.

> "But how can you control matter?" [Winston] burst out. "You don't even control the climate or the law of gravity. And there are disease, pain, death—"
>
> O'Brien silenced him by a movement of his hand. "We control matter because we control the mind. Reality is inside the skull. You will learn by degrees, Winston. There is nothing that we could not do. Invisibility, levitation — anything. I could float off this floor like a soap bubble if I wish to. I do not wish to, because the Party does not wish it. You must get rid of those nineteenth-century ideas about the laws of Nature. We make the laws of Nature."

The truth is that no belief is true, and to say that any belief is true is to open the floodgates and say that all beliefs are true. No untruth is more or less true than any other untruth. When we are lucid within the dream-state, we see that two plus two equals four, but when we are non-lucid within the dreamstate, no such restrictions apply, and even two plus two equals four is just another belief. Anything plus anything equals anything. Two plus two equals whatever we say it equals. It can equal different things to different people at different times for different reasons. In the sleeping dreamstate, your two twos can be seven, and mine can be one. Maybe the 2+2=5s and the 2+2=3s hate each other and have been warring for centuries. Maybe they're barely aware of each other, or maybe they're uneasily allied against the 2+2=7s. The world belongs to the 2+2=4s at the moment, but as *1984* helps us see, that can change. That's life in the non-lucid dreamstate, where truth is arbitrary and reality is only an 'opeless fancy.

23. The Three-Legged Stool of Delusion

His mind slid away into the labyrinthine world of double-think. To know and not to know, to be conscious of complete truthfulness while telling carefully constructed lies, to hold simultaneously two opinions which cancelled out, knowing them to be contradictory and believing in both of them, to use logic against logic... to forget whatever it was necessary to forget, then to draw it back into memory again at the moment when it was needed, and then promptly to forget it again: and above all, to apply the same process to the process itself. That was the ultimate subtlety: consciously to induce unconscious-ness, and then, once again, to become unconscious of the act of hypnosis you had just performed. Even to understand the word 'doublethink' involved the use of doublethink.

—George Orwell, 1984

I T'S BOB'S LAST DAY IN Mexico. He appears at my table and eyes the advance reading copy of his book sitting in one of the piles, but doesn't ask me if I've looked at it yet. In fact I have, but not for long. It doesn't take me long to detect and assess ego, whether in people or in their works. I could easily and confidently separate a hundred "new thought" books into a reject pile and a further-look pile in ten minutes, (eight, if I didn't have to neatly stack the rejects), and then winnow the small further-look pile down in another couple of minutes, leaving me with, probably, two or three books I'd want to spend another minute with, of which maybe one, but probably none, would prove a rewarding find.

I mentioned in *Damnedest* that I could meet a person and know very quickly, within a few words, where they were currently located in the spir-itual terrain. This is that. This ability to make fast, accurate judgments, especially about printed material, is something I developed early in my own process, which is why I mention it here; anyone with a strong grasp of enlightenment theory could do it. I found it to be a very valuable tool. It saved me from wasting time and energy treating books and their authors with respect based on the respect in which they were held by those whose respect I didn't respect. Also useful was manifestation; the ability to ask for and receive and recognize what I needed when I needed it. Between these two budding talents, I was able to get what I needed and not get lost in the mountains of books and teachings and groups and philosophies competing for my attention.

With Bob's book, I made a greater than usual effort to be appreciative and constructively critical. I went through it with a highlighter at first, marking phrases and claims that seemed particularly underwhelming, that he might wish to revise or reconsider or rephrase, but I only got a few pages before the futility of the task sank in. I spent another few minutes scanning through the rest of the book and set it aside.

It was essentially a rehash of the same old gurus and teachings, the same old ideals and platitudes. Plenty of heart and soul and equanimity and serenity, plenty of peace and compassion, love and beauty, but not a sharp or pointed thought to be found. Just the standard New Age prattle; a soft, sweet marshmallow of a book. In other words, I realized, Bob just wants to be a teacher. He's put in his time, he's learned the talk, and now he wants to move to the next level.

Bob's book will probably be popular and catapult him up into the ranks of successful and respected spiritual author/teachers. It has all the right elements. It's nice and fuzzy and warm. It demands nothing of the reader except to recommend that they perform the usual techniques and practices; meditation, journaling, witnessing, etc. It assures the reader that they can achieve profound liberation in a moment, just by realizing something or releasing something, or something like that. No real change is necessary, no renunciation or sacrifice is called for, nothing difficult or demanding or even inconvenient is required. It promises the world and it has a pretty moral: We are love.

In short, standard have-your-cake-and-eat-it-too boilerplate. Of course, market forces are at work and you have to give the people what they want if you want them to want you. It didn't used to be this way, with all this unseemly pandering to opinion and competition with all manner of contenders and wannabes. Blame it on Gutenberg with his printing press and Al Gore with his internet. Catholics, as one example, held a monopoly for centuries in parts of the world, and so firm was their grip that they could, in the name of suppressing heresy, torture and kill their own adherents. Nowadays, in our climate of informed alternatives, they can barely get away with suppressing heresy by sodomizing young boys. How the mighty have fallen.

Bob has asked me to discuss his book with him on a point-by-point basis, to address the particulars of what I consider its merits and shortcomings. He sounds reasonable when he says it, but there's no getting around the fact that the transition Bob writes about is one that he himself has not undergone. Lisa has undergone it, or *is* undergoing it, and that's what it looks like, not the pretty picture Bob paints about how love is our true nature and all we have to do is go into the silence and let go of our negative whatever and embrace our positive whatever so our inner whatever can... whatever.

Bob wants to give enlightenment back to the people. Yes, enlightenment is the word he uses, although quiet reverie or mild trance or grinning stupor is usually what he describes, and a shallow, undeveloped Human Adulthood is, at the very most, what he means. He feels enlightenment has been unfairly taken from the people and made the exclusive province of, well, the enlightened. He sees an injustice in that and seeks remedy by acting as the self-appointed spiritual Robin Hood who steals it back from the elite and returns it to the unfairly deprived. He wants to bring enlightenment down from the mountaintop to the valley where everyone can enjoy it. Spiritual socialism.

The enlightenment of which Bob speaks and writes is of an ordinary, everyday quality. He provides a list of myths and misconceptions about enlightenment which serve to rule out anything that would make it seem other than a minor, garden variety epiphany. His book is a who's who of spiritual authors and teachers who hold the same or similar views, about how being awake and being enlightened and being happy are all the same thing, and how the reason no one can ever find any of these things is because they're looking for them, and how the great paradox is that in order to find what we're searching for, we have to stop searching for it. That kind of thing.

And it's probably true. If what someone is searching for is contentment, then it seems like a good idea, at least on the face of it, to tell them to stop being discontent; that their problem isn't that they lack something they want, but that they want something they lack, and that as soon as they stop wanting it, they'll stop lacking it. That would be fine if they were just talking about contentment and happiness, but they—and by they, I mean the roster of authors and teachers who make their livings and their reputations espousing this line of jailhouse orthodoxy—keep making it about enlightenment, awakening, Buddhahood and truth.

There's nothing new or surprising in all this. This is the standard operating procedure of protective ignorance; just another day at the office for Maya. How do you keep people in a jail without locks? By keeping them from becoming discontent. Easily done.

The problem, as they see it, is that spiritual seekers think they must climb to the mountaintop where, they assume, such peak individuals as Buddha and Jesus reside, but the seekers aren't making a very good job of it, which is a pretty safe way to interpret total failure. Rather than revisiting their ideas about Jesus, Buddha and mountaintops, Bob's breed of spiritual solution-provider seeks to fix the problem by switching labels. Now the valley *is* the mountaintop, and everyone *is* enlightened, *if* they go along with the switch. The new goal is right here, right now, and need only be recognized as such. *Voila!* Total failure is now total success.

Peace is war. Captivity is freedom. Ignorance is knowledge.

Asleep is awake.

This is so Orwellian, so brazen yet subtle, so elegantly representative of the self-deceit of which the fear-based mind is capable, that it arouses in me powerful feelings of admiration and respect for Maya. I say this without any trace of irony. I can't think of anything more fascinating or lovely or worthy of appreciation than Maya; the architect of delusion, the intelligence of fear. Our beloved Big Brother.

✧

Bob wants to talk, but it's time to take Maya for a walk so I invite him to come along. My knee still needs help on these hilly excursions, so I grab a hiking staff and the ball-flinger and a water bottle and we head out.

Early in Orwell's *1984*, protagonist Winston Smith is sitting in a cafeteria contemplating the various personality types around him. They're different, but what they have in common is that they're all managing to believe what is, to Winston, unbelievable. One manages to believe through sheer stupidity, another through zealotry, and a third, the most intelligent, through the mental complexities of doublethink.

And sitting in their midst is poor, hopelessly sane Winston, who knows that two plus two makes four, but who is surrounded by people who know with greater certainty that two plus two makes five. All of them living in a world where you get tortured and killed for believing—even in your most secret heart—that two plus two makes four. Believing the lie is absolutely necessary to their survival, and Winston's fatal flaw is that he can't do it.

Bob is a unique blend of all three types; stupid, as in protectively ignorant; zealous, as in the emotional reinforcement of ignorance; and intelligent, as in capable of the strenuous mental contortions necessary to believe the obviously untrue. That is the three-legged stool of delusion, and Bob, like everyone, sits squarely upon it.

*Un*like everyone, however, Bob has declared himself an authority on truth and has written a book on the subject. Regardless of what comes from it, his hope when writing it was that it would be well received and that he would rise from the swollen ranks of students to the less puffy ranks of teachers; from sheep to shepherd, from common inmate to respected trustee.

We exit through the north gate and follow roads and trails up into the hills toward an old chapel. For the first ten minutes it's all uphill and not conducive to talk. Maya is off prowling around, sniffing every third rock. There are perils for a dog out here and I'm only semi-ready for an emergency, but she's a smart girl and hasn't come close to getting into trouble yet.

Once leveled off, we walk and talk for a few minutes, circling around the edges of tricky subjects. The problem with talking to Bob has been that we don't have a workable dynamic. If we were student-teacher, that would be fine because I could muscle him around a bit and he would know not to resist too much. As it is, he wants to think we're having a peer-to-peer dialogue, which leaves me in a bit of confusion as to what to say and why to say it.

The world is full of false and artificial authority. To my casual observation, true authority comes from knowledge and false authority comes from might. Badges and guns, titles and offices, money and rank, these are a few of the things that bestow upon people a power and privilege to which they have no independent claim. They are the outward sources of a power for which there is no inner source. In spirituality, titles and garb and fancy names serve a similar purpose. With Bob, even though we've had a few hours together every day for almost a week, there is still this slight friction in our conversations because he wants his authority recognized and I have no capacity to do so. He has written a book. That's his badge, the tangible symbol of his authority. He has found that most people respect the badge and grant the authority, but this is a place of sharp blades where skill and mastery are everything and costume and showmanship are nothing. I like Bob and he is very useful to me, so I have to remember when I talk with him that he has consigned himself to a sort of gray area where he can neither speak nor listen.

✧

"Do you have a question?" I ask when the terrain permits.

"What should my question be?" he says. "What do I need to know?"

Not a bad question on the face of it, but actually a strategic evasion.

"The short answer is Human Adulthood," I tell him.

"What's the long answer?" he asks.

"The books," I say. "Read the books."

"Okay," he says, "I plan to read them, but while I have you here, while we're walking along together, anything you say, regardless of my feelings, I'd be very receptive—"

I sigh. He's learned to play me over the last few days.

"That's very commendable, Bob. I understand that you're a person of deep learning and uncommon spiritual refinement. I've known a lot of people who were very spiritually refined, but they were all still ego-bound, so—" I shrug.

"You mean, like me?"

I scoop up a tennis ball in the ball-flinger gizmo and give it a long toss. Maya ignores it.

"Okay, like me, I get it," he says. "Sorry, please go on."

"You want me to tell you what I think you need to hear," I say, "so I will. Spirituality is the most insidious form of self-delusion, and it's got you. Spirituality is Maya at her most cunningly self-preserving; ego at it's most deeply entrenched. That's what you're up against, that's what has you trapped. Spirituality hangs over the world like a pall, like an oily black smoke being pumped into the atmosphere by smokestacks sticking up from millions of churches and universities and monasteries and temples, from bookstands and magazine racks and websites. I look at you and I see a lifelong consumer of this smoke who now wants to get into the manufacturing and distribution end of the business."

He's silent for a minute.

"I just have a really hard time believing all that," he says.

"Yes," I say, "I think that's my point."

"But it doesn't *seem* like an oily black smoke," he persists. "It seems like people trying to find meaning and happiness, trying to live life in accord with higher laws, trying to live in harmony with the earth and their fellow man, trying to raise children, to be better people, better custodians of the planet. I don't know how you can compare the kind of evolved, life-positive, non-denominational sort of spirituality I'm describing with an oily black smoke. I just don't see it."

"That's my perception from the outside looking in," I say. "From within, I know, it seems sweet and pleasant and good; something desirable and comforting. Naturally so. Nature of the beast."

He ponders. I limp. Maya sniffs.

"So," Bob continues, "I'm saying there are all these people who are living these harmonious, spiritually elevated lives, and you're saying they're living in some sort of smoke?"

"I don't mean it in a bad way," I say. "This is what Maya does. This is how she holds the whole thing together. This is the critical service she performs."

"You endow Maya with a great deal of power and intelligence."

"Actually, you do. I cut her off years ago."

"I was speaking figuratively," he says.

"I wasn't."

He doesn't reply.

"Maya is inside you, animating you, right now," I continue. "If I seem impatient with you at times, it's because you think I'm talking to *you* and I know I'm talking to *her*. You believe you're awake, and I see that you're asleep. What's the point of us having this conversation? I don't know, but it's what I do, and you asked, so here we are."

"So, I'm standing in this oily—?"

"It's not just that you're standing in the oily black smoke, it's that you've been breathing it in deeply for years, and now it suffuses your entire system from the inside out. In through your lungs and your pores so that now you radiate it back out in the form of your words and your writings. It has seeped into every cell of your being so completely that you have no awareness of it, like the air, like water to a fish. It's the medium in which you exist. You don't know anything else."

"Well," says Bob with an uncomfortable laugh, "I must be in here somewhere."

"Must you? Then maybe that's what you want to be looking for; this alleged self of yours that must be in there somewhere."

"Well, maybe that's what I'm trying to do; find this inner self."

"Or maybe that's what you're trying *not* to do."

I keep throwing balls for Maya, but she's more interested in scents, so I have to chase them down myself.

✧

We take a break on a hilltop with some nice views. I pour some water in a folding bowl for Maya, then Bob and I drink.

"You know," he says, "there are a lot of myths about enlightenment. They say that anyone who claims to be enlightened automatically isn't, or that there's no such thing as enlightenment."

"I agree with that," I say.

"You do?"

"Sure. Enlightenment is untruth-unrealization, and self is an untruth. You can't have both, it's one or the other, so who does that leave to be enlightened? No-self is true self. Despite the apparent paradox, being enlightened means there's no one left to be enlightened."

"But you claim to be enlightened."

"Within the context of our current metaphor, I claim that I'm not in the blinding smoke. The thing to remember is that, regardless of any and all claims to the contrary, there is no visibility in the smoke. No one can see anything, and the most significant thing no one can see is that no one can see anything. Some people say they can see, and if they tell a good story and if they believe it themselves, then they can get others to believe it as well. That suits Maya's purposes and there are rewards for doing it. Nearly all spiritual teachers fall into that category; the blind leading the blind. Once you can see, you can easily see who else can and who can't. There's no room for debate."

"Me?" he asks.

"You what?"

"I'm in this smoke pretending I can see?"

"Of course," I reply.

"But not you?"

"I'm not a teacher. I have no students. I have no teaching."

"But what's the difference then? You're here with the rest of us. You see what everyone else sees."

"I'm not and I don't."

"But we're here together right now," he says. "I'm looking at you. You're looking at me. You see me."

"You're a mirage, Bob. I see through you. I'm a mirage, I see through me." I gesture to indicate the lovely view. "It's *all* a mirage, I see through everything. Just to clarify; this oily black smoke isn't just the medium in which the spiritually benighted ego resides, it is the ego itself; the stuff of which ego is made. There is no distinction to be drawn between deceiver, deceit and deceived. Until we understand the egoic condition, there's really no chance of making any actual progress."

"You know," he says, "there are quite a few highly respected teachers who say there is no progress to make, that *that's* the illusion, that we're already fully awake, already enlightened, and that we just have to stop struggling and searching. What we seek is what we already are, and it's only our searching that blinds us to that truth."

I can't find the heart to respond to that. Everything Bob is saying about modern spirituality dovetails with my own views, only with a reverse spin. Where he sees tranquility and equanimity, I see docility and unconsciousness. Where he sees advancement, I see entrenchment. Whenever I venture to take a look at what's current and popular in New Age and spiritual thought, all I find is the same dumbed-down, watered-down, sickly-sweet slop. It's as if everyone was dining from a common trough and the special of the day is just a matter of who regurgitated last. I try to tough it out, but the experience is ill-making, like radiation exposure, and only tolerable in small doses. When I get over my sour reaction, I remind myself that if I can't stand the smell, I shouldn't stick my head in the sewer.

There are exceptions, of course, which is why I go back and check once in a while, always looking for someone with true authority and direct knowledge and the power of expression.

I put the water away and we continue walking. I pay silent tribute to the supreme and subtle mastery of Maya; the goddess of delusion, not the dog. This is her show, she has it locked down tight, and nowhere is her influence stronger than where you'd expect it to be weakest.

24. Alternative People

There seem to be two kinds of searchers: those who seek to make their ego something other than it is, i.e. holy, happy, unselfish (as though you could make a fish unfish), and those who understand that all such attempts are just gesticulation and play-acting, that there is only one thing that can be done, which is to disidentify themselves with the ego, by realising its unreality, and by becoming aware of their eternal identity with pure being.

—Wei Wu Wei

B OB PICKS UP SOME STONES and tosses them off into the brush as we walk. To me this is just idle gab. To Bob, it's an assault on the foundation of his carefully crafted and heavily fortified egoic structure; his Bob-ness. After a few minutes he tries another tack.

"Jed, seriously, I think you've got it wrong about the present spiritual climate in the world. You're being very contemptuous of something you don't really seem to understand. Human spirituality isn't this dinosaur trapped in the past; it's an evolutionary process and it's happening right now, all over the world. We can change the world, make it a better place for everyone. Maybe I'm not talking about people who are fully enlightened the way you think of it, but people who are awake in their own right, all sorts of very inspired people: artists and musicians, teachers and parents, people full of loving kindness and open hearts and fundamental decency who've seen that the path of the heart has its own riches and rewards. Intelligent, successful, thoughtful people—"

I try to cut him off but he cuts me off.

"Let me continue," he continues. "I'm talking about deeply, authentically spiritual people who live life in the moment while adapting to a changing future; who create art and green businesses and wholesome, happy families; people who aren't part of the great herd of humanity mindlessly squandering their lives and our planetary resources; people who've escaped the rat race and found a better way. These are people of awareness and vision who understand the predicament in which humanity finds itself—socially, politically, environmentally—and are leading this revolution, Jed, they are leading the way into a—"

"A new world order?"

"Yes, okay, a new world order, a new kind of humanity, of human community. That's what I'm trying to tell you, I understand what you're saying about the old ways, but what you're not seeing is—"

"That it's already happening," I say.

"Yes, that this revolution is taking place right now, and it's not about Buddhist or Hindu or New Age ideology, or any particular school or doctrine. It's not limited to any one viewpoint, but embraces all ideologies in the sense and to the degree that they respect the individual and the family and the rights of people to follow their own path and pursue their happiness. It's about a new approach to life based on deeply held universal values and principles common to all. There's a global spiritual—"

"Renaissance?"

"Exactly, a global spiritual renaissance taking place—"

I stop walking and scowl at him, but he has some weird glow of righteousness that makes him immune. The theme he's expounding is prominent in his book and seems to call for the uniting of many different fringe belief systems—those falling into the gray zone between major religions and whacko cults—into a cohesive movement which would lead mankind into a better tomorrow. As far as I can make out, the common trait shared by these people and groups is their tolerance for all points of view. Two plus two equals whatever anyone says it does. Everyone is right.

All beliefs are true.

In any event, what he's talking about, even if it were true or likely, has nothing to do with me and what I talk and write about. Except that both our subjects fall under the broad rubric of human spirituality, they are unrelated. I am completely indifferent to all of his stated ideals, and he is completely unacquainted with my views. I've made several attempts to impress this upon him, but people seem to have a special place within their framework for things that are outside their framework, and that seems to be where he has put me.

We continue walking. He continues talking.

"I'm talking about an approach to life that is open and receptive," he goes on. "An approach that encourages the processes of growth and creation and heart expansion. It's all about living lives of love and peace in a way that no society before has been able to accomplish. Do you know how most people live in society today? Like slaves, like mindless automatons going through the motions of life, but not really alive. We enjoy this wonderful level of abundance and prosperity that allows us to realize the dream of a new dawn for mankind, a transformation of consciousness. All of the great wisdom teachings point to this. That's why I think of it as a revolution, Jed, an ideological realignment. Together we can bring about real change, an evolutionary shift. Have you ever heard of the hundredth monkey? This is a radical awakening of the species and it's happening right now. Many thousands of people throughout the world are taking part in this transformation. Millions, probably. This is a very exciting time, Jed, and I don't think you fully realize—"

✧

But I do.

Bob is talking about alternative people. Alternative beliefs and outlooks, alternative business and politics, alternative lifestyles and health-care, alternative foods and fabrics, alternative child-rearing and schooling, alternative fuels and energies—alternative everything, basically, but not *very* alternative. These are alternatives with*in* the established paradigm, not alternatives *to* it; a subherd running in parallel to the main body. Rather than detaching from their ego structures, alternative people merely reshape them along more heart-felt and self-centric lines, their multivarious goals and ideals reducing to personal happiness via the removal, avoidance, and denial of unhappiness.

In short, they make the minor course adjustment from orthodox to somewhat less orthodox beliefs, and the one reason underlying the many apparent reasons for this change is always the same; survival of ego. A chameleon-like adaptability is one of Maya's most effective maneuvers. Paint some trees on the walls of your cell and some clouds on the ceiling and you're free as a bird.

This is the status of the would-be spiritual aspirant in the world today. Spirituality is merely an alternative religion; the same lines filled in with similar colors from a slightly different palette. It fulfills the same needs as religion, makes the same undemanding demands, and offers the same vague promises and rewards. It also enjoys the same curious immunity from accountability enjoyed by the religions and whacko cults it falls between, such that users blame failure on themselves and not the belief package they bought, or the people who sold it to them. In the end, all three groups—major religions, whacko cults, and the gooey middle—are just minor variations of the one true religion of man: Agnosticism.

Without Knowledgism.

Bob's alternative people have convinced themselves that they have escaped from incarceration when they have merely burrowed from one cell into another and labeled the new one Freedom. In this prison of ego, world-view and cell decor are synonymous. Many live in perpetual dissatisfaction with their cell and seek remedy by introducing new and exciting decorative touches; a swatch of Buddhism here, a dab of Sufism there, a little mystic poetry to brighten a drab corner, and maybe a little Native American splash to give it some local color. Always shopping, always looking for that perfect thing to fill that empty space, finding it and then growing tired of it and returning to the search. This chronic urge to spruce up one's surroundings provides the lifeblood of the spiritual marketplace, which is, at all levels, nothing more than a prison cell design boutique. Whether you're in the market for Christian Gothic, New Age Eclectic, or Apocalyptic Chic, they've got what you're looking for.

Being an alternative person is a luxury not available to everyone; it takes disposable time and disposable money. Welfare moms and migrant workers aren't the ones buying organic tofu or chakra tuning forks or hemp luggage sets or, frankly, my books. Peasants only do Tai Chi where it's mainstream. Not everyone can afford to take off for a month of energy healing at Esalen, or a week of swimming with dolphins, or even a day to skinnydip in the Dalai Lama's vast ocean of wisdom.

Of course, anyone can meditate for free. Even if you're poor you can sit down and close your eyes and repeat a mantra or count your breaths for a few minutes, but realistically, without a dedicated sacred space stocked with imported incense, hand-tufted cushions, authentic-replica temple bells, and an alabaster Kuan Yin statue on a museum-quality mahogany altar where, clad in loose-fitting, vegetable-dyed, organic cotton yoga robes you can work toward your spiritual salvation in a manner befitting so austere a pursuit, what chance do you really have? Sure, you can put on flannel jammies, lock yourself in the bathroom, light up that old Boysenberry Delight candle that's been in there since the fan broke, scrunch some towels under your butt and place the Snoopy bath toy reverently upon the porcelain altar, but seriously, who's that gonna fool? Not you, and that brings us to the Golden Rule of all spiritual practices:

If you're not fooling yourself, what's the point?

The true goal of all spiritual practices is to keep yourself fooled, to maintain the self-deception, to see what's not and not see what is. That's why the stated goals are always unverifiable and ill-defined; it's not about attaining them, it's about pursuing them. Who wants to wake up? When we have a little itch that threatens to awaken us in the night, we want to scratch the itch and make it go away, not let it evict us from our slumbers. Same thing here. In this sense, spiritual practice—meditation, for instance—is one hundred percent effective. If a spiritual practice satisfies your urge to do something spiritual, if it makes you think you're making progress, if it scratches your itch without disturbing your slumber, then it's doing exactly what it's supposed to be doing.

✧

What to say and why to say it? I ponder these questions as Bob and I begin the downhill return leg of our walk. He keeps pushing his ideas of a spiritually elevated humanity and I keep pushing back, more from habit, I suppose, than from any hope or belief that I'll get through to him. I know our discussions will probably make it into the book, so I have that in mind. Otherwise, I'd be at a total loss as to what to say and why to say it.

"You and your alternative people seem married to this idea that we're playing by some sort of point system," I tell Bob when it's my turn again, "as if you're working toward a karmic degree, or prizes in a cosmic gift catalog, like some glorious eternal vacation package in a place where the rules you don't like don't apply. You're tinkering around on the surface with the petty cosmetic issues, but the real stuff you have to deal with is inside you, in as deep as you go, which is a lot deeper than you know until you *do* go. You asked me to tell you, Bob, so I'm telling you. I know these spiritual people you're talking about. I've known many spiritual people from many paths and systems; I see them with eyes you possess but have never used. They're dilettantes, dabblers, hobbyists; deserters from their own lives. This isn't measured in opinion but in progress. Their spirituality is on the surface only; an egoic embellishment, an evasive tactic. It's better to look different, they think, than to *be* different. Spirituality is something that's supposed to improve our lives, they suppose, not derail them."

He's shaking his head as if I'm still not getting it. He starts to protest but I press on.

"You disagree with me," I continue, "because you've never seen where real spiritual battles are waged, where spiritual progress is like slowly and methodically skinning yourself with a straight-razor, one layer at a time, each more painful than the last. You've convinced yourself that ego is something small and trite, like it's a habit you can kick. Imagine having your head cut off. Then imagine it not in a single chop, but in small pieces. Then imagine doing it yourself."

He grimaces.

"You don't even know about such things. The money and the crowds flow toward pretty fairy tales where everything is beautiful and everyone lives happily ever after. A fairy tale is what everyone wants, so that's what everyone gets, and it's ego that lives happily ever after."

All the while we're walking and I'm throwing balls for Maya who gives joyous pursuit before being lured back to all the strange and exciting scents along the path, leaving me to hobble around collecting the balls and throw them again.

"Your assessment seems unduly pessimistic," he says half-heartedly.

"I wouldn't characterize it that way," I say, "because I don't see anything as wrong, but yes, ultimately, my assessment is that people exist in such a marginal state that it's more like coma than life, so I guess that sounds pessimistic. I'd be happy to stop talking."

"Go on, please," says Bob in a quiet voice.

We're getting into a curvy area of the path with limited visibility.

"Do you see Maya?" I ask.

"Not the way you do," he says, "but from what I understand—"

"My dog, Bob, do you see my dog?"

I let out a short whistle and after a few seconds she comes bounding around a corner behind us and straight into hot tennis ball pursuit.

"For many sincere people like yourself," I continue, "spirituality is a walk in the park on a sunny day, bubbling with pretty notions of peace on earth and good will toward men. It's softcore spirituality, full of soft focus and soft lighting and soft music, everything soft and fluffy, all moving towards some earthshaking climax that never seems to materialize. Anyone involved in the actual process of awakening would view such frivolity the way men on a bloody battlefield view children playing war in backyards. You talk about a revolution, but revolutions aren't like afternoon tea parties with fine china and extended pinkies, they're hellish nightmares from which you can't wake up. Real spirituality is a savage insurrection, the oppressed rising up in a do-or-die bid for freedom. It's not something people do to improve themselves or earn merit or impress friends or to find greater joy and meaning in life. It's a suicidal assault on a foe of unimaginable superiority."

"Like David and Goliath," he suggests.

"Actually, yes, good parable. Our Goliath is large and powerful and cunning and all-seeing. Our David is puny and weak and stupid and blind. He has no advantage in this fight whatsoever, except the heart to fight and his rock. We can think of the rock as truth, and truth is the giant-killer. Truth destroys everything. Goliath has every power and advantage except truth, and that's why we can fight and win; we have truth and Maya doesn't. Still, it's not a one-shot deal where David throws the rock and Goliath tips over dead. It's a long, ugly struggle because we are both friend and foe; both David and Goliath reside within. Every inch of ground takes everything we have. Lessons aren't delivered as quaint little parables and allegories, but as irreparable losses; lesson after lesson, loss after loss. Every step is a loss and as long as there's more to lose, there are more steps to take. Everything is lost. Nothing is gained."

"So you're saying I should—"

"Not at all, Bob. I'm not inciting you to revolt or to launch an insurrection. The dreamstate is a big amusement park and I would never encourage anyone to try to escape. That would be as absurd as suggesting that you commit suicide for your own good."

Bob is silent for a few moments.

"Gosh," he says.

25. Carnivalesque

> A child-like man is not a man whose development has been arrested; on the contrary, he is a man who has given himself a chance of continuing to develop long after most adults have muffled themselves in the cocoon of middle-aged habit and convention.
>
> *—Aldous Huxley*

D EATH WAS IN THE AIR.

I've had two people in my life who were critical in helping me handle my modest financial concerns. Neither actually did anything or charged anything as far as I could tell, yet between them they got everything done and got themselves paid for doing it. Clark was a lunch man and Norman was a phone man. Both were from a different era of New York City, both were already in semi-retirement and practically like family when I was a kid. Clark died a few years ago and Norman, the winking, brandy drinking, cravat-wearing Gin Rummy champ, died shortly before I was to travel to Virginia with Lisa's help and eulogize Brett.

It was Norman I called when I wanted to buy the Ajijic house and needed to convert my few assets to cash with the most speed and least loss and tax consequence. I gave him legal power to act for me and he devised and implemented a solution that gave me what I needed in the timeframe I needed it.

But Norman's passing left some loose ends, so I had to make a trip to New York and New Canaan to finalize things. I was staying in a bed and breakfast in Connecticut when my newly acquired and much-despised disposable phone started chirping. It was Lisa, calling to let me know her dad Frank had passed away. A heart attack in his sleep, she said. She had to get the body back to the states for services and burial in the family plot alongside her mother, who had died the previous year.

Naturally, I excused her from any obligations she felt regarding our trip to Virginia, but she assured me she wanted more than ever to make that trip and that since we were both already in the states, maybe we could get together a few days early and make a more relaxed trip of it.

✧

We manage to hook up at Reagan National just outside DC. I had asked her to rent a comfortable sedan, but she upgraded us to a very stately black Lincoln Navigator, explaining that she wanted this trip to be special and that she'd pay the difference. It's only a few hundred miles and we could make it in a straight shot, but we decide to stretch it out to over five hundred miles and two days by heading east first, then leisurely southward and westward, stopping and taking sidetrips as we felt like it, avoiding larger towns and highways and Civil War tourist hotspots as much as possible. Due to time constraints, our drive back to DC will be a straight shot up through the Blue Ridge Highlands and the Shenandoah Valley, driving at night the whole way, which I much prefer.

Not only are Lisa and I saying goodbye to other people in our lives at this time, we're saying goodbye to each other as well. Once we get back to the airport I'll be getting on a plane and that's probably the last we'll see of each other.

We drive most of the morning, not in any hurry. We stop for a late lunch and wash down Chesapeake oysters with cold beer on a veranda overlooking the docks of a quaintly rundown marina.

I can't say it to her, but I am aware that Lisa has become, over the course of the few months I've known her, a very attractive person. That doesn't come as a surprise to me; I've seen many artificially attractive people become authentically attractive as they underwent the early stages of the transition from artificial to authentic personhood. When we met, Lisa was very pretty in the professional woman, urban/suburban, always-on-the-go, soccer mom sense; everything just so, make-up subtle but ever-present, hair in a low-maintenance cut and always done, outfit always carefully selected and accessorized. Now she has left all that behind, and at the same time, it has all become unnecessary. She has come into herself, and now her attractiveness radiates from within rather than from department stores and health clubs and from a morning hair and makeup routine. She looks great in jeans and tennis shoes and a t-shirt, hair pulled back or loose. She's happier and healthier and she looks it.

During the first few weeks of her stay with me in Mexico, she underwent a profound physical transformation as her body saw a rare opportunity and seized it. She was initially distraught to find herself battling a whole slew of low-grade symptoms, her discomfort worsened by overall anxiety. It was all quite normal in my experience and I reassured her and encouraged her to relax into the process and trust it. Her body was taking advantage of this opportunity to bring itself back into alignment after years of being over-stretched in all directions. She was releasing a lot of stored up toxins and dealing with the compounding effect of processing them all at once. For someone who has been eating and sleeping poorly, who has had their nerves frazzled by ever-present electro-magnetic fields, who's been bombarded from all directions by deranging images and messages in all forms of media, who has been constantly suffocated under the pressures of work and family and the clock, for whom even vacations are structured madness, and who, above all, considers this state normal and healthy, for someone like this, true relaxation can be like its own rebirth.

The most noticeable thing is sleep. The first thing the body wants to do is shut down, and people who haven't slept more than five or six straight hours in years or decades are shocked to find themselves sleeping deeply and untroubled for ten or twelve hours at a stretch, night after night, in addition to long naps during the day. They assume it's something mystical or spiritual, and it is, but not the way they think; just in the ordinary mystical and spiritual way of things. They're not just sleeping, but sleeping well and waking up deeply rested and content in a way that feels new and wonderful and surprising to them. They are revitalized and rejuvenated. It's something they may not have experienced since their childhood, and may not have thought possible.

This seems to be mainly a matter of how severely bent out of shape they've gotten themselves. Once the body is allowed to repair and heal itself back into its natural state, a whole host of dramatic changes begin taking place. Tastes change and bad habits naturally fall away. Years fall away from the appearance. Pounds fall away too, and healthy skin tone and muscle tone return. Not all on the first day, of course, but surprisingly quickly. It's amazing how resilient and forgiving the body can be.

In Lisa's case, there were also some chemical challenges to overcome. Her body had developed an over-fondness for coffee and diet soda and a few prescription medications, and it took about a month for her to be comfortably weaned off them to the point where she could have a cup of regular octane coffee with me in the morning and leave it at that. I don't know what her alcohol habits were, but I got that sense that a couple of glasses of wine a couple of times a week represented a reduction.

This, quite naturally, can also be a very challenging time emotionally and Lisa looked to me for answers, so I gave her a mantra; Rest, breathe, water, walk. Rest, breathe, water, walk. Rest, breathe, water, walk.

The mind is much slower to rid itself of toxic thoughts than the body is to reclaim its health. Lisa underwent an inner conflict stemming from her deeply ingrained attitudes about productivity and time management. Sleeping half the day was lazy and unconscionable. Naps were an affront to her work ethic. Not doing something at all times was a major challenge for her. Just getting to the place where she could see that it might not be necessary to be in a constant state of busyness was a struggle. In the first week I knew her, just to actually sit still for five minutes would have made her crazy. Simply agreeing that doing nothing now and then might not be too horrible was a major concession. She's much better now, but the productivity bug still infects her system.

This just gives a small idea of the transformation people undergo when they stop subjecting themselves to the endless barrage of assaults and stresses so many people find normal. I'm sure there are plenty of good books about the benefits of getting the hell out of that mess and back into one's natural element, so I won't pound on it here except to say that it has been particularly good to Lisa. She is, in virtually every respect, a different, healthier and more youthful and poised and radiantly attractive person than she was when we met. Still a work in progress, but coming along very nicely.

✧

"I still don't see why you need a travel assistant," she says, "not that I'm not grateful for this opportunity. You just seem perfectly capable of handling all the arrangements for yourself."

During this journey with Lisa I make an effort to be more talkative than I usually am. I share things about myself, little anecdotes, stories from my life; not biographical in content so much as process-related. I'm trying to show her something, to give her a glimpse of how the world really works and how we work in it and with it. There are a few books she'll find useful in the early stages, but she'll quickly move beyond those and then she'll be alone. For me, this process of discovery was and is a very delightful thing, but our circumstances are very different. I want to leave her with a sense of the spaces she herself can be moving into so that when we part ways she'll have a sense of her new self and her new place in things, and what she is and where she is.

"It's mostly the dealing with people part. I realized years ago that my contact with uh, you know, normal people, should be kept at a minimum."

"It was indicated?" she asks in a playful tone.

"Actually, it was," I say.

She smiles and nods to encourage me to explain.

"Okay," I say, "let's see. Well, it was in Mexico, actually, in some little dirt town an hour from the border, I don't remember where. I was at the counter in a hotel trying to arrange a replacement for a broken down rental car and the woman behind the counter said something about the terrible heat. Anyway, I was trying to dial a call and without really thinking about it, I said, '*No diría eso si era muerto.*'"

Lisa barks out a loud, shocked laugh.

"'You wouldn't say that if you were dead?'"

"Uh, yep."

"Jesus, you *said* that?"

"Uh, yep."

"Oh my goodness Jed, you shouldn't say things like that. People might not be real thrilled to be told something like that."

"I wasn't thinking. I was just saying what I'd say to any student back then who complained about trivialities, the point being that every day is the best day, that this isn't a dress rehearsal and all that. I happened to know the phrase in Spanish. I thought it was amusing."

"I bet that's not how she took it," she says.

"I didn't mean anything by it," I say, feeling a need to explain the blunder. "I never try to be witty or sagely or insightful with strangers. It just popped out, like a standard response you don't even think about. Even to this day I don't really understand why she was offended, which is why I need a travel assistant, I guess. I can't speak honestly and I hate talking bullshit, so I'd just rather avoid dealing with people whenever possible. Sonaya saw that I'd rather drive non-stop cross-country than deal with ticket agents and hotel clerks and make phone reservations and stand in lines and all that, so she just started sending someone with me and travelling got ten times better."

This is just one small example. This disconnect between me and normal people comes up all the time in many ways, always stemming from the fact that I am no one thinly disguised as someone. In order to be out and about, interfacing, I have to impersonate myself. I'm very uncomfortable doing that, and not very good at it. The disguise is unconvincing, the deception easily detected. People don't know what it is they're detecting, but they know something's not right. They sense in some way, even if they don't understand it, that I'm an imposter. Bit of irony there, I suppose.

"Was she offended?"

"Sonaya?"

"*La mexicana.*"

"Oh yeah, she freaked out. She thought I was threatening to kill her. Within five minutes the whole town was involved. This was just some impoverished little crossroads town and here's this gringo threatening to kill a local abuelita. A bar next door emptied out to see what was going on, her boss comes out of the office carrying a steel pipe, the local police chief shows up and it turns out he's the woman's brother. They're all yelling at each other, gesturing, consoling the woman. It was quite a scene. Emotions were running remarkably high. Carnivalesque."

"Oh my God. Did you explain?"

I laugh. "I couldn't have gotten a word in. The whole scene was crazy. This went on for half an hour. The whole thing had the feel of a Hollywood backlot, all the people seemed straight out of central casting. That's pretty much how I see everyone anyway, but here it was quite pronounced. I just relaxed and tried to enjoy the spectacle."

"Are you crazy? They thought you were threatening to *kill* her. I'm surprised they didn't gut you and dump you in the desert."

"We are in God's hands, brother, not theirs."

"Brother? Excuse me?"

"Oh, it's just one of those nice cultural references. In *Henry V*, the Duke of Gloucester is worried that the French will attack when the English are at their weakest, and that's what Harry replies: 'We are in God's hands, brother, not theirs.' Harry was an adult; a king in a state of surrender, threatening to rape daughters and smash old people's heads and spit babies on pikes while marching his ragtag little army against an overwhelming force because to do so was clearly indicated. You don't see that represented in books or plays very often."

"And what does that have to do with you getting gutted by an angry mob?"

"You're subscribing to the belief that they had the power, that the choice was theirs. The idea that someone with a knife or a gun or money or a nuclear arsenal has some sort of power is beyond my powers of make-believe. I couldn't pretend that was true even hypothetically."

"You're saying you weren't in any danger?"

"I'm never in any danger, whether an angry mob—what is it? guts me?—whether an angry mob guts me or not. Whether I break my neck in a motorcycle accident or not. Whether all the peoples and nations of the world rise up against me or not. If the universe wants me gutted and dumped in the desert, I'm all for it, and if it doesn't, no mob or government or law of physics is going to make it happen. Those are the fixed and absolute terms of my existence. It's not what I believe, it's just what is. I don't know how to say it any better."

She shakes her head in dismay.

"And this is normal to you?"

"This is *life* to me, and to you too, now." I set my plate aside and push back a few inches from the table. "As you've probably noticed, I'm not a gabby guy. These stories I'm telling you are your new stories. I'm a grown-up in a world where you're just a kid, and I'm telling you these things to help you grow up and make your own stories. The world isn't set up for you now; wherever you go, you'll be an outsider. There are no families or clans or tribes out there waiting to welcome you and show you around and explain how everything works. There's no apparatus in place to receive you and teach you and protect you. You're going to move beyond the point where anyone can help you because you're an adult now and this is a children's world. You won't have me and you probably won't have anyone older than yourself, not even in books. I'm telling you things, making an effort to be a little open and conversational, because you're going to be alone in the world and it will be very easy for you to just find a rut and stagnate."

"That can happen?"

"That's practically the only thing that *does* happen. Everything is set up for that. The world is full of warm dark holes for you to fall into."

"I won't have anyone?" she asks in a forlorn tone. "I won't have you?"

"You'll have yourself. That's all you need."

"Am I going to do that?" asks Lisa. "Go crawling back? Find a hole to hide in?"

"Despite the statistical near-certainty of it, I'd guess you won't. I could be wrong, it's not really my thing, but from what I can tell, you're being groomed for something more. You have to try to understand what fear is or it will get you and you'll never even know it."

✧

We leave the restaurant and go for a stroll along the shoreline.

"So what ended up happening?" she asks.

"When?"

"With the mob? In Mexico?"

"Oh, nothing. The police chief drove me up to the border and told me never to return to his country."

"They kicked you out of Mexico?"

"Well," I shrug, "it seemed pretty informal."

"You seem to get into a lot of trouble with the law."

I shrug again. "No trouble at all."

"And what did you do after?"

"After he dumped me at the border? Cancelled my credit cards. Reported my passport and traveler's checks stolen. Had money wired."

"They stole your wallet?"

"Sure, everything I had on me and the knapsack I left in the car."

She shakes her head, fed up with petty corruption.

"Bastards," she says.

"Everybody's just playing their role," I say. "No reason to take any of it personally."

She gives me a long sideways look.

✧

We get back in the Navigator and get back on the road. We drive for an hour in silence, though I sense that it's quite loud inside Lisa's head.

"I don't think I'll ever look at people the same way again," she says at last. "I don't think I'll ever be able to trust anyone again."

I watch the changing scenery in silence for a few minutes; happy to be here, happy to be with Lisa, happy to be heading toward Brett's farewell, happy to be. Is this my last day? Are these my last moments? Is death's ever-hovering finger about to come down? The thought fills me with a gentle rush of joy and bathes the world in beauty.

"People are dust-bunnies," I finally respond, "little bundles of lint and cobwebs that collect in shadows and dark corners, held together and drawn together by fear. Once you see them clearly, trusting them becomes very easy. I trust everybody and I'm never disappointed. It can be the same for you."

"That's very hard to believe."

"You don't have to trust people not to betray you or break your heart or steal your purse; you just trust them to be who they are. Once you under-stand fear, get a little distance from it and see what it really is and how it operates in the world, then you can understand everything about people. In an eyes-closed being, everything flows from fear; good and bad, courage and cowardice, love and hate, all flow from the same well."

"How can you trust someone who you know would betray you?"

"You answered your own question; because you know. Everything that's so mysterious and unknowable with eyes closed becomes clear and obvious once we open them. It takes time and experience and effort, just like it took you time and experience and effort to become the adult you are. That's what life is; a process of constant becoming and renewal; a motion toward clearer seeing and greater simplicity and reduction in the perceived division between I and not-I. This is the world, this is the way it will be for you if you continue forward. It's a whole different thing."

"*If* I continue," she says flatly.

"When you begin gaining some altitude and seeing the larger picture, people's personal traits will become a blur and you start to categorize people by what hole they're hiding in."

"That sounds a little cynical."

"Try this on for size: Life has no meaning and no belief is true."

"That sounds a *lot* cynical."

"My point is that cynical is an eyes-closed word. You don't need it anymore. Your buffered, thought-based relationship to your environment is outmoded and much of your vocabulary is obsolete. You've made this enormous transition, a true paradigm shift, but your infrastructure hasn't caught up with you yet. You've had your revolution, you've overthrown the oppressive regime, and now it's time to govern, to rule wisely and to lead this newly-emerged island-nation into a future of growth and prosperity. You have others to think about; Maggie and DJ and maybe Dennis. Maybe others as well. You were a wife and mother before, what are you now? Maggie's at a critical age and she's had quite an unusual ride already; watching your meltdown, working with her grandfather, interrogating me. What are you going to do with her?"

"Maybe I *should* find a hole," she says glumly, "go find Jesus. Maybe that would be best for everyone."

I nod.

"Maybe so."

✧

"Thank you for talking," she says. "Thank you for telling me things."

"De nada."

"I can't believe how my life has changed. Look at me, here with you, off on this bizarre adventure, whatever it is. It's completely surreal. I feel like I'm going to wake up in my old bed next to Dennis, turning off the alarm and starting a new day and forgetting all about this crazy dream of a new life." She gets a little shaky. "What am I doing here?"

"Why do you think you're here?" I ask her. "Step back from events and ask yourself impartially what's going on? A few months ago you're a lawyer and a wife and a suburban mom and all that, and now here you are driving this big black hearse across Virginia—"

"With Jed McKenna," she supplies.

"With one awakened being on the way to eulogize another. This would be a very good time for you to reflect on what's going on and why."

She's quiet for a few moments.

"Do you know?" she asks.

"I know for me."

"Do you know what you're going to say at the eulogy?"

"In the broadstrokes. Maggie gave me the idea of show-and-tell, so that's what I'm going to do."

"Really? What are you going to show?"

"Two things. One, as you know, we're hoping to find waiting for us in the hotel safe."

"And the other? What else are you going to show?"

I reach into my pack on the floor behind her seat. I pull out her day-planner and set it on the console between us.

"You."

26. Postuterine Gestation

Magnifying and applying come I,
Outbidding at the start the old cautious hucksters,
Taking myself the exact dimensions of Jehovah,
Lithographing Kronos, Zeus his son,
   and Hercules his grandson;
Buying drafts of Osiris, Isis,
   Belus, Brahma, Buddha,
In my portfolio placing Manito loose,
   Allah on a leaf, the crucifix engraved,
With Odin, and the hideous-faced Mexitli,
   and every idol and image;
Taking them all for what they are worth,
   and not a cent more;
Admitting they were alive
   and did the work of their days;
(They bore mites, as for unfledg'd birds,
   who have now to rise and fly
   and sing for themselves.)

–Walt Whitman

LISA GETS US PLEASANTLY LOST. We're in no hurry so she maintains the correct general heading and whenever there's a choice she takes the road less travelled. We've meandered along this way for nearly two hundred miles. Now it's getting late in the day and we're both a little tired of driving, so we stop in a small river town to find a place for dinner and a hotel with a couple of rooms.

Lisa wasn't happy to be told she'd be speaking to the group at Brett's place. She actually refused on the basis that she had no knowledge or understanding of spiritual matters, and was therefore an inappropriate choice to address a group of dedicated spiritual aspirants. I pointed out that, in her short journey, she had already gone far beyond them all, but she was still adamant that she would not address the group.

"I understand that you won't do it," I tell her, "but I'm pretty sure you will. It's simply the pattern, there to be seen."

She finds a nice old hotel and we park but neither of us is very hungry so we decide to stretch our legs and check out the town.

"How does it feel to be an orphan?" I ask her.

"God, I hadn't thought of it that way," she laughs. "I'm an orphan. What a strange thing to say, like I'm married, or I'm not a virgin anymore."

"Maybe it's not so much a new status as a non-status."

"Hmm, I'm not sure it feels that way. I'm not sure how it feels."

"Not to be insensitive, but you might want to take a moment to appreciate the way the universe is accommodating this transition of yours; it's pretty impressive. I don't know if it's very clear to you right now, but the way your past is being picked up and your future is being laid down—"

"You're right," she says abruptly, "it's not very clear to me. I guess it's more clear to you."

I take that as a grudging invitation to continue.

"All forces are being steadily employed to complete and delight you, to borrow from Whitman. It's you who set all this in motion. You demonstrated clear intent, not merely through words or ideas, but through actions. When we do this, the universe naturally becomes more pliable than our usual experience of it. It starts reshaping itself to us and we to it. This is what happens as the perceived division between self and non-self begins to erode. That's what's happening with you, and this much more responsive, pliable universe is your new reality."

"It sounds like you're saying my parents are dead because of this situation I'm in."

"Are you saying that if you weren't in this situation, your parents wouldn't have died?"

"I don't know," she answers after a pause.

"I don't know either. I just know what I can see from the outside looking in, and that's that here in your first stages of life as an integrated being, you're getting the star treatment; massive quantities of biographical baggage whisked away, having me around, your future life of ease and comfort and continued growth being laid out for you like a royal banquet—"

"A royal banquet?" she asks with a trace of bitterness.

"No waitressing in Corpus Christi with big hair and a fat ass," I explain. "No damage to your credit rating, should you still care. You're in for a nice little inheritance from what your father said."

We walk in silence for a while. I feel an unusual urge to meddle. Lisa's not going to have me around much longer and it would be nice to scoot her through this uncomfortable teething stage and get her to a point where she can fend for herself a bit. It's hard to believe, but most people who go as far as she's gone dig in and refuse to go further. They curl up in a fetal pose, scrunch their eyes closed and live in the world as if they were still in the womb. It sounds too weird to be true, but among those who make the death/rebirth transition it's so common as to be the norm. I wouldn't like to see Lisa stop before she starts. I usually don't invest myself, not because I have a rule about it, but because I feel no urge, but now I do so I do.

"I'm going to tell you what you need to hear even though you didn't ask. You've had your death and birth and you've experienced major changes and losses, but now that part is over and it's time for you to open your eyes and start getting things figured out. It's a whole new world and you're a whole new being. This is what it's all been about since that picture first stabbed you in the heart; all this pain and suffering and loss, the wrenching decisions, the personal betrayals, it was all leading to this. That part is over now. You're not that person anymore. Now you have to let it all go and move forward, or else it was all for nothing."

She stops abruptly, pissed, I imagine. I keep walking. I head off into the surrounding neighborhoods, wishing I had my dog with me.

✧

Think of a man who loses his job and sinks into despair because he personally identified with his work to such a degree that loss of job means loss of self or loss of manhood. Think of a woman who undergoes a similar crisis of identity due to divorce, with the attendant loss of her primary identity structure. Think of parents whose lives lose all meaning due to the loss of a child, or someone who's lost all hope and joy due to some bad news from the doctor. Losses like these can make us feel like we've lost our core. We might feel we can't recover from them, and maybe we can't.

When we believe in the world outside of ourselves, gain is often perceived as good and loss as bad. When we stop believing in a world external to self, that reverses; gain becomes bad and loss becomes good. Nothing we can lose was ever ours in the first place. All we can ever lose is illusion.

Using the movie *Joe Versus the Volcano* as our parallel, Lisa has managed to make the transition from a mindless drone shuffling through a life of programmed drudgery to a vibrant and aware being charting a course "away from the things of man." As in *Joe*, the universe has gone to seemingly supernatural lengths to accommodate her transition. She could never have wished for such cataclysmic upheaval in her life any more than Joe Banks could have wished for a prognosis of a "brain cloud" with a life expectancy of a few months. Looking back, however, neither would change a thing.

✧

Emerson said a man is what he thinks about all day long. (Buddha supposedly said something similar, but any time you see the words *Buddha said...*, your bullshit alarm should start screeching, so we'll stick with Emerson.)

I don't seem to think about anything anymore. I can't even think of anything that needs thinking about. Sometimes I try to think about something, latch onto something and give it some thought, but it just fades after a moment or two. Thought for me is a tool, a weapon. The only reason to lug it out is if something needs to be killed. It's a sword, but I have nothing left to swing it at. I pick it up desultorily and cleave the air, but it's just the empty reminiscences of an old soldier. What would I think about? Religion? Politics? Business? The arts? I am blank. I am, by Emerson's reckoning, nothing.

My general state most closely resembles a kind of bittersweet gladness. I don't dwell in my memories, I'm not even sure if I really have any. It seems like I have a box of old Super-8 footage somewhere in my mental space, but the idea of hauling it out and reminiscing over the clumsily spliced scenes of a life with which I feel no connection holds no appeal. I know that I was once a warrior, but it's not the memory of that state of being, just the recollection of a fact. There's no pleasure or displeasure in it. It's like something you know about someone else.

Once in a while I climb up into the belfry and look around for bats. I head into my head to make sure that there are no messes anywhere; no pockets of darkness, no tracks in the dust, no piles of droppings. Like an old, unarmed night watchman making his rounds, I do a quick tour of the joint. I don't do it in a very alert or cautious manner; I'm not too concerned that there would be anything to find or, if there was, that removal would pose any great challenge.

Death especially is an area where I want to remain a bit vigilant. I don't feel any fear or concern about my death, I don't attach any importance to it, but it seems like the kind of thing that could sneak something past me, so I keep an eye out. I've been in a dozen situations in the last decade where I figured it was all over, and never were there any unpleasant surprises about my reaction. In every situation I felt intrigued, ready, grateful. I didn't panic or react fearfully, so I'm reasonably sure that I don't have much in the way of death demons lurking about. It would be interesting if I did, but I don't think I do.

Refusing the fat sergeant's invitation is something I find curious in this regard. It's not that I'm sorry I didn't turn around and yell *Boo!*, it's that I'm not sure why I didn't. I'm not concerned about it, just curious. You don't get an offer like that every day, so it seems appropriate to review your response.

My day-to-day persona is another thing I keep a lazy sort of awareness about. I interact, I have a presence in the lives of other people and I have my own life to navigate through; my dreamstate existence. That's something I pay attention to, but again, not much. It doesn't take much thought or effort. I have this teacher/author thing going, but there's no real danger of that pulling me back down into the peri-natal states commonly mistaken for waking life. I don't think anything could pull me back down, but there's no harm in this minimal sort of mindfulness.

A lot of it comes down to the books. I have a very enjoyable interest right now in Orwell's *1984*, for instance, but if it weren't for the context provided by the writing of the third book, I wouldn't have a care for it. It's of no interest to me personally because there is no personal me to be interested. The time I spent in Frank's library and listening to his encyclopedic knowledge on the methods of transcendence used by various cultures through the ages, and his views on a dystopian corporate world state, is the same way. It was interesting insofar as it served the book, but beyond that, nothing. I have no genuine, independent interest in anything except going for walks, preferably with my dog. This is what it is to be fully awake, enlightened, truth-realized. This is what it would be for anyone. A Buddha of Compassion, for example, is an oxymoron, an irreconcilable contradiction. It sounds nice, but it's a complete absurdity, as anyone who has worked through the theory part of this subject can easily see for themselves.

It amuses me to think that there are people in the world who consider the truth-realized state something to be devoutly wished for and fought for. The contradictions start piling up immediately. It can't be wished for because there's no it, nor an I to inhabit it, and yet I, who reside in this state, wouldn't trade it for any amount of wealth or power or beauty or kids or grandkids or anything else. I want to shy away from marketing buzzwords like bliss or love because I don't feel they accurately describe this state, at least not as these terms are understood by those not in it. I am happy, content, usually either amused or cheerfully engaged, and yet if I were to receive a message informing me that my death would occur in exactly five minutes, I would have no reaction except to clear my mind and shift my attention to what a nice time I've had here and allow my gratitude to well up and engulf me.

Maybe that was the missing piece when the sergeant made his offer; I wouldn't have had the chance to say thank you and good-bye to this fun, lovely, challenging existence. Slipping out the back door like that might have had an irresistible comic charm, but it would have left this large reservoir of gratitude unreleased. That would have made for a poor death, and that twinge of regret would have been the second to last thing to go through my mind. That's what I decide as I stroll around the little town in Virginia. When it's time to go, I'd like a minute or two to say good-bye first. I set my desire on that wish and release it, confident that it will, when the time comes, be granted.

✧

Lisa and I get back together an hour later and make our way to the hotel restaurant's outdoor dining area. We settle in and order iced teas and look out over the water.

"I don't think people can simply make their past go away as if it wasn't there," she says, picking up from our last exchange, "as if it wasn't a part of them."

The drinks come and we order.

"You don't make your past go away," I tell her, "it just fades away, like when you wake up in the morning, the dreamworld in which you were just immersed fades away and is forgotten. When this happens, we know directly, see for ourselves, without intermediary people or processes. For the rest of your life you'll look at the person you were and virtually everyone else as inferior and defective."

"Inferior and defective," she repeats with distaste.

"Inferior in the developmental sense that a child is inferior to an adult, and defective in the sense that developmental stagnation is abnormal. What else would you say about a creature that grows and develops into physical adulthood without ever exiting the womb?"

She makes an expression of distaste. "That's gross," she says.

"That's another thing you can expect to change," I say, "that egoic need to judge and categorize and label everything. That will fade as otherness gives way to is-ness. It's a much more relaxed, low-maintenance perspective."

"Isn't that what intelligence is for?" she asks. "Judging? Weighing? Determining value and worth? Am I supposed to just relinquish my powers of discrimination? That doesn't sound right to me."

"What you call intelligence is the intelligence of rats in a maze, of chimps stacking blocks to get to the higher bananas. Once you see the real intelligence at work in all things at all times, you'll never think of it in human terms again. Thought, as you understand it, as a tool of navigation and understanding, is just another non-necessity that gets dropped and forgotten. All our opinions are just mini-beliefs; rubbish we haul around with us at the expense of our life energy. Your tendency to judge things as good or bad, right or wrong, and so forth, just naturally falls away and that energy is freed up. You'll soon begin to find all opinions and beliefs rather noxious and you'll naturally tend away from their source, which is ego."

"I can't imagine," she says, sipping her iced tea while I dig around in my Caesar salad looking for signs of Caesar. Iceberg lettuce, tomato wedges, orange cheese and mystery dressing from a can; the only ingredient that belongs on this plate are the croutons, and they're chewy.

"You seem to be judging your salad," she observes wryly. "Are you not content with its is-ness?"

I laugh.

"I have likes and dislikes, personal preferences, things that please me and displease me. No one's talking about acting a certain way or trying to adapt to some preconceived notions of how you should be. That's a trap, and a very effective one judging from the number of people in it."

"I don't see you falling into many traps," she says.

"We're not talking about me," I say.

She sighs heavily.

"Why are we having this conversation, may I ask?"

"Because I want to make you uncomfortable," I say. "I want to irritate and annoy you."

"You're succeeding."

"What's the context in which this conversation is taking place?"

"Meaning?"

"What are we doing?" I ask. "What are you doing?"

"I'm delivering you so you can deliver Brett's eulogy, I thought."

"No. My context is the book. I'm writing a book. What's yours?"

She shakes her head.

"I don't know. I guess I haven't thought about it."

"You don't have to think," I say, "you just have to look."

✧

We eat an uninspired meal and they take away our plates. We turn our chairs to the view and sip our iced teas. It's a few minutes before she speaks again.

"I don't know how *not* to distinguish good from bad and right from wrong," she says after the long interval. "How do you not judge? It's like I'd be forfeiting my intellect, my personal sovereignty, my moral compass. How can you do that?"

This is a tricky question to answer because it would be so easy to over-answer. I like to help people take their next step and to gently discourage them from looking beyond it. In *Damnedest*, there was a brief dialogue between me and Maya (the architect of delusion, not the dog). I had remarked on her beauty and she asked if I would prefer her other face and I said either was fine. That playful exchange concealed all the horror and evil and suffering in the world; Maya's other face. I am awake *from* the dreamstate, so I can no longer be fooled by either face; not good or evil, not beauty or horror. I know it all for what it is, that it's all one thing. It's not necessary or even possible to show Lisa at this stage that there's no differ-ence between any two extremes, but it *is* time she started to rethink her deep-rooted belief that there is. She doesn't have to see Maya's other face to take the next step, but she does have to start questioning her practice of sorting the world into piles like laundry.

Yes, we're going to deliver Brett's eulogy, but that's not our context. My context is this book, and Lisa's context is that of a crawling infant; to start moving around and interacting with her environment; to figure out where she is and how things work and how she fits into it all.

✧

Trees grow weak in biospheres because there's no wind for them to contend against. Artificial wind is generated to let the trees develop their strength, not to be cruel, not to bully them. Spare the wind, spoil the tree.

"I watched a young girl on television," I tell Lisa as we stroll a wooded biketrail a little later. "She'd undergone this horrendous tragedy. She'd been trapped in a burning car, I think, and sustained more damage than you'd imagine a body could. She'd been through many surgeries, but her disfiguration was virtually total. At one point during the interview she looked at the nubs where her fingers had been and said: 'I used to cry when I broke a nail.'"

It's a moment before Lisa responds, her voice a whisper.

"My God, that's so horrible."

"Is it?" I reply. "I thought it was one of the most beautiful things I'd ever heard. What poem could compare? What art? War and disaster photography is the only thing I know that comes close, but that doesn't compare with the image of a real live girl, once a pretty little high school kid full of hopes and dreams, but now as physically ruined as it's possible to be, looking at her ravaged hands and saying, 'I used to cry when I broke a nail.'"

"You have a very peculiar idea of beauty," says Lisa sourly. "That poor girl. Her poor family."

"To me, it wasn't about the girl, it was about me, about life, about being. This is where we are, these are the rules. That dead body receiving a Y incision on a stainless steel table tomorrow morning is me. That woman plummeting from the World Trade Center is you. That burned girl is Maggie."

Lisa stops and turns to face me. I stop too. She has a very level and steady gaze that's hard to read, but I don't have to read it. I speak my next words slowly and clearly.

"Do you know where you are?"

Nothing.

"*Mires. Ábrase los ojos.*"

"Jed—"

"Do you know what this place is?"

"Please don't, Jed," she says. "I know you're trying to help me somehow, but it's such a nice evening. Can't we just relax and enjoy it?"

⁂

Too much? Am I pushing Lisa too hard? I could go into any library or bookstore and fill boxes with books from the poetry, religious, spirituality, self-help and philosophy sections written by people who made it as far as Lisa is now and never an inch further; people who have undergone the death-rebirth transition, but stayed in their eyes-closed, imagined reality instead of opening their eyes to the new world into which they've emerged. I wouldn't have thought it possible, but I see it all the time. It seems that once we were set in motion we would stay in motion, but this is plainly not so. The same fierce determination to stay rooted in place we exhibit while in the womb, we continue to exhibit after we emerge. When we cross-reference the metaphors against each other and index the observable cases, we discover an intermediary stage between two worlds, a sort of hypnagogic, purgatorial state in which a person has left the womb but still calls it home, in which they have entered the world, but not yet opened their eyes.

This is not the same thing as the faux-rebirth so common in pop Christianity and twelve step programs, these are people who have truly made the transition out of the womb, but not beyond the grip of fear. Nor is it simply the removal of one's chains in Plato's cave; it's undeniably more than that, but undeniably less than lucid. It seems almost unnatural, but as people who go in for freaky sex assure us, the only unnatural act is the one you can't perform, so we have to look at these in-between states as rungs on the evolutionary ladder out of the subterranean levels of dark consciousness in which mankind crouches in self-imposed damnation.

And that's where Lisa is now; emerged from the darkness, but eyes still closed. And that's how she could stay, between two worlds, an alien in both. It would be easy for her to mistake this starting point as a final destination and put down stakes, maybe even put out a shingle once she figures out how she got here; write a book, give talks, make a career of aiding others through an incomplete transition.

The temptation to rest must be great after the struggle it takes to get this far, but I'm eager that Lisa should keep going. Maybe that's what that delivery room slap on the ass is for. Maybe that's what I'm trying to do for Lisa. The next thing she has to do isn't easy, but it's not that hard either, and if she can do it, then she can go and keep going. I feel like it would be quite a shame for Lisa to have made it this far and to go no further. This is where it starts getting good. I don't have a lot of experience of working with people at this stage, but what I do know is that I should be encouraging Lisa not to get too comfortable just yet, even if it means pissing her off a bit.

✧

We walk in silence for ten minutes before I start in on her again.

"You lived thirty some-odd years of your life in the womb, born of the flesh but unborn of the spirit," I say. "Who wants to leave the womb? No one. Regardless of what they say, no one wants out. You *can't*. It's warm and comfortable and safe in there, and to leave means the end of the world, the end of the only life you've ever known. The only way anyone gets out of there is if some sort of disaster or toxicity drives them screaming out into the world."

"Which is what I went through," she muses, "like a gradual toxification that eventually became unbearable."

"Yes, and now here you are, but you still want to deny and reject all that's not pleasing and nice. That's the old way, the eyes-closed way. Now it's time to look, to see everything, to behold the creation of which you are a part. That's what honesty is, that's what living with eyes open is. Acceptance of what is. Acknowledging where you are and what the rules are. Seeing how it works, how to participate, how to live without fear."

"This is all so dark and depressing," she says.

"It's not that it's dark," I continue, "it's that you're squinting. It's okay to look. It only seems dark because we don't look at it, don't go into it, but we can. *You* can. We wall off all the bad scary stuff because that's what children do; they shut their eyes real tight so they don't have to see the monsters. This is a children's world and it's full of reward-and-punishment religions and pick-and-choose spiritual systems that embrace the pleasant and pretty while excluding the dark and ugly, but the only reason for that is fear. When you open your eyes and see where you are, you see everything and only then is fear vanquished. Right now, you're still living in your imagined realm. You're not a part of that anymore, but you haven't moved on yet either. It's time to open your eyes, to see where you are."

She lowers her head.

"So much for a nice evening," she says.

"Long enough have you dreamed contemptible dreams," I quote Whitman again. "Now I wash the gum from your eyes, you must habit yourself to the dazzle of the light and of every moment of your life."

"I'm getting a lot of Whitman today," she observes.

"Whitman, at his best, is all about where you are now, all about this transition, this rebirth."

She looks over at me.

"Really?"

"You shall no longer take things at second or third hand," I recite, "nor look through the eyes of the dead, nor feed on the spectres in books. You shall not look through my eyes either, nor take things from me, you shall listen to all sides, and filter them from yourself."

"That's Whitman?"

"Most mystical poetry, when it's not just flowery gibberish, is about the two elements of the death/rebirth process; leaving the Segregated State and entering the Integrated State."

"Not enlightenment?"

I chuckle at the thought of it.

"No, there's no art depicting nondual awareness or poetry celebrating the truth-realized state or anything like that. It's not that kind of thing."

"Well, Whitman sounds nicer than the story of that poor little girl."

But it's not a time for nice.

"Here's something from my own experience, a little *aha!* event. I was in school in New York in the early eighties. One day, a news radio station was on. Standard news items, the kind of stuff you only half hear, and then, after something about the mayor and before something about the Yankees, in the same mechanical tone, the announcer says: 'A man broke into an Upper West Side apartment today and threw a baby against the wall for no apparent reason.'"

"Oh Jesus," she says, hands over her mouth. "Please Jed, no more. Let's just walk. *Please?*"

✧

I've always thought of that as the perfect haiku, despite its form violations. I call it *Fuck Basho's Frog*:

> A man broke in
> to a west side apartment today
> and threw a baby against the wall
> for no apparent reason.
> *Plop!*

✧

Even much later as I edit this chapter beside another pool in another part of Mexico, I don't know whether this material will go into the book. Is it too dark? Fingerless girl, baby thrown against a wall? Does it serve the book or detract? The answer, as I well know, is that it's not for me to decide. I am unclear and clarity will come, I need only be patient and the answer will appear. The universe will make itself known.

I wasn't trying to shock Lisa for the sake of shocking her. If I just wanted to be shocking, I suppose I could have hit her with some truly high-voltage horror and really fried her circuits. My thought was to deliver a few light zaps to her heart, just enough to make her aware of this whole area she kept dark and walled off.

That's what I'm idly musing when this New York Times headline appears on my laptop: "Man Stabs Baby Girl in Her Stroller."

The universe has made itself known. The material goes in.

✧

One final note. On the night of what would have been my final edit of this chapter, I was reading something unrelated to any of this and I came across the term *postuterine gestation*. I'd been struggling with this whole concept of people getting just as stuck after their emergence as they were before it, and from the most unlikely of sources, an essay on Cormac McCarthy's *Blood Meridian*, I was provided with this term, postuterine gestation, and it seemed to capture this bizarre phenomenon we've been looking at in these pages. This term suggests, as my observations have found, that emergence into the world is not the clear formative demarcation point one would naturally assume. The processes of growth and development that are at work before and during this emergence are still at work after, and if we abort these processes, or fail to recognize and nurture them, we are likely to entomb ourselves outside the womb as effectively as those still in it.

Weird.

27. Casus Belli

Yet now, forsooth, because Pierre began to see through the
first superficiality of the world, he fondly weens he has come
to the unlayered substance. But, far as any geologist has yet
gone down into the world, it is found to consist of nothing
but surface stratified on surface. To its axis, the world being
nothing but superinduced superficies. By vast pains we mine
into the pyramid; by horrible gropings we come to the central
room; with joy we espy the sarcophagus; but we lift the lid —
and no body is there! — appallingly vacant as vast is the soul
of a man!

—Herman Melville, Pierre

A S WE DROVE, LISA TOLD me about her husband, Dennis. Dennis
was a dentist. Dennis the dentist. She told me he secretly hated
being a dentist, or maybe he just hated being Dennis, she wasn't sure. He
became a dentist because that's what his father was. He was so desperate to
please his parents, she said, that his life was a constant losing struggle to
live up to their expectations and win their approval. Lisa said he hated a lot
of things about his life so he was never happy and often angry. He suffered
from depression and alcoholism, though to outward appearances he seemed
happy and successful. Projecting that image, especially to his parents, was
the driving motivation of his life.

Our relationship to our parents is a very important thing to look at,
not because we want to heal the relationship and any wounds we may have
suffered or inflicted, but because most of us are still stuck at that level. If
our basic understanding of life is similar in the broad outlines to that of our
parents, then we have not yet begun our own journey. We are the children
of children who are the children of children who were the children of children and so on all the way back. Quite a chain to break, but breaking
chains is what liberation is all about. Anyone who ever wants to do

anything in life, to become a person in their own right, must begin by killing their parents. (*Metaphorically!*)

When we kill our parents, what we're really doing is sloughing off the inmost layer of false context in which we are encased and by which we are defined. That's what we're doing any time we take a step; sloughing off the next layer of enshrouding delusion. We'll see another variation of this theme when we look at Brett's past and her relationship with her father and how she dealt with it. Dennis, according to Lisa, hasn't dealt with it. Maybe he will. Maybe he'll go into counseling and talk it out or have a primal scream or take some MDMA in a therapeutic setting and have a cathartic healing event that lets him finally move beyond this spiritual constipation that has rendered him a perpetual and chronically ill child.

Cathartic means purgative, as in purge, as in evacuating a toxin or obstruction, as in taking a massive mental/emotional dump and restoring free flow system-wide. All progress can be understood as a matter of flow and obstruction. Lisa, after suffering a prolonged illness, finally managed to have her own cathartic, purgative, healing event, and we can see where that got her—so far, anyway. She lost all of her primary definitions. Maybe she would have preferred to just take a pill and make the pain go away so she could remain in her life circumstances. There are many such pills, and they take many different forms, but she didn't take a pill, she took the pain.

"He has a morbid fixation on pleasing his parents so they'll be proud of him," she told me of Dennis, "but they're never pleased. Nothing he does is good enough, so he keeps trying to do more and he just makes himself crazy. He's still just a little boy to them. I don't think I ever realized it before, but it's like a sickness with him, and a lot of his problems are like symptoms. Drinking, high-achievement and low self-esteem, chronic unhappiness, always dissatisfied, always pretending he's happy and successful, and all because he's so eager to please his parents, which he'll never do because they're never impressed by anything. No matter what he does, he's trapped. Even after they're dead they'll still have this hold over him. There's no way out for him."

The unexamined life, said Socrates, is not worth living. That's some serious shit. Most people wouldn't want to examine that statement, much less their own lives. If we take it to mean the stagnated, entrenched life is not worth living, then we are saying that most people's lives aren't worth the bother, which is pretty much how Human Childhood looks from the perspective of Human Adulthood. You can still make a case for Human Childhood, but it has that dissatisfying feel of winning on a technicality.

Socrates makes quite a damning indictment: The unexamined life is not worth living. Who lives a conscious, examined life? Everyone probably thinks they do, but virtually no one actually does. Who *decides* to spend the hours and days and weeks and months and years of their life as they do? Who, by conscious decision, with informed thought aforethought, *decides* to pair up and have kids and buy a house and work a job and spend the very coin of their life filling in the lines of a hand-me-down, coloring-book life? Where are the people living examined lives? Lives worth living? Where are the people who made a choice? Not just the secondary choices made within an unchosen framework, but the principal choices, the choice of the framework itself. Where are the people who chose their lives?

Who consciously chooses to wrap themselves in chains? Who chooses marriage and children and career? Who chooses to join the ranks of debt-ridden consumers and spend the fruits of their lifelong labors as a slave to possessions and corporations? Who chooses to spend their free time running errands and doing chores and watching television? Who chooses to eat toxic foods, to live in toxic environments surrounded by toxic people? Who chooses to live a pre-programmed life from birth to death? Who dreams such sordid, vile, life-negative dreams?

Sure, maybe a life of drudgery and carrot-chasing is exactly what we'd choose if we *did* choose, but we don't. That's what it means to be unconscious; to be asleep within the dream. We slip into the lives that are laid out for us the way children slip into the clothes their mother lays out for them in the morning. No one decides. We don't live our lives by choice, but by default. We play the roles we are born to. We don't live our lives, we dispose of them. We throw them away because we don't know any better, and the reason we don't know any better is because we never asked. We never questioned or doubted, never stood up, never drew a line. We never walked up to our parents or our spiritual advisors or our teachers or any of the other formative presences in our early lives and asked one simple, honest, straightforward question, the one question that must be answered before any other question can be asked:

"What the hell is going on here?"

That's how you kill them. Not with guns and machetes, but with thought and honesty and directness. That's how you look, how you see. That's how you draw a line.

This isn't a peppy little halftime speech meant to whip us all into a *carpe diem* frenzy and send us screaming out onto the field with victory in our hearts and a life-positive, freedom-loving, first-day-of-the-rest-of-your-life bloodlust pumping through our veins until the alarm blares Monday morning and sends us shuffling back to prison routine. Seizing the day just ain't gonna cut it. That's like encouraging an inmate to pursue their life-long dream of singing in the prison choir. If I had a son or daughter, someone for whom I cared deeply, I would encourage them instead with the words *carpe vitae*; seize your life. And if I knew the Latin word for *fuckin'*, I'd stick that in there too. I'd tattoo it on the backs of their hands so they had to look at it all the time and feel a healthy shame and self-loathing for every minute they pissed away as a spectator instead of a player.

Speaking metaphorically (!), the first thing we must do in our bid for freedom is kill our parents. We kill the Buddha (or equivalent) last on the way to truth-realization, but we kill our parents first on the way to anywhere. There are a whole lot more people who need killing before freedom is achieved, but that's how it must begin. Until we kill our parents (*metaphorically!*) we remain unborn.

That's what the movie *The Graduate* is about; the death and rebirth of Benjamin Braddock as he smashes out of his life, killing his parents—their world, their hopes for him, their society, the person they had molded him into and the future for which they were fitting him—and struggling through his own self-birth process.

There are no good guys or bad guys in *The Graduate*. The parents aren't evil, just vapid, and there's no law against being vapid or we'd all be locked up (rather, there is and we are). Elaine exhibits no will and is just a prize to be won or lost. At the end of the film she has not been set free, she has merely had her pattern disrupted. Ultimately, the movie is about the time-bombs among us. Ben didn't want to explode and ruin everything around him. He didn't do all that hard work at school while plotting his escape. He is as much a victim of his own spontaneous detonation as anyone. *The Graduate* is not about love, it's about breaking away.

If they did a sequel to *The Graduate*, we'd probably find that Ben didn't go a whole lot farther than what we saw in the original. Like most of the few that make the transition, he would probably treat his new state as a destination rather than a departure point and be quickly repatriated with the herd. Never fully, but fully enough.

That's what I'm trying to help Lisa get beyond.

Ben's transition was relatively mild. He was still just a young sapling, his roots shallow and sparse and easily yanked from the ground. At twenty-one he had no family but parents, no kids, no mortgage and debt, no friends or extended family, no established career, none of the many complex roles he would have played had he been more established, more deeply rooted in his life. In short, he had his breakdown at the ideal time, when there was very little to cut away from, very few people to betray, very little to lose.

But what happens when the same crisis occurs twenty years later when the root system runs far deeper? When it's much stronger and much more intertwined with surrounding root systems? Then, instead of *The Graduate*, we'd be watching *The Partner*. At forty-one, Ben is no longer a sapling that can be easily ripped from the ground. Now he's a tree and that same single step of progress at this more advanced stage of emotional arborization requires a tremendously greater amount of explosive energy, and a far more powerful source of discontent to fuel such an explosion. It's not tidy or surgical or contained. It's not spiritual or compassionate or blissful. It's going to make a huge mess. It's going to do damage to all surrounding and intertwined growth. If Ben had continued on his trajectory for another two decades before his epiphany occurred, then instead of just rebelling against tragically unhip parents, he'd be cutting ties with wife and children, with friends and extended family, with work and community and church. His career and finances would be reduced to a shambles, everything he'd worked so hard his entire life to build would be smashed to rubble, and all for what? You don't ride away from that in the back of a bus, grinning like you beat the house and stole the life-sized trophy.

Who's the hero in *The Partner*? Who's the good guy? How do we see an older Ben in that situation except as a psycho-spiritual terrorist? A guy who infiltrates people's lives and, when he gets in nice and deep, goes off like a bomb? A mole under such deep cover that he doesn't know it himself until the wake-up call comes and triggers his detonation. Who's he sitting with in the bus at the end of *that* movie? What would he have to smile about then?

If the movie *The Graduate* continued for another fifteen minutes we'd see where Ben and Elaine were really headed. They've smashed heroically out of the prison cell of parental constraint, and now we'd see them crawling through the sewer pipes on their way to—where? They have to find a place to settle; to be. They have to find another cell to crawl into. First they would go to a seedy motel, then Ben would have to go out and buy Elaine some cheap street clothes. Then what? Ben has to get a job. They have to crawl back to their betrayed parents for their belongings and for help. Elaine gets a job or gets pregnant. Twenty years later Ben and Elaine would be playing house, dealing with their own rebellious kids and bitter parents and jobs and bills and a crumbling marriage—everything they thought they were breaking out of when they were only digging deeper in. No one lives happily ever after.

What happens when that same awakening comes late in life? For that we are fortunate to have the film *About Schmidt*. Warren Schmidt's color-by-numbers life was in perfect order. He did everything right. Then it all comes undone as every layer of his carefully constructed identity is stripped away until even Ndugu, a starving Tanzanian child he sponsors and writes to looks upon Schmidt as an object of pity. One by one, all his emotional attachments and layers of selfhood dissolve; job, wife, home, friendship, family, alma mater, history, future, options, and with no happy ending tagged on because the clock has run out. The film ends honestly, with a man who played by the rules and did everything right, sitting alone, weeping.

Dear Ndugu... Relatively soon, I will die. Maybe in twenty years, maybe tomorrow, it doesn't matter. Once I am dead and everyone who knew me dies too, it will be as though I never existed. What difference has my life made to anyone? None that I can think of. None at all. –Warren Schmidt

That's a great realization for young Benjamin Braddock, a cataclysmic one for thirty-something Lisa, and a very sad one for old Warren Schmidt.

✧

Lisa had a much rougher go of it than Ben Braddock. What for a twenty year-old kid is like plucking a daisy is, for her, like dynamiting a well-established tree from the ground. Not pretty, but effective. She was very fortunate to find so much unhappiness in her life for those three years, which is something she's starting to understand now. She killed her parents, which is just another way of describing the transition from Childhood to Adulthood. There are no books in the self-help or parenting or New Age aisles called *Kill Your Parents (Or Never Grow Up)*, but there should be such a book, and in a world where the inhabitants weren't all developmentally arrested, it would be handed to every child, by their Adult parents, at the age of ten or twelve.

But then again, in such a world, there'd be no need.

After Lisa tells me about Dennis, I tell her my thoughts about *The Graduate*, *The Partner*, and *About Schmidt*, and use them to help her understand the developmental status of her husband, of Brett, of herself, and of virtually everyone she knows. We talk about vertical versus horizontal progress, and the critical importance of the word Further. We discuss some other movies as we cross the state, seeing how old stories function as new stories. She asks if there has ever been someone like me in a movie she might have seen; an awakened being.

"*The Razor's Edge?*" she suggests.

"No," I say, "that's about you, not me. Larry is going through this same transition to Adulthood you're going through. Instead of a picture of a woman falling to her death, he had the war and the memory of a dead friend: 'The dead look so terribly dead when they're dead,' he says. He's going through this process of self-birth, exiting one life and entering a new one. In the end, he has broken with all aspects of his former life, even cutting himself off from his own family money, as I recall, and starting a new life in New York as a humble taxi mechanic."

"But he doesn't end up enlightened?"

"No, he ends up where you are now, at the beginning of his life, and if he's perceptive, he'll be thankful for all the forces that conspired on his behalf to get him there—death, war, murder—blessings disguised as tragedies. You should read the book and see how it compares to your own experiences; you'll find some very interesting parallels."

"So you think there was a real guy?"

"Had to be, it's too accurate—his initial break, his confused searching, his pattern and stages of progress, his final vanity, the way the universe facilitates his journey—Maugham couldn't have made it up."

"So Larry only did what I did?"

"There's no *only* about it, kiddo. Where you are now is where all the great sages and wisemen and seers and mystics are. They're just a little further along."

"I could be one of them?" she asks. "A mystic or a sage or something?"

"They're just roles. You can play whatever role you have an authentic desire to play. The recognized and respected wisefolk are seldom very advanced in their development. You can go beyond them. You'll see."

She seems pleased and says nothing for a few minutes.

"Then what would be a movie about someone like you?" she asks.

I think about it. The character of Tech Support in *Vanilla Sky* is a close representation of me in my role as teacher; someone who explains the option of either staying in the dreamstate or jumping off a high-rise roof to awaken from it, and waiting patiently, available but disinterested, while his client struggles with the decision to wake up or stay asleep. But that's just a minor character I play in other people's dramas.

"*Cast Away*," I say after a few moments.

"Really? Tom Hanks? On the island? I don't get it." She pauses. "This isn't going to make me sad, is it?"

"Maybe, I don't know."

"I'm feeling a bit raw today, I guess. You're saying the Tom Hanks character became enlightened through his experiences on the island?"

"No, he just found himself thrust into the unadorned paradigm of the awakened being. Being alone on a desert island is a good metaphor for the awakened state. By getting stranded on that island, he has effectively died to his life, but without physically dying. Prior to the crash, the Tom Hanks character, Chuck Noland, had everything we think of as a life—friends, career, family, fiancé—as well as the countless other big and little things we take for granted until they're gone. It's all about context. Chuck Noland, at the beginning of the movie, has a full, rich context. He fits in his world, he has a robust belief-set, he is a part of things and things are a part of him. And then, *bam!*, his plane crashes and it's all gone. Suddenly, simple survival is his only context. What does that leave? A man without a context. A man who is in all respects, except physically, dead. A man with twenty-four hours a day with nothing to do but sleep, eat and stare at the waves. The differences between him and the man he buries and eulogizes with such Zen-like succinctness are negligible."

"And that's what it's like to be enlightened?"

"That's what the truth-realized state is; the absence of context. There's no artificial framework in which to say one thing is better or worse than another."

"He had his friend," she says, "Wilson, the volleyball. I guess he had to go a little soft in the head to make that relationship work."

✧

Actually, that's a relationship I can understand. Yes, he had to go a little soft in the head to make it work. He had to bend or else he'd break. He had to play a life-or-death game of make-believe. He had to believe the untrue and disbelieve the true. He had to perform an act of Orwellian doublethink: "The power of holding two contradictory beliefs in one's mind simultaneously, and accepting both of them." Chuck Noland *knows* Wilson is just a volleyball, but he must *believe* Wilson is a fellow being because he cannot *not* have a fellow being in his life. Wilson provides the context Chuck can't live without. Without Wilson, Chuck will snap, but with Wilson, Chuck can bend. Before the plane crash, Chuck's context was reflected back to him by virtually everyone and everything in his very meaning-rich and clock-centric environment. After the plane crash, all that's gone and there's just one thing left to reflect it; a volleyball with a bloody handprint that kind of looks like a face. It's not much, but it's all he needs to pretend he's not completely alone on an island in the middle of nowhere. That's what context is and that's what it does; it tells us that we're not completely alone on an island in the middle of nowhere. It provides the illusion of a populated environment in which meaning and values can be perceived and applied; where it matters what we do and what choices we make. All context is artificial. There is no true context.

Cast Away, reduced to its allegorical structure and stripped of everything after Chuck's rescue, provides us with a powerful vehicle of philosophical inquiry. Chuck Noland had his attachments severed, but he never wanted that. He's been forcibly liberated from a prison where he was perfectly content. Someone slipped the red pill into his drink, and he woke up outside a matrix he never knew he was in. All he wants is to get back in, but he can't. He's locked out of his own life, not really dead and not really alive.

Who *wants* to be cast permanently adrift on a shoreless sea? Who *wants* to spend the rest of their life tumbling through infinite space? No one, of course. What's the point of pointlessness? How can you want nothing? Words ascribed to the Buddha are often fraudulent, but there's one very clear exception and it's the quotation at the beginning of this book: "Truly, I have attained nothing from total enlightenment." That statement is like an optical illusion; it can be viewed two ways, the less obvious one the more correct. It's not so much that he *didn't* gain anything as that he *did* gain nothing.

"I see," says Lisa after we've discussed it for awhile, but she doesn't. She doesn't see that what Chuck does to survive is what everyone does to survive. She doesn't see that she herself is alone on an island in the middle of nowhere, that she's gone a little soft in the head and that her mind has reshaped itself to fit her needs, that her life is given shape and form and meaning only by her capacity for doublethink. She doesn't see that Chuck

Noland's soft-in-the-head relationship with a volleyball wasn't unique; that it's the same tactic employed by all people all the time in order to maintain the state of denial necessary to continue a meaningless existence in a fictional universe.

But Lisa is feeling a bit raw today, so I don't bother her with all that.

✧

Writing the books has provided me with an artificial context within which there are things to do and reasons to do them; within which one thing can be better or worse than another. Once the book project is over, once I'm done scribbling words in the sand, then I'll turn around and face my desolate island of near-total contextlessness, really for the first time. It's been nice to have something to do and a context within which to do it. When the teaching and writing thing is over and I'm moved into the new house with my new dog, my last remaining layers of artificial context will have vanished. If I want them after that, I'll have to generate them, if I can.

I pondered this in the first book: *Idly, soggily, I wonder what comes after.* The island is what comes after, as I've always known. A secluded oasis, devoid of contrivance and fabrication. Chuck Noland didn't like his exile. He didn't want it and he spent his time on the island wanting to get off and get back to his former world. That's a significant difference between his condition and the awakened state. I can't return to the world from which I am self-exiled and I have no such desire. Maybe I'll continue with this curious act of writing words in the sand since I'm in the habit, but probably not as part of any agreement with the universe, so it will be a different sort of enterprise; a hobby, not a vocation. My dog will be my Wilson, and I'll have to go a little soft in the head to make it work.

I have no problem with that.

28. Come What May

Alice came to a fork in the road.
"Which road do I take?" she asked.
"Where do you want to go?"
responded the Cheshire cat.
"I don't know," Alice answered.
"Then," said the cat, "it doesn't matter."

–Lewis Carroll
Alice in Wonderland

I PACE BACK AND FORTH in the sand where I've paced back and forth on a dozen previous visits, like I've paced back and forth in front of many other groups on many other nights. The difference this time is that this will be my last time.

Lisa is seated with Dr. Kim in the front row and another seventy or eighty people are seated in the sand and in the bleachers. They all appear interested to hear what I have to say. So am I. My threefold task, the way I see it, is to eulogize Brett while saying what these assembled people most need to hear in a way that best serves the book. I have a piece of paper with some quotations in my back pocket, but I haven't given much thought to what I'll be saying beyond that.

Everyone was told to bring twenty dollars each tonight to go towards a memorial gift to be presented to Brett's daughter Melissa later in the evening. Some of them paid more and Dr. Kim would later make a generous contribution. The gift itself will be a surprise to the group, but not to Melissa who has known about it for several months, since the beginning of the planning for tonight. The gift was in the hotel safe waiting for me, as hoped, and now sits in my pocket.

"We're going to sit in here and listen to me for a few minutes," I tell them when they've settled down, "then I'm going to leave you in the hands of my designated guest speaker, Lisa. Later on, we're all going down to the lake where we'll have a fire and say a proper goodbye to our—let's say friend—to our friend Brett. I don't know how we're all going to squeeze in down there, but these things have a way of working out. When we go down there we'll hook up with Brett's daughter and maybe her granddaughter, and we'll have a little surprise that might knock your socks off; a gift for them that you've contributed to. Anyone have any questions at this point?"

Some do and we end up killing half an hour with casual conversation that serves to get everyone settled and comfortable. It's a beautiful, early Autumn evening. The lights are on low and there's a misty rain falling that creates a soft patter on the aluminum roof and lends a coziness to the riding arena. Tonight's activities will actually run, off and on, for more than four hours. After a period of pretty relaxed discussion I start veering into the reason we're all here.

"I'm told the last time you all came here and met with Brett was about a year ago. Who was here for that?"

About twenty hands go up.

"What happened? What did she say? Nicole?"

Nicole is a professional woman about Lisa's age who worked with Lisa and Dr. Kim to organize tonight's meeting.

"Well, you know how she was, pretty loud, always cussing and getting in our faces?"

"Yes," I reply and everyone laughs at the memory of the fiery Brett.

"Well, she wasn't like that. It was the only time I ever saw her kind of as herself. She was very softspoken, not so much accent. She was very polite and a little sad. She just sat down with us and explained that the meetings weren't doing what she thought they would, that she felt like she was acting more as an enabler of our denial rather than as an agent for positive change. She said maybe that was what we really wanted, but she didn't want to serve that purpose. It was pretty sad. Some of us were crying."

I nod and pace back and forth in front of the bleachers and nod some more. How do we manage not to find the one thing that can never be lost? How do we manage not to see the only thing there is to be seen? Why do people who say they want to see, refuse to open their eyes? These are the questions that must have been tormenting Brett. This is what she couldn't understand as she looked back at these eager, alert, intelligent faces from where I'm standing now. How do these people, who say they want to escape from delusion, manage only to dig themselves deeper in? And how have I, someone who knows where they want to go and how to get there, been turned into just another sleep-aid?

Brett couldn't answer these questions, so she shut it down. That's very understandable to me. What's not so understandable is why she opened it up in the first place. Dr. Kim is the answer, I suspect. Now these friends and students and admirers of Brett want to know something about her, something she didn't share. They want to know why she terminated this thing they had together. They want to know why, before she died, she turned her back on them.

I start talking. I start delivering my final lesson: Brett's eulogy.

✧

"Why are you here?" I ask the group in a rhetorical, sermon-like tone. "What do you want?"

I hold out my hands as if to receive an answer, but none is forthcoming.

"I said right at the beginning of the first book, *Damnedest*, that you have to know what you want. You have to have a clear desire, a strong and specific intent. If you don't know where you're going, then there's no basis for judging one direction better or worse than another. I don't want to single anyone out, so just let me ask; can any of you stand up right now and say, in a few words, what it is you want? Why you came here to see Brett?"

No one stands up. I keep pacing and let the silence hang there so everyone can grasp its meaning.

No one knows what they want.

"How would you have answered that question?" one of the guys, Ronald, asks.

I stop pacing. I face the group squarely and answer.

"It's not how I *would* have," I answer, "it's how I *did*. I said that I want to stop being a lie. I want to stop *not* knowing who and what and where I am. I want to stop being confused and unclear. I want to stop pretending lies are true and that I understand things when I don't. I want to stop playing make-believe and find out what's real. I will give anything to do it. I will cut off my hands or pluck out my eyes or chop off my head. Nothing is too much and no price is too high because a life of ignorance and self-deceit has no value to me. There is nothing I won't do or give because I would rather be dead than continue in this blighted, benighted condition. I set no terms or conditions, I relinquish all opinions and preferences, I just want to know what's true, whatever it is, come what may."

They stare back at me in silence.

"Live free or die," I say. "That's the motto of escape. It's just that simple."

I repeat the one simple question none of them have an answer for.

"What do you want? Why are you here?"

They continue to stare. Ronald stands up.

"I think we're all intelligent people," he asserts, feeling some need to mount a defense. "I guess you don't seem to think so."

I wonder if he got uppity like that with Brett. No matter. I like uppity.

"Not true," I say. "I know we're all intelligent people, but intelligence is a curious thing in the dreamstate; can't live with it, can't live without it. It's like an icepick in a balloon store. We have to push it into a cork or things are gonna start poppin'. That's the real point of all spirituality and religion and philosophy; they are the safe corks into which we can bury the sharp points of our minds. This self-inflicted dulling of the wit is how we constantly cast our own sleep spell. No one else is doing it to us. There is no magic behind our delusion except the magic we conjure with our own emotional energy. If we stop weaving our enchantment, we start waking up, and that is the last thing we want to happen, even though it may be our stated intent. Whatever we might say, we don't want things to start poppin'."

I pause. I pace. I ponder.

"If I talk about food poisoning or stomach flu, does everyone know what I mean? From personal experience?"

This is met with a chorus of groans which I interpret as a yes.

"What?" I ask in mock dismay, "no one likes violent stomach flu? Cramps, nausea, vomiting? No? Diarrhea, fever, chills? Nobody? Jeez, tough crowd. Curled up on the bathroom floor all night? Your body wracked and heaving? No one? Wait a second, I haven't told you the good part. How about a violent stomach flu that lasts for a year and a half, maybe two years? Any takers?"

Nope.

"Come on, seriously, what would it take?" I prod them. "What would make two years of violent stomach flu worthwhile for you? What would make that worth enduring? What would make you *want* it?" I pass my gaze over the entire group. "A million bucks? An extra twenty years of life? The return of a loved one who died?" They sit in motionless silence. "Or wait, I've got it. How about nothing? Anyone? Two years of gut-wrenching purging for absolutely nothing? The line forms to the left. Who's first?"

They're unsure as to how amused they should be. Am I being funny or gratuitously gross? Am I dishonoring Brett's memory or am I making a valid point? I think they're giving me the benefit of the doubt because they're used to Brett's wild, off-color orations. Brett could be an earthy woman.

"Stay with me, please," I say. "This analogy is tight. Violent stomach flu is very much the physical counterpart of the spiritual awakening process, and it's one of those great metaphors that just gets better the more you play with it. I see how you're all looking at me, like even if it's a good metaphor that doesn't mean you want to hear about it, especially when we're all here to commemorate Brett. Trust me, this is about Brett and it's about all of you. It's about why she had these meetings and why she decided to stop having them."

They settle in to a more attentive mood.

"The main feature of both of these processes, spiritual awakening and physical stomach flu, is the violent and indiscriminate evacuation of all contents; physical in one case, mental and emotional in the other. By indiscriminate, I mean no picking and choosing; if it *can* go, it *does* go. Upheaval, downheaval, every-which-way-heaval. Emergency purge. Blow all tanks."

I'm aware that this is all just talk to them. They haven't gone through this process I'm describing and I doubt any of them will in this life, but this is my last time addressing a group and it's a great analogy and I'm not going to let it—sorry—go to waste.

"Both processes come in waves," I continue, "cycles of agony and relief. You finish one bout of violent retching and for a little while you feel okay, you think maybe it's over, but then it starts again. You feel that first twinge of not-rightness, that first subtle rumbling that tells you all is not well, and you know what you're in for and there's nothing you can do but ride it out. It builds from bad to worse to unbearable and then explodes out in all directions, leaving you weak and trembling, unable to endure any more. Then there's that brief period of respite and the glimmer of hope that it's finally over, then you feel that twinge and the whole cycle starts again. On and on it goes, wave after wave, far past the point where you're sure there's nothing else to come out. But there is."

I pace back and forth and study their faces.

"Didn't your other spiritual teachers explain about this part? The year or two of gut-wrenching expurgation?" No response. I spend the next few minutes pacing back and forth and pronouncing the names of a few dozen well-known spiritual teachers, gurus and authors, living and dead, with a pause after each in case anyone wants to raise a hand and vouch for any of them, and so they can take note of the fact that no one does. I end the list with a single name.

"Brett?"

All hands go up.

I really wanted to be clear about that. Now we can continue.

"Something else that's important to appreciate about this analogy," I say, "is that when you have the stomach flu or food poisoning, it seems like your system is going totally haywire, but it's not. There's an intelligence at work. It's a process. The organism is putting itself through this terrible ordeal for a reason. These same things can be said about the awakening process. It looks like total mental and emotional chaos, but it's a process and there's an intelligence at work. The process works a certain way and there are reasons for it."

And now for the cherry.

"And the analogy is still incomplete," I say. "I've said many times that no one really wants what this really is. The prize at the end of this two-year bout of violent illness isn't just nothing, it's nothingness. That's what it means to say that it's not just something we *don't* want, it's something we *can't* want. There's no *it*."

No one looks in the least bit happy.

✧

"How would someone make it happen if they wanted to?" asks Nicole. "How would someone, uh, induce this process?"

"Excellent question," I reply, "very close to the heart of the matter. Can you make it happen? What can you do? You can't just take an emetic like some spiritual ipecac to induce the vomiting of a lifetime. You can't just shove your mudra-shaped fingers down your throat. You could try sitting in zazen for a few years, try to puke up that ball of molten lead they talk about; let me know how that works out for you. To really make something happen, you have to become poisoned, you have to introduce some foreign agent into your system that's going to grow and spread like it has a life of its own. Maybe this foreign agent is already inside each of us, maybe it's that little voice that urges us to come to meetings like this, some seed of discontent, and it just needs to be nurtured and encouraged. Maybe this foreign agent is the only thing in us that *isn't* foreign."

I observe my thoughts to see where this goes next.

"Can you make it happen?" I ask. "Can you keep it from happening? I have no idea. My opinion is that it's not within your direct control. You have to pray for it and use Spiritual Autolysis to bring your desire and intent into sharp focus to find out what this little voice has to say and if you want to hear it. But what we keep coming back to is that if you don't want it, you don't want it. That brings us to the question at the very center of this entire subject: Why? Why make yourself want something you don't want? Why try to initiate a two-year bout of violent illness for nothing? That's a tough one because there is no sane reason to do it. You have to become *in*sane, you have to go out of your mind. What it takes to get out of Maya's funhouse is so extreme and so counterinstinctual, so unwantable, that it can't happen within the mindset we think of as sanity."

I pause for a drink of water. The group looks a little wan.

"I know it's an unsavory analogy," I continue, "but that's part of its merit. Waking up is an unsavory process. It's the ultimate detox program, as the term Spiritual Autolysis implies; spiritual self-digestion. And just a reminder, when you take away all the metaphors and analogies, all we're really talking about is unbelieving what is untrue, about not seeing what's not really there, about getting back to our clean, uncontaminated, uncorrupted state. It's really as simple as that."

I turn out my hands again.

"So, I repeat my question. Why are you here? What do you want?"

✧

We take a short water break. When we pick up again, I speak in a more conversational tone.

"Brett had the wrong idea about what was going on here, about what her role was and what your roles were. The really puzzling question is why she had the meetings at all. Here's the thing Brett was wrong about. She thought you were all coming here every month because you wanted to catch the flu. She thought you wanted to be infected and to go through this violent stomach flu I've just described."

This stirs up some response. I pace while they quiet down.

"She thought you understood this," I say "and that you wanted to undergo this severe and protracted illness, just as she had."

A young musician-type named Justin stands up to ask the question they all want to ask. "She thought we came here because we wanted to be sick for two years like you're talking about?"

"Absolutely."

"But you said it was all for nothing."

"More like nothingness; it's all for nothingness. Totally spent, hollowed out, the contents of your mental-emotional alimentary canal completely evacuated, leaving you cored out like a fruit rind. Anyway, yes, it's an easy thing for someone like Brett or me to believe."

Justin doesn't believe.

"You and Brett think people would actually want to go through all that? Like, for nothing?"

"Good question, and the answer is an emphatic yes. I know that's hard to believe, but it's a natural thing for people like me and Brett to believe. From our perspective, it's a no-brainer. If anything, it's hard for us to believe that everyone isn't on their knees begging for it. I know that sounds equally incomprehensible to you, but there it is. For one thing, we consider this experience I'm describing to be the birth process from fantasy to reality. To our way of thinking, there's simply no alternative. For another thing, here you all are. You came here asking for something, even if you didn't know what it was. So yes, we take you at your word. Finally, thirdly, I'll say that Brett and I are not completely incorrect in our assumptions. I have known quite a few people, and have received a small mountain of correspondence from other people, who received this message in the spirit in which people like Brett and I deliver it. Only a very small percentage, but strong and clear in their desire and intent."

"In your first book," says Nicole, "you said one or two people a year were waking up with your assistance—"

"That number has grown surprisingly now with the books out, but I see far more people who just want to stop lining up for every spiritual dog-and-pony show, and approach the major questions of their existence with some maturity and common sense."

✧

I take a break to drink some water and let that last bit settle in. A bunch of private conversations spring up, but everyone quiets down when I return to center front.

"Why should such extreme measures be necessary? Why should we have to go through such an agonizing ordeal just to become who and what we really are?"

I don't expect an answer. I turn it up a notch.

"Flow and obstruction," I say, "are the basic operating principles of life in the dreamstate. For most people, though, it's all obstruction and no flow. They say we are spiritual beings having a human experience, but really, we are mortally constipated spiritual beings having a sub-human experience.

The pandemics of obesity, diabetes, heart disease and cancer that ravage the Western world are merely the outer manifestations of a far-progressed inner condition. While only some of us are physically fat and diseased, virtually all of us are spiritually fat and diseased. Morbid spiritual obesity is a plague that has decimated the human race, leaving this lovely planet little more than a terminal care facility in which we sit glassy-eyed and slack-jawed, wiling away the hours of lives we didn't ask for and don't know what to do with; a world of moribund hospice patients mainlining on flavored morphine and running out the clock."

That leaves a few moments of silence in its wake.

"But maybe that's all that people want to do," suggests an older fellow named Henry, rushing to smear some lipstick on this pig, "to be spiritual couch potatoes. Go to work, raise their families, zone out in front of the TV or whatever. It's not hell, it's just life."

"I agree," I agree. "No one is kicking down doors and dragging people out of their beds. You all came here to see Brett. She didn't seek you out and lure you in, did she? You came to her asking for this, right?"

Henry nods in agreement, as do others.

"Did Brett ever talk about how great enlightenment was? How it would solve all your problems, fill you with love and peace and happiness, elevate your soul, let you transcend the human plane and even death, give you special powers, anything enticing like that?"

No one responds. This is another important thing to make clear.

"Did she ever try to talk you into anything? Did she try to convince you of anything except to think for yourselves, to look and see for yourselves? Was she like some gladhanding salesman or baby-kissing politician, making promises about how much better life would be if you bought into her special brand of spirituality? Was she running some sort of get-bliss-quick scheme? Did she espouse any teaching? Did she irradiate you with her shakti energy?"

There's a bit of laughter because everything I'm saying is so obviously *un*-Brett. I wait and let the questions hang for a moment. I don't want anyone thinking we're here tonight to say goodbye to some beloved prison-trustee, just another of Maya's legion of flunkies and toadies, a cheerleader for a message of niceness and passivity and contentment; a hypnagogue. Hypnagogue is defined as an agent that induces sleep. Maya has unleashed an army of hypnagogues into the world to induce and maintain the sleep state. All well and good. I have no issue with that. I just don't want people here tonight to think that's what Brett was.

"Most of you know that I have a pretty strong contempt for the spiritual marketplace. A pornographic mockery of man's desire to know the truth, I think I called it. Do you all understand who and what I meant by that?"

Nods and grunts of general assent.

"Do any of you think that applies to Brett? Was she someone who was pushing an agenda? Trying to get rich? Building an organization? Publishing a newsletter or a blog? Going on tour? Did she want to be popular? Did she need her self-image as a spiritually superior being reflected back to her? Did she ever even *smile*? Christ, was she ever even *nice*?"

They are alert and attentive. They know something important is being said, something near the scary edge of things.

"Did she ever ask for money? Try to sell you anything? Invite you on a cruise or to a coastal retreat? Did she ever dress up or adopt a title or a spiritual name? Did she ever claim a teaching or lineage? Did she ever utter a Sanskrit or Japanese term? At the meetings, did she turn down the lights? Play music? Light candles? Begin with a prayer or meditation? Anything like that?"

The only response is some gentle laughter. This is an important point to make, like listing all the teachers and authors. We have a very nice show planned for this evening, but none of it means anything if these people come away from it lumping Brett in with the world of spiritual whoredom.

"Brett was the real deal," I say, "and that's such a rare thing that it's very easy for us not to know it when we see it. That fiery temperament you saw wasn't her. That quiet, thoughtful person some of you saw in that last meeting was closer to how she was away from all this. This is a very challenging message to deliver and she became the person she had to be to get it across. She stopped the meetings when she realized the truth of what I told her every time we talked; that there's a total disconnect in this teacher/student relationship. A total disconnect. We don't have what you want and you don't want what we have. Brett didn't want to believe that, but finally she couldn't help but see it was true, and that's when she stopped having the meetings. I have other reasons for doing this teaching thing, but she didn't."

✧

"So now, with the help of the Dalai Lama, I'll answer this question I've been asking: The question is, why are you here? What do you want?"

I take a piece of paper from my back pocket and unfold it and read one of the quotations I scribbled down.

"'In the final analysis,' said the Dalai Lama, 'the hope of every person is simply peace of mind.'"

I refold the paper and put it away.

"Does anyone disagree?"

No one does.

"Me neither," I say. "What do you want? Peace of mind. It's that simple. So you came here seeking this peace of mind from Brett, but she thought you were here for the exact opposite. She was a disruptor, an agitator, a metaphysical anarchist. She was all about smashing things up and burning them down. She was an iconoclast, a revolutionary. She thought you wanted war and the whole time you wanted peace. I agree with the Dalai Lama; peace of mind—Spiritual Consonance—is what virtually all seekers of all places and all times are really seeking. It all makes perfect sense when you look at it that way. Why is everyone seeking and no one finding? Because they're not seeking truth or growth or change, they're seeking peace of mind. The rest is just dressing."

"What's so bad about peace of mind?" asks Justin.

"Nothing's wrong with it," I answer, "it just doesn't register with someone like Brett."

"Or like you," he says.

"Or like me, right. Personally, I think about this idea of peace of mind and I shudder in revulsion. To me, it's just a fancy way of saying that people just want to keep munching their cud and plodding along, head down, surrounded by herdmates; unconscious, unengaged, unalive. To someone like me or Brett, peace of mind is the enemy. It's the worst thing in the world. It's the cow, it's the inmate, it's the hairless, fetal thing that's still plugged into the matrix. I mean, peace of mind," I make a gun of my finger and blow my brains out. "What's the point?"

That seems to get them a little agitated.

"Don't be insulted by any of this, it's certainly not your fault. This is the universal seeker dynamic. You can go to practically any spiritual teacher or clergy member and they'll help you in your search for peace of mind. Brett was the one who didn't get it. It's not just that she didn't know you wanted peace of mind, it's that she would have found such a desire incomprehensible. Even if you guys had said it straight out, it wouldn't have computed for her. She would have equated peace of mind with being asleep, so it would be like you were coming to her and asking her to put you to sleep. That's the disconnect. Just as it doesn't make sense to you that we think you come here to have your lives incinerated, it doesn't make sense to us that you come here asking for sleep."

✧

I signal a break and everyone gets up and stretches. After fifteen minutes we all return to our places and speak casually back and forth for a few minutes. After awhile, I introduce a reluctant Lisa. She comes out, holding her dayplanner. She is visibly uncomfortable and embarrassed. She doesn't really understand that she, a spiritual neophyte, has succeeded where legions of spiritual veterans have failed. She agreed to speak. I didn't try to convince her. She understood what I was trying to show her, that she still had a big thing to do, and she decided she wanted to do it and that standing in front of these people and telling her story might help her do it.

She opens her dayplanner to the photo and hands it to someone in the front row to be passed around. She has a hard story to tell. She starts slowly, in the clipped fashion of a painful emotional confession, but then, eyes down, voice soft and wavering, she finds a quiet, heartfelt rhythm of expression and the story begins to flow. I step out so my presence won't make things harder for her. Twenty minutes later, from out in an adjacent field, I hear loud and sustained applause, and I know she did good.

Brett and I never got any damn applause.

29. Epitaph for a Friend

AS I lay with my head in your lap, Camerado,
The confession I made I resume—
    what I said to you in the open air I resume:
I know I am restless, and make others so;
I know my words are weapons, full of danger, full of death;
(Indeed I am myself the real soldier;
It is not he, there, with his bayonet,
    and not the red-striped artilleryman;)
For I confront peace, security, and all the settled laws,
    to unsettle them;
I am more resolute because all have denied me,
    than I could ever have been had all accepted me;
I heed not, and have never heeded, either experience,
    cautions, majorities, nor ridicule;
And the threat of what is call'd hell is little or nothing to me;
And the lure of what is call'd heaven is little or nothing to me;
Dear camerado! I confess I have urged you onward with me,
    and still urge you, without the least idea what is our
    destination,
Or whether we shall be victorious,
    or utterly quell'd and defeated.

—Walt Whitman

30. Duckspeak

"You remember when I said how I was gonna explain about
life, buddy? Well the thing about life is, it gets weird. People
are always talking about truth. Everybody always knows what
the truth is, like it was toilet paper or somethin', and they got
a supply in the closet. But what you learn, as you get older, is
there ain't no truth. All there is is bullshit, pardon my
vulgarity here. Layers of it. One layer of bullshit on top of
another. And what you do in life like when you get older is,
you pick the layer of bullshit that you prefer and that's your
bullshit, so to speak."

–Bernie LaPlante, Hero

I RETURN TO THE ARENA half an hour later and find everyone spread
out in small groups, standing and seated, drinking and munching on
treats from a well-stocked snack table that has mysteriously appeared,
engaged in a variety of conversations. I exchange smiles with Lisa who is in
close conversation with the mysterious Dr. Kim. I stroll from group to
group and listen in and hear talk of Brett, talk of the story Lisa just shared,
talk of the critical differences between the Rinzai and Soto schools of Zen,
talk of boyfriend shortcomings, talk of an exciting new spiritual teacher in
Maryland who has her students roll their eyes up during meditation so they
can see their third eye, and talk of local restaurants. I move on.

I respond to questions when asked, but mostly listen. Lawrence, the
fellow holding forth on Zen, I find out, has spent twenty years meditating
his "ass off" under several different Zen Masters in New York and out West,
and is currently writing a book about his experiences. He informs me that
my views on Zen are far too simplistic, that there is infinitely more to Zen
than the hot and narrow pursuit of enlightenment. I thank him without
irony and drift back over to the folks I heard talking about local restaurants, but they're talking about something else now.

Zen, I have to admit, really grinds my nuts. It has been a subject of confusion and frustration for me since forever. When I think about Zen, I know there's something there, but when I look at Zen, I can't seem to find it. Churchill said that democracy is the worst form of government, except for all the others. Similarly, I'd say that Zen is the worst path to enlightenment, except for all the others. It's not just that Zen has been Westernized, bastardized, homogenized and commercialized beyond all recognition. I've looked back over the centuries into the history of Zen and have found that it has long since drifted safely away from its dangerous center. I have looked at many highly revered Zen Masters, East and West, and one thing is very clear; Zen Master is not synonymous with awakened, truth-realized being. Frankly, I don't know what the hell a Zen Master is if he's not awake, or what the hell Zen is if not the annihilation of the ego, but anyone who uses those criteria to refine their personal Zen search will instantly see their results plummet from millions of strong hits to a dubious handful, with very few of the big names surviving the purge.

The sincere aspirant could spend the next decade in a Zen monastery, sit at the feet of a revered Zen Master, perform zazen with perfect discipline, endure the pain and the stick and the agonizing hours and the selfless toil, soak up every word, every parable, every drop of teaching, and ultimately know nothing more about Zen than the cabbie who picks him up when he finally calls it quits. And here's the funny thing; even as he's leaving, knowing that the whole thing was a total waste of time, he'd also know that he wasn't wrong. He'd know he picked right and that what he wanted was in there somewhere, he just never found it. All that *other* Zen got in the way.

Zen is a race car without an engine. It looks very cool, but without an engine it can't take us anywhere. We can slip in behind the wheel and make engine sounds and turn the wheel and shift gears and pretend we're rocketing across the spiritual landscape, but when we get tired of it in ten minutes or ten years, we'll get out of this sexy little hotrod exactly where we got into it.

So why go on about it?

I hadn't actually thought about Zen much since writing the first book, but over the summer and on the trip here, I have given a lot of thought to Lisa's experience, and it occurred to me that in her I was seeing the real Zen; a force so powerful and inexorable that it can reach into someone's life unbidden and hurl that person like a rag doll into the furnace of disillusionment.

That's some crazy shit. I mean, there she was, a perfect housewife, super-mom, career gal and all-round high-achiever, and all of a sudden, out of nowhere, *Bam!*, her perfect little connect-the-dots life gets nuked back to infancy. Not into enlightenment, but into and through the death-rebirth process that marks the beginning of the journey. Of *any* journey.

What I was seeing in Lisa was the real Zen, not the long-dead Zen of myth and marketplace. Not the sideshow corpse of Zen that still lures in the rubes, or the tapdancing Zen zombie selling energy drinks and lawn ornaments at the bidding of the dollar-eyed Svengalis on Madison Avenue, but the inferno at the very core of Zen. Without training, without middlemen, without stated desire or specific intent, Lisa had somehow managed to plunge straight into the heart of things.

Why Lisa, I wondered. Why was she different? Millions of people saw that picture of the falling woman, and many others like it. The world is full of seemingly senseless tragedy. We're all dangling by a thread and everyone gets a reminder of that now and then. Not everyone does what Lisa did, though. Most of us turn away from such an unsettling revelation, but Lisa didn't. She turned toward it. She wouldn't or couldn't let herself turn away. Was it destiny or free will or the timeless, spaceless other? I have no idea, but what I *do* know is that what she did is what virtually all spiritual aspirants, to all appearances, should be doing and aren't; relinquishing the illusion of control. But appearances can be deceiving and spiritual aspirants don't always know to what, if anything, they aspire. That's what Brett was figuring out when she stopped having these meetings.

In Zen terms, what Lisa managed to do in three difficult years was empty her cup; an impressive and remarkably uncommon feat, especially for one so deeply-rooted in life as Lisa was. She never asked for it, she never wanted it, but it came and she dealt with it.

Impermanence had become Lisa's own personal koan, and those thousands of minutes she spent staring at that blurry photo of the falling woman was her zazen practice. This is real Zen, burning from the inside out of a real person. Who cares about one hand clapping or your face before you were born or any of those quaint little mindbenders? What's more mindbending than your own looming death? What could be more devastating to ego than the contemplation of meaninglessness and insignificance? Of nothingness? Of no-self? Here was Lawrence, a clever, dedicated man with twenty years of Zen study under his belt, writing the obligatory book and already signed up for the next twenty years, and he's made as much real progress as anyone I might pick out of a crowd, or a lot less, depending on how you reckon anti-progress. And here was Lisa, with no interest, no motivation, deeply established in her well-worn, circular path, and she had achieved a level of success a seasoned veteran like Lawrence wouldn't even recognize as such.

✧

"We can use the opportunity afforded by Lisa's experience to take a closer look at Zen," I tell the group after calling them back to order. "In spite of itself, Zen is what we're talking about when we talk about peeling away the many-layered fabric of false identity. If you take away all the trappings of Zen—the teachings and the ceremonies, the different schools, the postures and the koans, everything you think of as Zen—and throw it all into the fire, what survives? What is the true core of Zen after all the veils and vanities have burned away?"

I pause because I want them to think about it.

"The fire," I answer. "The fire is what's left. The fire is Zen."

Lawrence is shaking his head.

"You're free to speak, Lawrence," I say.

He sighs in exasperation and stands up. He addresses not just me but the entire group. He talks about the real Zen that I seem to be ignoring. He talks about patriarchs and ancient roots and Zen today, he pays homage to his own teachers and their teachers. He talks about heritage and philosophy, training and lifestyle, practice and dedication, personal struggle, tradition, commitment, sacrifice. He is intelligent, eloquent, and expert on his subject. I let him continue for a few minutes because I'm optimistic, on Brett's behalf, that some of the people here tonight are looking at Lawrence and seeing what I'm seeing; a little boy who is scared of the dark and has spent his life burrowing into the fortress of Zen; the grown-up version of huddling under blankets, hiding from some imagined boogeyman.

Parents tell their children that there is no such thing as the boogeyman, but that's because they themselves have never thrown off the covers and turned on the lights. There *is* such a thing as the boogeyman. He *is* out to get you, and he will. The boogeyman is real. He is the most real thing in the dreamstate, and real Zen, if there is such a thing, is about turning toward him, not away.

While he speaks, Lawrence tries several times to engage me, to draw me in, but I know better and gesture for him to continue without me. The first rule in this business is never let them drag you down into their imagined realms. He wants to pull me down into the muck and mire of words and concepts and debate, into the warm ooze of perpetual stalemate. That is his element, that's where he and many like him are most comfortable, making their engine sounds, busily going nowhere.

I watch the group as Lawrence speaks. It's not always easy to remember that these people aren't like me; they look and sound awake, but they're not. They are asleep and dreaming, sleepwalking and sleeptalking. Their words make sense to them, inside their dreamworld, but from my perspective it's mostly mumbling. They seldom express a lucid thought or formulate a coherent question. In several minutes of uninterrupted discourse on Zen, Lawrence has not said anything that I recognize as being related to the topic of awaking from delusion.

> As he watched the eyeless face with the jaw moving rapidly up and down, Winston had a curious feeling that this was not a real human being but some kind of dummy. It was not the man's brain that was speaking, it was his larynx. The stuff that was coming out of him consisted of words, but it was not speech in the true sense: it was a noise uttered in unconsciousness, like the quacking of a duck.
>
> —George Orwell, *1984*

So how can we communicate across this great divide? Metaphors and well-known stories like books and movies provide a common ground where ideas can be expressed, but if we drift away from that shared territory in either direction, it's like a radio tuner drifting away from a clear channel into static.

If you're standing out here in front of these people and you're attached to results, as Brett was, then it's only natural that you'd get a little aggravated and finally give up. The gulf that separates these states is very real and all attempts to communicate across it are inherently quixotic. It's not until a student or aspirant or reader starts closing the consciousness gap from their side that any real communication can start taking place. Until someone understands what it really means that their eyes are closed and begins the process of unseeing what's not, nothing Brett or I might say could really make much difference. The wall separating the awakened and unawakened states is not conceptual or theoretical or metaphorical. Intelligence can't pierce it, piety can't melt it, fervor can't smash it. It is a forcefield empowered by the emotional energy of fear, so everything we hurl against it is rechanneled into it. Only ego-death defeats this barrier because the barrier is ego itself. The segregated self must recede for the integrated being to emerge.

✧

The whole evening will last more than four hours, less than two hours of that time spent with me addressing the group. Mostly it's just easy conversation and quiet remembrance.

We speak casually for another half hour. Together, we talk about the *Bhagavad Gita* to see if Krishna isn't actually Maya and if the Song of the Lord isn't actually a lullaby. We talk about *The Matrix* and lay it like a template over our own world to see how it fits and where everyone fits in it, including us here tonight in this horse arena. "Are you Morpheus?" one person asks me. "Brett was more like Morpheus," says another, "Jed's more like a program." "No, he's the red pill," another answers and everyone laughs. Many of them have brought their copies of *Damnedest* and *Incorrect* with them tonight, so a lot of their questions come from the books. We talk about *1984,* with which they're somewhat familiar; about *Moby-Dick,* which many own but few have read; and about Whitman and Thoreau and U.G. Krishnamurti. It's all very nice and pleasant in the arena, with only a few lights on and the soft rain falling outside and a gentle breeze passing through. As long as we stay on the subject of the books, or within the frameworks of metaphors and allegories, we are able to enjoy an interesting and instructive exchange.

Of these seventy people, I know that maybe one, but probably none, will actually do anything. They're mostly just tourists, which is fine with me, but it was a tough realization for Brett. Of those I have observed, Dr. Kim seems the most sincere, and I know he's not going to blast out of his holy trinity—work, home, family—due to the minor technicality that he's playing a fictional character in a fictional world. Lawrence is so deep into his role of dedicated Zen adherent that he'll never get another glimpse of daylight. There are others who seem equally sincere or dedicated, but a closer look reveals that it's written into their character to seem sincere or dedicated, or that their spirituality has been clumsily retrofitted, like a pressure-relief valve not specified in the original design.

Of course, there's always the one that surprises you. Maybe there's a Lisa or a Brett up in these bleachers somewhere. If there is, it probably won't be any of the most likely candidates but one of the quiet ones, sitting in the back, slowly building up some heat, starting to burn from the inside.

❖

I take a break and wander down to the lake. When I get there I see that my concerns about fitting in all these people have already been addressed. More than an acre of lakeside field has been cleared and mowed. A medium-sized white canopy has been erected and there are at least a hundred folding chairs set up in semi-circle facing the fire pit and the lake. I had hoped to be able to scare up a dozen logs and a pint of gas for the fire, but that's been taken care of too. A large, well-kindled bonfire is waiting to be touched off. The area around the fire pit, which was cramped with twenty people in the past, was now mown and groomed to handle a hundred.

I knew all this lakeside tribute part would work itself out, that we could get a fire built and squeeze everybody in somehow, but I had no idea it would be taken care of like this.

Dr. Kim.

I am sure right away that he put all this together, as Nicole would confirm for me later. Dr. Kim arranged landscapers and day-laborers, got the chairs, tent and a few tables from his temple and had the whole thing ready in three days.

I have the last cigar I got from Frank. This is a bit pre-planned. I wanted to create a pause in tonight's events in which I could come down to the lake alone, light a cigar, walk a quiet lap around the lake and just think about things. I've done a lot of cool things in my life, more than just jumping out of planes and writing some books and escaping delusion, but I know no greater pleasure than taking a nice walk in a nice place on a nice night. I wish Maya was with me.

"I'm always with you," she says.

"I meant the dog," I reply.

The rain has stopped, the clouds are parting and a nearly full moon is peaking through. Perfect. I light the cigar and begin my walk. This little stroll around the lake is supposed to be quiet and reflective and soaked with meaning as I pay silent tribute to Frank and Brett and many others who have played important roles in my own journey. I know things are winding down for me and this is supposed to be like my victory lap where I look back over one life and, perhaps, forward to another.

I should know better than to try to pull such a schmaltzy stunt. The cigar tastes like crap. It needs the booze for counterpoint and I have no booze. The lake path Brett walked so many thousands of times is now over-grown with brambles like razor-wire. I get about fifty feet before chucking the whole thing as a bad idea. The cigar goes in the lake and I go back to the riding arena.

Sentimental bullshit.

31. The Demon Tamer

"The only thing that burns in hell is the part of you that won't let go of your life: your memories, your attachments. They burn them all away, but they're not punishing you, they're freeing your soul. If you're frightened of dying and you're holding on, you'll see devils tearing your life away. If you've made your peace, then the devils are really angels freeing you from the earth."

—Louis, Jacob's Ladder*

"MOST OF YOU PROBABLY KNOW that I managed to arrive at the truth-realized state through the writing process, Spiritual Autolysis. I talked about that in the first book. Anyone who manages to do it has a *way* they managed to do it. Does anyone know how Brett managed to do it?"

A few hands are tentatively raised. I point to a guy in front.

"Something to do with her father," he says.

"A *lot* to do with her father," I confirm, "though it was a few years after he died. He was a military guy, an officer, so Brett was an army brat; she lived in a bunch of different places, different countries. Her father was an extremely critical person; found fault with everything, always very judgmental. That's what Brett told me about him. Even after he died, he was still a constant presence in her mind. You all know what it's like to have a critical voice in your head? Some person or thought or emotion that has taken up residence in your head and tends to be a bit on the obnoxious side?"

Everyone raises a hand and nods with grim familiarity.

*Attributed to Meister Eckhart.

"Well, those are demons. Demon is a useful way to describe anything in our heads that we don't want there and which seems to have a mind of its own; something that haunts us or has power over us, has its hooks into us; memories, people, addictions. They torment us in a variety of ways, but the main thing demons do is hold us back, restrict our progress.

"This is Brett's final lesson for you, by the way. This comes from her. She explained all this to me one night last year. We were sitting down at the lake after a meeting, the fire was dying down and she told me about what a fierce presence her father had been in her mind. Always there, always critiquing and belittling; a real cancer of the spirit. Normally, I'm not very tolerant of that sort of disclosure. If Brett had been a student of mine, I would have encouraged her to stop dawdling over childhood grievances and maladies; to leave it behind and move on."

Sounds of disapproval rise from the bleachers.

"Maybe that sounds cruel," I continue, "but problems of this nature are solved by transcending them, not by dealing with them. We are in the business of slaying demons, not feeding them."

This is getting me a lot of scowls and dubious stares, so I have to say more. I'd planned to keep it simple by limiting my discussion to Brett's father—as extreme an example of demonhood as you're likely to find—but now I see that demonology is something we should take a few minutes to look at.

"Imagine you're climbing out of a dark sewer and some beast has its teeth sunk into your leg, making a lot of noise and tearing at you and weighing you down; a demon. Are you going to jump back down into the sewer and fight it? A lot of people think that's the answer, but why do that? It's tough to slay demons because they're symptoms, not causes, and even if you kill one, there are always more. What's next, a fight to the death with your obsessive neatness? Pistols at dawn with your love of chocolate? The only real result of these little battles is that you haven't gone anywhere; you're still in the sewer. All you've really killed is time, and time is all you really have. You haven't killed a demon, you've lost a piece of your life, and that means they've won; the part of you that's afraid to move forward has won. You have to ask yourself, what's your objective? To achieve mental equilibrium in a sewer or to climb out of it? To slay every little demon or to rise up out of the realms they inhabit? Don't laugh like it's obvious, everyone seeks solutions within the sewer rather than escape from it. Battling demons is the ultimate form of shadow boxing. You're just punching at an empty projection of yourself. For our purposes, if demons aren't demonizing you, then they don't exist; it's as simple as that."

"Sounds like a cop out," says Justin, "like a way of not dealing with your issues."

"Who agrees with Justin?" I ask the group, and many people nod or raise their hands.

"So do I," I agree, "it does sound like a cop out, but dealing with our issues is the real cop out. It's our way of avoiding the real war by engaging ourselves at the level of minor skirmishes. Who wouldn't prefer to struggle against their addiction to caffeine instead of their addiction to mindless conformity?"

They laugh.

"As we develop a subtler and more refined understanding of what a demon is, identifying them by what they do, not how they look, we begin to see that demons aren't limited to addictions and critical voices. It's not just negative attachments that hold us captive within ego's sphere, it's all attachments. The approach to life and spirituality where we decrease bad things like sins and addictions, and increase good things like love and compassion, never has and never will move anyone a single step in the direction of awakening."

They look half dubious, half confused.

"For example," I explain, "if I were a gambling addict, then a large portion of my life energy—my time, my thoughts and emotions—would be spent either gambling or fighting my urge to gamble. But for our purposes, feeding my addiction and fighting it are really the same thing. Whether my gambling demon is beating me or I'm beating it doesn't matter, all that matters is that I'm sitting in my prison cell fully engaged in processes that will never move me one inch closer to liberation. That's what demons do. They're like Maya's army of winged monkeys. They always fight a delaying action that expends our resources and prevents us from making forward progress. That's their objective, to occupy us, not to defeat us."

✧

There's an interesting parallel in *1984*. The country of Oceania has the power to create a high standard of living for everyone, but the ruling party wishes to keep everyone impoverished and thereby enslaved:

> The problem was how to keep the wheels of industry turning without increasing the real wealth of the world. Goods must be produced, but they must not be distributed. And in practice the only way of achieving this was by continuous warfare.
> —George Orwell, *1984*

Continuous warfare. People toiling in factories producing ships and tanks that are destroyed in a perpetual war that is never won or lost. People stay busy and production stays high while their standard of living stays low and their hope of overthrowing their oppressors stays nonexistent.

Demons are similar in that they don't exist to win or lose, but only to keep us busy. Say, for instance, that after twenty years of fighting my gambling addiction, I finally manage to overcome it. What would I have to show for that victory?

Twenty years gone.

✧

"Demons keep us unfocused and distracted," I continue, "which is something the Spiritual Autolysis is very effective at cutting through. The need to deal with tormenting demons comes up again and again as we progress, so you have to know what to do as a matter of policy; keep climbing or jump down and fight? My advice: Fight when you have to, climb when you can. Further is everything. Use the writing to keep yourself in tight focus and the demons will die from lack of attention."

"Isn't it possible that these demons could be used in a positive way?" asks Shanti. "You talk about how dark emotions can be useful, is there any way demons might be useful too?"

"Yes," I say, "and that brings us right back to Brett. This father-presence in her mind was much more serious than any of us can probably imagine. I'd never heard of anything like it before Brett told me about it. I've looked into it since then and I found out that for some people, these critical internal voices can be really shattering."

No one moves or speaks. I don't think Brett ever got too touchy-feely in the meetings. She was as naturally indifferent to mundane emotional, psychological and biographical content as I am. The point isn't to study and understand and cherish the bags of rocks we carry, the point is to drop them.

"This is all back when Brett was just a normal person, before any sort of awakening at all, no interest in any of it. The presence of this father-demon in her mind was constant and highly toxic. Whatever she was doing or thinking, it was there; loud, contemptuous, undermining. She spent an hour telling me what this was like for her, and I found myself intrigued because she wasn't sad or sobbing or self-pitying, she was smiling with that air of a warrior recounting tales of battles won and lost. Even when she was quiet and thoughtful, she could tell a good story."

Everyone laughs and smiles.

"What she told me was that it just got to be too much. She couldn't stand the presence of this hyper-critical asshole in her head any more. She said life had no pleasure. Nothing she did was good enough. She couldn't enjoy anything. She was trying to find relief in alcohol and drugs. I assume this is a more severe case than most of you are familiar with?"

Eyes are wide. No one responds to the contrary.

"This was her whole life since she was a kid. Twenty years of this negative, nagging voice in her head. She was suicidal. Think about that. That's how bad it was. That's how serious this was for her. She knew it would never go away. She knew she couldn't fight it. She knew that no matter what she did in life, this voice in her head would always be there sucking the joy out of it, ruining everything, and once her father died there was no way she could ever confront him in person and make a meaningful change in their relationship, which left her even more hopeless. She was trapped, no way out. That's how she described it to me through that hard smile. Did you all know she had cancer?"

That jolts them. I was pretty sure they didn't know. Dr. Kim knew, but not the rest.

"Not a big surprise, I suppose, that a malignancy of the mind and spirit would eventually manifest as a malignancy of the body. This was in her late twenties, before any of us knew her. By the time they caught it the prognosis was bleak and it got her thinking more and more about the larger issues."

I pause and pace and let my thoughts get out of the way.

"She told me that at her lowest point she was in terrible shape. Low weight, her musculature was seized up, migraines, poor sleep, always tense and hunched, doped up on meds and sick from chemo. She lived here on the farm, but not as a going concern; no animals, no crop or gardens. She still had this critical voice in her head mocking every thought, and she had a pretty dire prognosis from the doctors."

"She beat it though, right?" asks Justin. "I mean, that was more than ten years ago, right? She beat the cancer?"

I look at all the faces looking eagerly to me for this answer.

"She kicked its ass," I reply to Justin. "You saw her, you knew her. Did she seem sickly? Seized up? Weak? Fatigued?"

"No," he says. "How did she beat it?"

"How do you think?" I ask back. I turn to the entire group. "How do you think Brett beat cancer? Chemo? Alternative medicine? Power of prayer? Positive thinking? A Mexican clinic? A visualization technique?" I pace back and forth and give it time.

"Anyone? How do you think Brett defeated what was diagnosed as advanced stage terminal cancer?"

Finally I stop in front of Dr. Kim.

"Sir?"

He looks up at me and speaks in a choked whisper.

"She stop fighting," he says.

✧

"She stopped fighting," I say after an extended pause. "She stopped resisting. Everything she'd been pushing against for so many years, she now began to allow. She knew she was defeated, she knew she had nothing to lose. She wasn't finding the support she needed in church or in medicine or anywhere else, so she just stopped fighting."

I pause for a minute to let them get the wrong idea.

"I know this sounds counterintuitive," I continue, "like giving up, like weakness, but when I say she stopped fighting, what I mean is that she stopped routing all her energy into her shields. This one simple act is the key to everything. It's the transition point from segregated to integrated, from Childhood to Adulthood. Ego is obstruction, surrender is flow. Surrender is the basis and precursor of growth. It is of the essence. There is no shortcut or workaround, no substitute or alternate route. You can fake it and many do, but you're only cheating yourself. There is no growth possible within egoic constraints, only the illusion of growth. Prior to surrender there's ego; the puny, ignorant, segregated self. Once we free ourselves from that noxious and artificial puniness, we come into alignment, *Bam!*, just like that. It may take days or months or years for the various aspects of our lives to make the adjustment, but the initial impact is as dramatic and distinct as climbing out of a dark, fetid sewer into clean air and dazzling sunlight. Before that, we're just silly, self-absorbed, rat-like little beings, but after that transition, after we have stopped asserting a false apartness, we are of the same dimension and magnitude as the ocean of being into which we merge. Virtually all of religion and spirituality is about being happy and ignorant in the sewer because that's what people want, but this is about climbing out. If you're happy in the sewer, then it's not a sewer to you. If you don't think it stinks, then that's fine, but then, why are you here? The assumption when you stand in front of someone like me or Brett is that you know it's a sewer and you want out."

I turn and walk away from the group. Nice to have so much space to move in. I turn and walk back.

"You're pretty hard on religion and all the spiritual and New Age teachings," says a woman I don't recognize. "There's a whole world of knowledge and wisdom out there, do you really think it's fair to tar it all with the same brush?"

"It doesn't matter what I think, I'm just telling you what I see, and what you'll see if you open your eyes and look. If you disagree, open your eyes and tell me you see something else. I promise that if you do that, you'll be my new favorite person."

"I don't necessarily agree with your premise," she says, "that my eyes are not open. I think I see the same things you see."

"Okay, then. Again, no offense, but you're here as a tourist, with no vested interest; a spectator, not a participant. That's the case with most people, but most of you here tonight would probably be nursing some degree of healthy self-doubt. Anyway, I'm not trying to convince you of anything, I just don't know why you're here."

She looks sour. I return my attention to the full group.

"I'm working backward from the complete and total failure of the world's spiritual and religious teachings to facilitate awakening, even those that claim to be dedicated to that exact purpose. Especially those. I see this failure and I see Maya and I understand everything clearly. The intellectual and emotional power of ignorance is fully visible to me, and I can tell you that all the compassion and meditation in the world won't drag you up out of that sewer. No breadth of knowledge or depth of understanding translates into a single rung of upward progress. No one can push you, pull you, or go with you. All thoughts, ideas, feelings, concepts, and systems of knowledge and belief boil down to this one unequivocal distinction; sewer or sunshine, dungeon or daylight, ego or surrender, obstruction or flow, segregation or integration, vertical entrenchment or horizontal progress. This isn't about spirituality or enlightenment or anything lofty, it's just about living your life honestly or dishonestly."

They sit quietly, attentively.

"Fear converts every inward thought and impulse right back outward. Maya turns everything to her purpose. That's what you're up against. It's a deathmatch and there's only one way to win and Brett found it. She stopped fighting. She surrendered. It's ego that fights, that resists, that sucks all our energy. Brett dropped her armor and exposed her breastbone to her enemy, and in so doing, she destroyed the enemy. Maya is not outside of us. Ultimately, she's just another internal demon. Routing our power against her or to her are the same thing, and when we stop, we stop empowering her and she ceases to exist."

✧

These books would never be complete if I didn't get this said.

Within the context of living a long and happy life full of people and diversions, being stuck in a jail cell or a wheel chair or a hospital bed or an unresponsive body might seem like the very definition of hell, but that's a factor of the context, not the circumstances. Do I mean to say that terminal illness and physical disability and institutional incarceration are just minor nuisances? I mean *exactly* that. Within the context of growth, progress, development, motion, realization—liberation—the tables are turned and the physically constrained might actually enjoy a considerable advantage over the freely mobile. Focus, intent, vision, will, heart, clarity, maturity, seriousness, warrior spirit, that's what's needed, not the ability to run out to the market when we want a snack. We may not be able to change our circumstances, but we can change our context. A prison cell can be a zendo. From a wheelchair we can fight a war. If we are physically restricted there may be many things we can't do, but if we still possess the sword of mind and the heart of will, there is still one thing we can do, and within the context of this book, of these three books, it's the only thing worth doing. The *only* thing. This isn't physical warfare, it's spiritual warfare, and to fight it you need spirit, not arms and legs or a rosy future or wide open spaces.

I can't pretend to understand the plight of someone who is addicted to crack, or sentenced to life imprisonment, or confined to a hospice or an asylum or a wheelchair, but I can, with certainty and conviction, say this: In my own process, my own struggle and journey of awakening, of dying to the false and being born to the true, no physical encumbrance would have been any match for my will, and may, if anything, have proven quite advantageous. The very idea that my physical circumstances would have prevented my awakening, so long as my mental and emotional resources were reasonably intact, is, to my certain knowledge, absurd.

To further support this point, I repeat the words of Melville/Ahab that

I included in *Incorrect*:

> What I've dared, I've willed; and what I've willed, I'll do! They
> think me mad... but I'm demoniac, I am madness maddened!
> That wild madness that's only calm to comprehend itself! The
> prophecy was that I should be dismembered; and—Aye! I lost this
> leg. I now prophesy that I will dismember my dismemberer...
> Swerve me? The path to my fixed purpose is laid with iron rails,
> whereon my soul is grooved to run. Over unsounded gorges,
> through the rifled hearts of mountains, under torrents' beds,
> unerringly I rush! Naught's an obstacle, naught's an angle
> to the iron way!

✧

"What Brett did," I continue, "was instead of finding a way out of life, she found a way in. Like a judo master, she turned this father-demon's energy to her own advantage. She figured she was finished anyway, between the progressing cancer and this father-presence poisoning her existence, so she realized she had nothing to lose. If I might digress for a moment, I'd like to say that I have nothing but good things to say about this particular realization: Nothing to lose. It's perfectly true of everyone all the time, but it's the realizing part that's tricky. Once you get to that realization though, not just conceptually but fully absorbed throughout your awareness, then this whole thing just busts wide open. Walls come down and the universe opens up. Anyway, where was I? Who asked if there was a way to put a demon to good use? Shanti?"

She nods.

"Well, that's exactly what Brett did. As she explained it to me, everything was just coming apart. She had the cancer with gloomy prospects, and she still had this dumb father thing yapping in her head, blaming her for everything, blaming her for being sick. She sought help, she looked to religion and the self-help aisles of bookstores, but no matter what she did, no matter where she turned, no matter what book she read or what method or ideology she tried to embrace, there was still this voice in her head telling her it was all just nonsense, that she was too scared to face facts, that she wasn't brave, that she was being an idiot, a fool, all sort of nasty negative things, on and on like that, and all the while she's just getting sicker and her time is getting shorter. Then one day, her search for answers and meaning having yielded no fruit, she realized that this voice in her head might not be totally wrong. It was very cynical and abrasive, but not necessarily incorrect. The more her illness drove her to seek answers, the more she found herself agreeing with her father's voice. All the answers she was finding were nonsense. When it came to her search for answers, for meaning, for ways to cope with her disease and her mortality, this cynical voice in her head was saying things she not only couldn't deny, but with which she agreed. I wish she were here to explain this to you the way she explained it to me, but the main thrust is that this is how she processed herself into the truth-realized state. Instead of working through it with a tool like Spiritual Autolysis, she did it with the aid of this built-in, hypersensitive bullshit detector that had been plaguing her for so many years. She was operating under what she believed to be a sentence of imminent death, she thought she was in her final months, and she was intent on getting to the bottom of things, finding the meaning in things. She wanted to find something real, something true."

"Did she think she was possessed?" asks Ronald.

"No, rationally, she knew she wasn't possessed by a demon. She knew that this voice wasn't really her father, but her own creation, some part of herself speaking, some buried or subconscious part of her trying to express itself. That was part of her decision to stop fighting it and start trying to make sense of it. She told me that during this period, she walked around her lake thousands of times, sometimes twenty laps a day, and that's more than a mile around. I recognized that behavior right away. That level of intense, angry energy is common in the awakening process. And while she was doing that, walking lap after lap around the lake, she was arguing with this father-voice in her head. They were debating, out loud. She was vocalizing both sides of the conversation. Imagine what a headcase she must have looked like to the ducks and frogs." Everyone laughs. "That's another common feature of the awakening process, the loss of regard for convention and normalcy. All thought for keeping up appearances falls away.

"Hours at a time, walking the path around the lake, lap after lap, hour after hour, day and night, month after month. It started with Brett screaming at her father, but at some point they came into alignment and started working together until, after more than a year of this feverish walking and ranting, Brett absorbed this harsh critical voice, which was always, of course, a part of her. This father-demon was that small voice of reason in her mind, screaming to be heard, and she pushed aside all her emotional resistance and let it speak.

"Think about her situation for a minute. She never had any desire for spiritual attainment of any kind, in any sense. She never went in for any sort of belief system, she wasn't following a path or a teacher, she wasn't trying to evolve or burn karma or raise her consciousness, nothing like that. She was just trying to deal with her shit honestly—her words—and that's what it looked like in her case, like a very sick lady walking laps around a lake carrying on this lunatic dialogue, processing herself out of her own bullshit. This wasn't just her bid for freedom, it was her healing process. Over time she subdued this demon voice in her head, completely eradicated the cancer from her body, and found the answers for which she so desperately searched."

⟡

"Now, you're all being very nice and listening because you think that all this demon stuff was Brett's thing and doesn't really have much to do with you, but you're wrong. This is all about you. I've mentioned that I was going to share two techniques with you all tonight. One is what Brett did, Demon Taming, which is interesting and illuminating, but would only be useful for someone who has an unusually powerful and vocal demon raging in their head. The other, Memento Mori, is for everyone everywhere. Every living human being, regardless of religion or nationality or whatever, should begin practicing Memento Mori right away and every day."

"What is it?" asks Nicole. "What does Memento Mori mean?"

"It means we *do* have this powerful and vocal demon raging in our head, and not just any demon, the *king* of demons, the boogeyman, but we drown him out with every thought and feeling, every minute of our lives. We all have our own personal demon inside us and our lives are completely dedicated to denying it. But if we want to awaken, we have to stop hiding from this demon-king that lives inside us. We have to turn around and face this big, bad boogeyman. That's what Memento Mori means."

"So what do we have to do," asks Justin, "kill the boogeyman?"

Everyone laughs. I laugh too.

"Don't be silly," I say, "you can't kill the boogeyman."

The laughing dies down.

"Let's go down to the lake and light a big fire and tell some scary stories."

32. Memento Mori

> To begin depriving death of it's greatest advantage over us, let
> us adopt a way clean contrary to that common one; let us
> deprive death of it's strangeness, let us frequent it, let us get
> used to it; let us have nothing more often in mind than death.
> We do not know where death awaits us: so let us wait for it
> everywhere. To practice death is to practice freedom. A man
> who has learned how to die has unlearned how to be a slave.
>
> *—Michel de Montaigne*

W HAT'S THE LAST THING I want to say? What does it all come
down to? If I could only have ever delivered one lesson, what
would it be? What is the single-most important message I could share?
What is the diamond at the core of all spiritual aspiration? What topic is
befitting not just my own farewell to the teaching gig, but a farewell to
Brett?

These were the questions I put to myself when I decided to come meet
Brett's group and say goodbye with them, and as soon as I asked the question,
I knew the answer.

Memento Mori: Remember you must die.

✧

How bad can all this spiritual stuff get? What's the worst-case
scenario? These can be very scary and paralyzing questions to leave open-
ended, especially as we set out alone on a journey beyond the charted
regions of the map.

The answer to these questions, happily, is death. Death is as bad as it
can get, death is the worst-case scenario. That's where this whole thing
ends up. That's the full extent of the downside. You are going to die. And,
of course, you're going to die anyway, so it's really kind of a non-issue.

I have always found this simple observation both comforting and empowering. My own journey was made possible by having that question—How bad can this really get?—neatly tied off at the end. Death is absolute. Unlike anything else in the dreamstate, death is clearly seen and certainly known. It is where we are going whether we take this journey or not. No matter what you do, no matter how horrible it gets, it doesn't just keep getting worse and worse forever. There's an end to it. And since I'm going to die anyway, and it's only a matter of when, the simple fact is that it really can't get bad at all.

This casual treatment of death is not meant to minimize the agony of peeling off your skin in layers as you divest yourself of emotional content and connections. That's the gruesome part, but the fact is that these wounds heal instantly. Rather, no wound remains. Gone is gone, done is done. With every step we leave behind that which we move beyond. No baggage is carried because releasing baggage is the essence of progress. The pain-giving thing is the thing removed; when it's gone, so is the pain. All that's left in its place is relief and a mild, short-lived curiosity. It's like pulling a bad tooth or ripping off a bandage; the tough part is the fear before and the pain during. There's no phantom limb syndrome haunting us after we've amputated a gangrenous piece of emotional meat; there's just a pleasant nothing.

Until a new pain announces itself, and the next cycle begins.

✧

It is later now, nearly ten o'clock. While everyone made their way down to the lake to have some more snacks and get themselves situated for the shank of the evening, Lisa and I walked up to the house and talked to Melissa. We'd met with her earlier and given her the jewelry box containing the gift we'd be presenting her with later. She's known about it for months, but I still didn't want her seeing it for the first time in front of a crowd. Best to let her spend some private time with it first. Now I get it back from her and walk down to the lake to join the others. Lisa stays with Melissa. We have arrived at the heart of the evening. I will do some speaking, we will introduce Brett's daughter Melissa and make a small presentation, then Lisa and I will make our exit so we can take a nice drive on the Blue Ridge Parkway and I can catch a red-eye for Denver.

✧

Behind me is the fire, above me a bright moon occasionally obscured by silvery whisps of clouds, the lake is to my left, a large fenced field to my right, and in front of me sit nearly a hundred people in orderly rows of folding chairs, a large white party tent behind them. The light rain will stop and start throughout the rest of the evening, but we'll never need to take shelter from it. The orderliness of the seating, I realize, is unpleasant to look at. It creates an invisible proscenium where I and the fire are on stage and they in their chairs are in the audience. I tell everyone to pick up their chair and move closer, to form a semi-circle around me and the fire. After a minute or two it's done and the whole thing is more intimate. I throw more logs on the fire while they settle in. I await their attention and soon have it.

I pull the small box out of my pocket. It's made of black walnut with a glass window in the top so you can see what's inside without opening it. Inside, on a bed of black satin, is a single diamond, not small, on a thin gold necklace. Everyone who sees it oohs and aahs over it. I hold it up and watch it sparkle in the firelight. I hand the box and a small keychain flashlight to someone in the front row. "This is what we're giving Melissa in remembrance of Brett," I say. "I hope you'll all appreciate the symbology represented by the diamond. Pass it around."

Here we go.

"You heard Lisa talk earlier," I begin. "She showed you a picture, passed it around. She told you about a woman who got up one pretty September morning, got dressed, got her family's day started, and made the commute to work. Just another day, nothing unusual to indicate that on this day she would have to stand in a blown-out window and choose between an inferno and a thousand foot fall."

I have their attention. Some look around for Lisa but she's still up at the house with Melissa.

"What Lisa showed you was the real Zen, the unknown Zen, the Zen that doesn't sell. That photograph of a woman who had just jumped out of a burning skyscraper was Lisa's koan. Like a badass demon, it got its hooks into her and wouldn't let go. That time she spent staring at the picture and contemplating its meaning was her meditation, her zazen. Over the course of three years her koan devoured her. It got in and metastasized through her system like a cancer. Eventually, despite her resistance, it killed her."

I pause for a drink.

"Memento Mori means remember your death, remember you must die. That's what Lisa was doing. Her practice of communing with that picture for an hour or more every day is a perfect example of Memento Mori as a spiritual practice; death-awareness as a vehicle out of the state of death-denial in which we reside. Lisa's experience, what happened to her, the profound reorganization her life underwent as a result, is what happens when we make this transition."

I pace and watch the flames for a moment.

"We live in fear of death. We don't want to think about it, we don't want to look at it, we don't even want to acknowledge that it exists. We just want to go about our lives and not be reminded of our mortality, so we try to minimize it in three ways. First, we push death off into the distant future so it's not something we have to think about right now. We'll probably die when we're eighty or ninety and we'll probably be too soft in the head to know what's happening anyway, so we don't have to worry about it."

They laugh despite themselves.

"Another way we reduce death to something we can deal with is by stripping it of its finality through our afterlife beliefs; heaven, and rebirth, mainly. For most of us, these beliefs are just strong enough to serve the purpose of getting death out of our face. Out of sight, out of mind, right?"

No one says wrong.

"A third tactic we use in our practice of death-denial is constant distraction. We keep ourselves from thinking by keeping busy, by keeping our attention outwardly focused on the myriad trivialities of life. The holy trinity is home, work and family, but then we have others as well to fill the gaps as needed; sports, shopping, books and television, addictions, hobbies and so on."

I pause and pace, pace and consider.

"So one, death is not for a long time and we'll probably be too senile to care; two, it's not an end like it seems, it's just a transition to something else; and three, we keep ourselves perpetually distracted. Between these three denial tactics, death is not an important presence in our lives. It's with us every moment, but never in front of us where we have to look at it and think about it. This is how we keep death out of sight, behind us instead of in front of us. This is how we maintain the state of death-denial that allows us to go about our lives in a state of virtual unconsciousness."

✧

That was the establishing shot; an overview of our subject and our relationship to it. Now I'd like to provide everyone with a close-up.

"It's a well-worn cliché that we don't know how precious something is until we lose it. It's a cliché that when someone has a close brush with mortality, they develop a newfound appreciation for life. Suddenly everything is beautiful and glorious, each day is a gift, everything takes on new meaning and all that. Very powerful and eye-opening and perspective-giving. We call this a wake-up call, and that's exactly what it is. Is everybody familiar with this? Hands."

All hands go up.

"Maybe from TV and movies. Who's seen it up close?"

Most of the hands go down.

"And who's experienced it for themselves?"

Only two or three people keep their hands raised. I point to one, a young guy named Terry.

"What happened?"

"I fell off a scaffold at work," he says. "I heard the paramedics say I wouldn't make it, and then in the emergency room too I could tell they didn't think I'd survive."

"And?"

"Well, I survived, obviously, and then it was like you described, I had this really sincere, profound appreciation for everything. I couldn't understand why everyone wasn't that way all the time, like, how can everyone not see this?" He chokes up a bit but goes on. "I mean, it just changed the way I saw everything. It changed my whole outlook."

"And how long did that last?"

"Well, it's still with me—"

"But not really," I say.

That creates a hush. All eyes turn to Terry.

"No," he says with a sigh, "I guess not. It's just a memory now. It's nothing like it was, but I *wish* it was. I felt really alive for, well, probably less than a week I guess, but it was *real*. It was like the most real thing I've ever experienced, like that was real life and this is just sort of, well, like you say, I guess, like being asleep. I promised myself I wouldn't let it slip away, like Lisa talked about, but I did and now everything is just pretty much regular again."

"So this wasn't a cliché for you?"

"Oh no, no way," he says with palpable sincerity, "it's the most alive I've ever felt. Just like you talk about, like I woke up for a little while but I couldn't stay that way, like I just closed my eyes and drifted back to the way I was before the accident, or like life just dragged me back down. It's kind of sad to think about it now that I'm like normal again and everything. I felt like I was finally born, like I really knew what life was for the first time. That's what I thought life should be like all the time. I still do. That's why I started getting into spirituality and coming to see Brett in the first place. I was trying to recapture that sense of intense aliveness. I still am, I guess."

"And how's that going for you?"

He shakes his head.

"Not very good."

✧

"Only that day dawns to which we are awake," I say. "Thoreau said that. Only that day dawns to which we are awake. It sounds like just a pretty sentiment, but it's really a nano-bomb like Lisa's picture, like a virus, a tiny little bug that can slip in and spread and eventually topple a giant. Or so you'd think, anyway. The fact is that Maya's autoimmune system is quite robust and well able to fend off these pesky little microbes. You heard what Lisa did; she had the photo and it got damaged so she got another one and laminated it. That's the one she showed you. She developed a kind of an addiction to it. An unhealthy obsession is what I suppose the shrinks would call it; they'd try to put her in therapy and get her going on some meds. Fortunately, she didn't go to a shrink."

I throw some more logs on the fire and rearrange it with a shovel. Sparks shoot up into the night and fade and disappear.

"No matter how we might try to deny it, death is *the* fact of life. We can turn away from it, but we can't push it away. It's always with us. Brett was just returning some movies, just another errand. For that woman in Lisa's picture, and thousands of others like her, that was just another day at the office. But what that woman found out was that there is no such thing as just another day. Every day is anything-can-happen day. There is no day or hour or moment so mundane that it cannot play host to death. How's that for a scary story?"

A few somewhat uncomfortable laughs. The diamond is making it's way around. I pick up my water bottle and take a drink.

"I know this sounds simple and it is. It's the simplest thing there is. The title of the first chapter of my first book was *That Which Cannot Be Simpler*, and that's what we always come back to; simplicity. Burn it all and see what's left. When we do that here in the dreamstate, what we find out doesn't burn is death. That's what's left when everything else is gone. Death is what survives."

I pull the sheet of paper out of my pocket and unfold it.

"Here's something Emerson wrote:"

> One of the illusions is that the present hour is not the critical, decisive hour. Write it on your heart that every day is the best day in the year. No man has learned anything rightly until he knows that every day is Doomsday.

"Write it on your heart," I repeat, "every day is the best day of your life. Death gives definition to life. Death-awareness is life-awareness. Death denial is life denial. Here's something Mozart wrote in a letter to his father:"

> I have formed during the last few years such a close relationship
> with this best and truest friend of mankind that death's image is
> not only no longer terrifying to me, but is indeed very soothing
> and consoling, and I thank my God for graciously granting me
> the opportunity of learning that death is the key which unlocks
> the door to our true happiness.

I put the paper away.

"What we're talking about here tonight is what you all heard Lisa describe; becoming conscious within the dreamstate, waking up in life. She didn't talk about her years as an apprentice shaman in the Amazon, or the time she spent researching ancient parchments in the catacombs beneath the Vatican or the Topala. She didn't talk about figuring this out like a puzzle where you're always scrounging for the next piece. She talked about becoming death-aware; plain and simple. The reason we get bogged down in all the weird and exotic spiritual stuff is to avoid the up close and personal stuff. We search the most distant places and times because we don't want to deal with the here and now. We eagerly subscribe to arcane, intelligence-insulting belief systems because they are, by their very design, conducive to the sleepstate we wish to maintain. Religion and spirituality exist to serve our need for death denial. They serve as lullabies and drown out the ticking of the clock. We spend our lives and our lifeforce running away from this monster we call death. This state of incessant denial takes all our time and energy. That's where our lives go, that's how we spend them. That's what it means to be asleep within the dream."

✧

I take a question and that turns into other questions and we spend the next few minutes getting all this figured out together. I asked them what they thought we were so afraid of, why we were so desperate to deny the reality of our mortality, and they offered some suggestions and we discussed them, but found them all unsatisfying. No one seemed to feel that we were afraid of the actual state of being dead, or that it was the actual dying part that was so scary. Everyone seemed to agree that death sucked and they didn't like the idea of it, but no one could really say why until a strangely sagely teenage boy, sitting between his mom and dad, stated the answer like a pronouncement.

"Futility," he said.

Like music to my ears.

"Futility," I echo. "No belief is true, life has no meaning, nothing we do matters. All is vanity and a striving after wind. We're going to die and it will be as if we never lived. Everything we think is true is false, all our beliefs are delusions and everything we know is a lie. There is no such thing as success, nothing we do can make any possible difference, no matter how fast we go or how far ahead we are, we are not going anywhere. The best and the brightest are in a dead-tie with the worst and the dimmest. These are the facts of life, simple, obvious, plain to behold, yet universally unrecognized and unacknowledged. This is what it means to see what's not and not see what is, to be in denial, to be asleep within the dream, to reside in the womb of the unborn. We are madly, desperately, insanely afraid of the truth, and it is that fear that walls us off from our unbounded nature. It is the emotional energy of fear that erects and maintains the egoic shell."

"Then this sort of death-awareness you're talking about," says Shanti, "Momentum, uh—"

"Memento Mori," I interrupt. "Remember you must die. Death-Awareness."

"Okay, Memento Mori," she says, "but that's not what you did? This wasn't your practice, was it?"

"Yes and no," I say. "I began my journey, from the very first instant, with the knowledge that my life was forfeit. That was a lock, and I was unspeakably happy to make that bargain. My fogged-in little nothing of a life in exchange for clarity? Of course. Total no-brainer. There was never the slightest hesitation. Would you trade nothing for everything? By the time you understand the question, you've already answered it."

"But you're not dead," she says reasonably.

"The person to whom that happened no longer exists," I say, "and what

I am now lives in constant death-awareness, it is suffused throughout my dreamstate being the way fear and death-denial used to be. Death is always before my eyes. I never hide it or deny it or push it away. Death is the diamond heart of my dreamstate being. It is the defining feature that shows me the value of everything I see."

I let them think about that while I kick at the fire. I turn back to them.

"I've said this before," I continue, "I love the fact of my death. It has made my life possible. There could have been no awakening without it. It's how I know the value of things. It's how I know what beauty is. It's why I am gratitude-based instead of fear-based. It's also how I know child from adult, asleep from awake. It's how I can look at someone and know if death walks before them or behind."

I turn it back on them.

"This isn't about death in the abstract, it's about death in the most personal, intimate sense; *your* death. Death is the meaning in the dream, the dreamstate shadow of no-self. Death is the boogeyman. You can't kill him or hide from him or get away from him, you can only turn toward him or away from him. If you turn toward him, befriend him, fully embrace him, not superficially, but as your own essential truth, then death is the demon you can ride into every battle the way Brett rode her father-demon, the way Lisa rode that photo-koan."

"What do you recommend we do?" asks Justin with a touch of sarcasm, "hang out in graveyards?"

"Hell yes," I say, "cemeteries are wonderful places to walk and think. Buy yourself a burial plot and have your lunch there every day. Order your headstone. A glimpse of our own mortality really puts things in perspective, isn't that what people say? Well, that's what you want to do, see your own mortality, put things in perspective. There are lots of ways you could raise your awareness. Study photos of people like yourself, now dead. Read books about death and suicide. Carry poison in your pocket and contemplate it often. Walk along high ledges. Lie down on railroad tracks and read poetry. Put a loaded gun in your mouth and cock it. I myself enjoy sitting on the ledges of tall buildings at night, looking out over the city and down at the street below, my feet dangling over nothingness. I like walking in thunderstorms where lightning could strike me down at any instant. I guess all this sounds extreme, but I don't see how anything could be too extreme. The idea is right; put yourself in close proximity to death. Every hour, every day, you want to be taking time to immerse yourself in the mindset of death-awareness, of time-awareness, of the fact that the clock is ticking, that every day is one day less, that every breath you take is one breath less. Measure your life in weeks or months instead of years, and take somber note of their passing. Take time every morning to understand what it means to have a new day. Etch the words, *'Only that day dawns to which I am awake,'* into your bathroom mirror. The contemplation of death, of one's own mortality, is a real and powerful meditation. Death-awareness is true zazen, it's the universal spiritual practice, the only one anyone ever needs and the one everyone should perform, so yes, you'd want to do whatever you have to in order to bring this living awareness into your life. Develop the habit of thinking of death every time you look at a watch or clock, every time you sit down to a meal, every time you go to the bathroom. Take a walk alone every day and think about what it means to be alive, to walk, to see and hear, to breathe. It's not an exercise, it's not something you're trying to make yourself believe like an affirmation, it's something that's real and central to your every thought and act. If you knew you were going to die tomorrow, what would you do today? And why the hell aren't you doing it?"

33. To be, or not to be.

Awareness of death is the very bedrock of the entire path.
Until you have developed this awareness, all other practices
are obstructed.

HH The Dalai Lama

When you start preparing for death you soon realize that you must
look into your life—now—and come to face the truth of your self.
Death is like a mirror in which the true meaning of life is reflected.

Sogyal Rinpoche

For those who seek to understand it, death is a highly creative force.
The highest spiritual values of life can originate from the thought
and study of death.

Elisabeth Kubler-Ross

Without being mindful of death, whatever Dharma practices
you take up will be merely superficial.

Milarepa

For any culture which is primarily concerned with meaning, the study
of death—the only certainty that life holds for us—must be central,
for an understanding of death is the key to liberation in life.

Stanislav Grof

I went to the woods because I wished to live deliberately, to front only
the essential facts of life, and see if I could not learn what it had to
teach, and not, when I came to die, discover that I had not lived.

Henry David Thoreau

We say that the hour of death cannot be forecast, but when we say this we imagine that hour as placed in an obscure and distant future. It never occurs to us that it has any connection with the day already begun or that death could arrive this same afternoon, this afternoon which is so certain and which has every hour filled in advance.

Marcel Proust

To fear death, my friends, is only to think ourselves wise, without being wise: for it is to think that we know what we do not know. For anything that men can tell, death may be the greatest good that can happen to them: but they fear it as if they knew quite well that it was the greatest of evils. And what is this but that shameful ignorance of thinking that we know what we do not know?

Socrates

It is not the end of the physical body that should worry us. Rather, our concern must be to live while we're alive—to release our inner selves from the spiritual death that comes with living behind a facade designed to conform to external definitions of who and what we are.

Elisabeth Kubler-Ross

Someday I'll be a weather-beaten skull resting on a grass pillow,
Serenaded by a stray bird or two.
Kings and commoners end up the same,
No more enduring than last night's dream.

Ryokan

It's only when we truly know and understand that we have a limited time on earth, and that we have no way of knowing when our time is up, we will then begin to live each day to the fullest, as if it was the only one we had.

Elisabeth Kubler-Ross

I said to Life,
"I would hear Death speak."
And Life raised her voice a little higher and said,
"You hear him now."

Kahlil Gibran

Death twitches my ear. "Live," he says, "I am coming.

Virgil

They tell us that suicide is the greatest piece of cowardice, that
suicide is wrong; when it is quite obvious that there is nothing
in the world to which every man has a more unassailable title
than to his own life and person.

Arthur Schopenhauer

Let death be daily before your eyes, and you will never entertain
any abject thought, nor too eagerly covet anything.

Epictetus

The wise man's eyes are in his head; but the fool walketh in
darkness; and I myself perceived also that one event happeneth
to them all.

Ecclesiastes

By daily dying I have come to be.

Theodore Roethke

The world is so exquisite, with so much love and moral depth, that
there is no reason to deceive ourselves with pretty stories for which
there's little good evidence. Far better, it seems to me, in our vulnera-
bility, is to look Death in the eye and to be grateful every day for the
brief but magnificent opportunity that life provides.

Carl Sagan

Death is a friend of ours; and he that is not ready to entertain him is not at home.

Sir Francis Bacon

Death is our eternal companion. It is always to our left, an arm's length behind us. Death is the only wise adviser that a warrior has. Whenever he feels that everything is going wrong and he's about to be annihilated, he can turn to his death and ask if that is so. His death will tell him that he is wrong, that nothing really matters outside its touch. His death will tell him, "I haven't touched you yet."

Carlos Castaneda

Tell your friends, "Look, it's Spring, the buds are sweet, the water sparkles, everyone is joyful. We are going to die."

Krishna, Mahabharata
Jean-Claude Carrière

All men live enveloped in the whale-lines. All are born with halters round their necks; but it is only when caught in the swift, sudden turn of death, that mortals realize the silent, subtle, ever-present perils of life.

Herman Melville

In the last analysis it is our conception of death which decides our answers to all the questions life puts to us.

Dag Hammarskjöld

Since the death instinct exists in the heart of everything that lives, since we suffer from trying to repress it, since everything that lives longs for rest, let us unfasten the ties that bind us to life, let us cultivate our death wish, let us develop it, water it like a plant, let it grow unhindered. Suffering and fear are born from the repression of the death wish.

Eugène Ionesco

There is but one truly serious philosophical problem, and that is suicide. Judging whether life is or is not worth living amounts to answering the fundamental question of philosophy. All the rest—whether or not the world has three dimensions, whether the mind has nine or twelve categories—comes afterward. These are games; one must first answer.

Albert Camus

Live as if you were to die tomorrow.

Mahatma Gandhi

Rehearse death. To say this is to tell a person to rehearse his freedom. A person who has learned how to die has unlearned how to be a slave.

Lucius Annaeus Seneca

You want to live, but do you know how to live? You are scared of dying—and, tell me, is the kind of life you lead really any different from being dead?

Lucius Annaeus Seneca

Is not philosophy the study of death?

Plato

Death is an endless night so awful to contemplate that it can make us love life and value it with such passion that it may be the ultimate cause of all joy and all art.

Paul Theroux

There is no fundamental difference between the preparation for death and the practice of dying, and spiritual practice leading to enlightenment.

Stanislav Grof

34. The Ultimate Taboo

> Perhaps the whole root of our trouble, the human trouble, is
> that we will sacrifice all the beauty of our lives, will imprison
> ourselves in totems, taboos, crosses, blood sacrifices, steeples,
> mosques, races, armies, flags, nations, in order to deny the fact
> of death, which is the only fact we have.
>
> *—James Baldwin*

DEATH IS THE KEY TO life. Death defines life, gives it shape and meaning and context. Without a clear and honest relationship with our mortality, we live in a state of endless spiritual sprawl, a soupy gray fog that creates the hellish illusion of life stretching endlessly in all directions.

We've homogenized our lives by hiding the parts we're afraid of, and in so doing, we've removed all sense of urgency from life. We have taken death out of life and that allows us to live unconsciously. Death never left, of course, we've just turned away from it, pretended it wasn't there. If we wish to awaken—and that's a mighty big if—then we must welcome death back into our lives. Death is our personal Zen Master, our source of power, our path to lucidity, but we have to stop running from it in a blind panic. We need only stop and turn around and there it is, inches away, staring at us with unblinking gaze, finger poised, every second of our lives. That finger is the one true thing in the dreamstate, and it will, for a fact, come down.

Death-awareness is the universal spiritual practice. What we have sought in books and magazines, in teachers and teachings, in ancient cultures and foreign lands, has been breathing down our neck the entire time. It's not just another mood-making spiritual technique that you dabble with for a few weeks and blame yourself when it doesn't deliver. Death always delivers. Death is your only true friend, the only friend that will never abandon you and that no one can take away. It slices through every lie, ridicules every belief, mocks every vanity and reduces ego to absurdity. He's sitting with you right now. If you want to know something, ask him. Death doesn't lie.

✧

"The inverse of death-awareness is equally important," I continue, seeing both interest and wariness in their firelit faces. "Learn to practice death-*denial* awareness. Anytime you find yourself sitting on the couch watching TV, shopping in a mall, or trying to find amusement in some pointless book or idle pastime, remind yourself that this is exactly the habit you want to break. Try to catch yourself in all the situations throughout the day when you are not awake, not aware, going through the motions of your life in a virtually somnambulistic state. Remind yourself constantly: This moment, right now, I am in the sleepstate. This is the mindlessness I'm addicted to like a drug. I am an opium addict living in an opium dream. This is the coma; this slow oozing of my life down the drain. Right now my life is slipping away."

I grab my water bottle and take a long drink.

"Another powerful thing about the practice and cultivation of death-awareness is that it provides an accurate barometer of your own spiritual sincerity, though you may not want one. Anyone can go sour on main-stream religion and adopt a less orthodox belief system to replace it, but how many people are really sincere in their spiritual aspirations? Probably all of you think you are, but are you really? Are you willing to go wherever this leads? To do whatever it takes? Thousands talk the talk for one who walks the walk. The practice of death-awareness separates the walkers from the talkers. We can use this as a spiritual self-diagnostic to determine, once and for all, if spirituality is something we're serious about or if we're just tourists. Most of us are tourists, but which of us are sincere and which are dabblers? If you want to answer this question for yourself, here's your chance. Your relationship to your own mortality tells the tale. Everyone is either facing toward it or turned away from it, it's that simple. Toward or away. If you can't face the most fundamental fact of your own existence, what can you face? This is ground floor, entry-level awakening. It doesn't get any closer or simpler than this. If, based on this discussion, your life does not undergo major restructuring over the next few months, then you have your answer; you're a tourist with no real desire or intent to wake up. What you do with that knowledge is up to you. Maybe you don't want to know the answer to this question, but if you don't want to know, then you know."

I pace back and forth in front of the fire and wonder what Brett would think about what we're doing and saying here tonight. I think she'd be pretty amused by the whole thing.

"It's not easy to practice death-awareness, but you can do it because it's true; you're going to die. Vigilance is the key. We don't need one wake-up call in life, we need hundreds of wake-up calls every day, more and more until we actually break the surface and come awake. It takes thought, desire, willful intent. The odds are heavily against you. I doubt even one of you will break this addiction. The sleepstate is too comfortable, too hard to rip yourself out of. It's like swimming upward through a mile of mud. You just have to keep at it, keep going, constantly reminding yourself of what you're doing and why, because as soon as you stop you start to sink again and the next thing you know you'll be sitting in a nursing home thinking back to that long ago night when some crackpot stood in front of the dancing flames and shooting sparks and told you not to let it slip away, but you did, and now it's too late."

There's a long stretch of silence while I mess with the fire.

"Are you talking about dying well, like, how we should meet death when it comes?" asks a woman in jeans and boots and a sheepskin vest. "Something like that?"

"Absolutely not," I reply, eager to make this distinction. "The point is not to die well, the point is to *live* well. Who cares how you die? Die bravely or crying like a baby, who cares. Death-awareness is about life-awareness and life-awareness is all about waking up. It really has nothing to do with dying."

"It seems like a very negative, pessimistic way to live," she says.

"My experience is just the opposite," I reply. "Nothing really bothers me, nothing gets me down. If I lost everything in some tragedy tomorrow, so what? I'm still alive, still here in the funhouse. Who cares about the rest? It's all good. Where's the pessimism in that?"

"Nothing gets you down?"

"Well, that's too broad a statement," I reply. "Life could certainly take a downturn I wouldn't wish to endure. The time might come when I would want to grab the bastard's bony finger and give myself the tap."

Someone actually gasps.

"You're not talking about suicide, are you?" asks the woman who looks like a rancher. "Is that what you're saying we should think about?"

"I'm not saying what anybody should do, but I'd say that suicide would be a damn silly thing *not* to think about. If you can't even consider the topic of ending your life, then whose life is it? Suicide is one of the very few options we might actually have. It means we're not necessarily at death's mercy. It's scary enough to make you sick, but that's no reason not to think about it. Most people treat suicide as the ultimate taboo, as if it's not even on the table, but it *is* on the table, it's the centerpiece, and there's no reason not to give it the respect it deserves. You can still rule it out, I suppose, but at least it would be *you* ruling it out instead of having it ruled out for you."

Some of them look a little shocked by this.

"Maybe all this sounds morbid or depressing to you. Maybe you think death is the opposite of life, or that all this death-awareness stuff translates into the end of happiness and good times, but this is not the case. Death isn't morbid, fear is morbid. Death doesn't oppose life, fear opposes life. To close your eyes to death is to close them to life; what could be more morbid than that? From your perspective, death and suicide are horrific and unthinkable. From my perspective, they are empowering and life-affirming, and I would look at any person that doesn't have an open, honest relationship with these subjects as themselves nine parts dead."

✧

It's clear that for most or all of them, this is a distinctly taboo subject, a roped-off area into which their thoughts seldom wander. They equate suicide with misery and failure and cowardice; the act of moody teenagers and the weak and the ill. They view self-termination as an absolutely, positively last resort, and maybe not even then, whereas I, an eyes-open being, might view it as a third or fourth resort. I don't think I'd stick my head in the oven to get out of a speeding ticket, but I might do it to get out of a wheelchair or a year in jail or a bad case of the hiccups. It wouldn't, however, be based on a decision so much as an observation. Things come into a certain alignment, patterns emerge, rightness is perceived, and the clearly indicated course is followed. I've never *not* done something once I saw that it was the thing to do, and that includes much harder things than suicide. Despite not being a bushido warrior kinda guy, I do have a clear and abiding awareness that today is a perfectly good day to die.

Only that day dawns to which we are awake.

If this seems like a light treatment of a heavy subject, it's because from the integrated perspective, it's not so dark and dreary. There's no evil stink to death when it's out in the open where we can see it and hold it steadily in our sight. This is what it means to befriend death, to embrace it; that we acknowledge it's importance in our lives, not that we get to like it or look forward to it or develop some creepy resonance with it. The primary benefit of this honest relationship is the way in which it throws life open to us, but also important is the way it de-horrifies the spectre of death.

We're not talking about the commission of the act, but only the honest contemplation of it. The question of suicide—to be, or not to be—is at the very heart of philosophical inquiry, but Maya has rendered it virtually unthinkable with a logjam of highly charged counter-beliefs; we have no right to terminate our own lives because life is sacred, it's an unpardonable sin and an abomination against God, it's a cowardly act and a cheat, whatever life lessons we escape now we'll just have to experience in the next life, and so on.

Rather than being *un*thinkable, however, suicide should be supremely thinkable. It is the thing that most needs thinking about. At the very least, we would want to break the logjam and make some decisions about it for ourselves. If you want to have some fun with Spiritual Autolysis, begin with the question: Why shouldn't I kill myself right now?

✧

"When all is said and done," I summarize for the group, "all this talk of demons and boogeymen is just a way to slap ourselves into stark raving sanity; to sober ourselves up from the intoxicating effects of belief and wrong-knowing. The point is that wakeful lucidity is something we're all perfectly capable of achieving. If anything, it's seeing what's not and not seeing what is that's so amazing. All we're talking about now is a way to stop performing this miraculous feat of self-deception so we can see things as they really are. Spiritual Autolysis focuses the mind, and Memento Mori gives it a known point to focus on. In combination with a sincere desire, they can set anyone on the road out of the segregated state of Human Childhood. So, if you want it, here it is. The only question is, do you want it?"

"I've already decided I'm never going to die," jokes a young guy, but no one laughs.

"Get real," I almost reply, and I realize that this admonition is at the very heart of this whole crazy business. I could've just said that in the first place and saved myself the trouble of writing three books. That's what it all comes down to:

Get real.

35. That Which Cannot Be Simpler

Men fear thought more than they fear anything else on earth—more than ruin, more even than death. Thought is subversive and revolutionary, destructive and terrible; thought is merciless to privilege, established institutions, and comfortable habits; thought is anarchic and lawless, indifferent to authority, careless of the well-tried wisdom of the ages. Thought looks into the pit of hell and is not afraid. It sees man, a feeble speck, surrounded by unfathomable depths of silence; yet bears itself proudly, as unmoved as if it were lord of the universe. Thought is great and swift and free, the light of the world, and the chief glory of man.

But if thought is to become the possession of the many, not the privilege of the few, we must have done with fear. It is fear that holds men back—fear lest their cherished beliefs should prove delusions, fear lest the institutions by which they live should prove harmful, fear lest they themselves should prove less worthy of respect than they have supposed themselves to be.

–Bertrand Russell

W E'RE ALL JUST KILLING TIME in death's waiting room, distracting ourselves with some book or magazine, puzzle or game, waiting to be called and pretending we're not. We are, most of us, oblivious to where we are and what's going on; oblivious by the maternal grace and savage cunning of Maya. Every minute that we are unaware of our situation, of where we are and what's going on, is a minute of unconsciousness, a minute when we are asleep and dreaming of a life in a different place with different rules. Virtually everyone dwells in this imaginary state virtually all of the time.

Whatever game we play, whatever diversion we occupy ourselves with, we are comforted to think that it leads somewhere, moves us toward some desired goal, that there is meaning in it, but meaning is just a figment of the dreamstate, where everything is real, but nothing is true.

The dreamstate is an absurd fiction, and to dwell within it we must, despite being possessed of reason, be able to maintain a healthy level of absurdity. This is the vital function that belief systems play in our lives. Beliefs provide us with the emotional ballast—the artificial gravity—we need to stay earthbound. But by cutting away the ballast of ignorance—wrong-knowing—we can ascend to an altitude where we see the forest and not the trees, where the threads disappear and the tapestry is revealed, and where a universe previously thought to be composed of innumerable separate parts can be seen as one undifferentiated ocean of being. Wrong-knowing is the egoic regulator that governs this rise and descent. As soon as we think we know something, that wrong-knowledge acts to restrict our natural upward tendency. When we relinquish the illusion of knowledge, as right-knowing suffuses our being throughout and displaces wrong-knowing, then we come to reside at the loftiest of dreamscape altitudes. By transcending opposites, we awaken from the dream of many parts into the reality of the unified whole. Once seen, this vision of unity cannot be unseen. Thought, as a way of navigating through life, is rendered obsolete, and is replaced by an immeasurably superior way; a direct knowing free of intermediary processes. From this integrated perspective, everything we once called dark or false or evil is unmistakably known to be of equal worth and importance as the things we once called light or true or good. Balance and wholeness are restored and we are born to our rightful selves.

That's what it is to be fully lucid within the dreamstate.

That's what I tell the group.

✧

"So there *is* knowledge," says Ronald, trying to trip me up.

"Not that I know of," I say and everyone laughs.

"Scoop a jar of water out of the ocean and put a lid on it," I tell them. "Study it in its segregated state. Where is the ocean in that jar? Where are the tides and the currents? Pour it back into the ocean and it returns to its integrated state. The temporary entity no longer exists."

"Entity?" Ronald asks.

"By scooping it into a jar, you've created a new entity, a sub-ocean. It's not possible to subdivide infinity, of course, but try telling that to your new entity. It has all the properties of the ocean from which you scooped it, in no way greater or lesser than any other sampling you might take, yet it bears little resemblance to its authentic oceanhood. It has an independent existence, yet as soon as you pour it back, it merges seamlessly back into the integrated whole. Where is that particular sub-ocean entity after you pour it back in? The same place it was before; everywhere and nowhere. It didn't exist before you scooped it up, but you didn't create it. It doesn't exist after you pour it back, but you didn't destroy it. So what was born when you segregated that jarful? What died when you reintegrated it?"

I don't know where all this is coming from, but I'm enjoying it and I seem to have more.

"Our perception of time makes some things look permanent and other things look temporary, but in this dynamic ocean of being, everything is constantly swirling in and out of existence, just like that jar of water, just like anything you can think of—a mosquito, a mountain, a galaxy, a man— all fluid, all forming and unforming. A spark is born and dies in a split second, while the sun seems to last forever, but if your time perception shifted in one direction, that spark might seem to last forever, like the sun. Shift the other way and you could watch the sun flicker in and out of being like a spark. Which is correct? Both? Neither? You can make the same statement about spatial perception. Shift one way and the sun is the size of a spark, go the other way and the spark seems to fill the universe. I wasn't here a hundred years ago and I won't be here a hundred years from now, I'm just flickering in and out of being. I was scooped up and I'll soon be poured back, so what's the truth of me?"

No one answers.

"Who am I? That is the question. If you want to know, find out. Use Death Awareness with Spiritual Autolysis. Think as hard as you possibly can. Dare to be a fool. Unchain yourself from respectability. Take an oath. Declare war."

I pace, drink some water, let them mull.

"Burn it all," I say. "Burn everything. This is the answer to the question you're asking by coming here. That's what all this awakening stuff is about. That's what real Zen is about. Nuke your life. What gets destroyed was never yours in the first place."

That hangs in the air for a few moments before anyone speaks.

"What does that actually mean?" asks Nicole a bit timidly. "Where does that level of energy come from?"

"From you," I reply. "It's your energy, the same energy you have now, but instead of spewing it outward in all directions, dumping it out as fast as you can, you harness it, focus it, bring it to bear on a single target."

"Yes," she says, "but how?"

"That's a good question, and prayer and Spiritual Autolysis and Memento Mori are my answers. You have to start by bringing yourself into focus. Nothing can happen before that and no one else can do it for you. The fact is that no matter how you cut it, no matter what you believe, all you have is this tiny moment of being sandwiched between two eternities of non-being. If not now, when?"

Several hands go up. They want to assert their afterlife preferences, the broader-than-readily-apparent dimensions of the dreamscape, but no talk of egoic immortality can survive two minutes of honest scrutiny and I don't want to let Brett's farewell devolve into protestations of belief, so I press on.

"All you have is this window of dreamstate being which can slam shut at any moment. The question is, what are you going to do with it? Once you come to deeply appreciate this question, your life goes into a kind of cascade meltdown. Everything in your life gets dropped except your life itself. Then the game is on and all this stuff starts making sense. That's when you find out what it really means to think, and why most people never do. That's when you begin to see what it means to be asleep, and that virtually everyone is. That's when you begin to see what it means to say that people are all children, and insane children at that. That's when you begin to see that all emotions are energetic attachments and that they all stem from fear. That's when you begin to see Maya and understand who and what she is and where she dwells and how she works. That's when you begin to see that nothing is wrong, that wrongness isn't possible and that the wrongest thing you can think of is no less right than the rightest thing you can think of. That's when all these seemingly contradictory statements stop being paradoxical concepts and start being the most simple and obvious of observations. And that's when you're going to want to be able to focus yourself like a laser, and *that* requires processes like Spiritual Autolysis or Memento Mori. That's what it takes to succeed in an enterprise where failure and mediocrity are so celebrated that no one remembers what success looks like."

I turn to watch the fire and take a drink. I turn back.

"No one's saying this stuff is easy," I continue, "actual progress is never easy. You heard Lisa; three years of suffering to get her eyes open, and they're still not really adjusted to her new environment. It tore her life all to hell, and she's just getting started. She didn't make pretty sand mandalas and sweep them away to remind herself of her impermanence. She didn't try to figure out what her face looked like before she was born. Maybe she didn't do anything more than lower her defenses, a little at a time, over the course of three years, like a slow dying. But fast or slow, that's what it is; a dying. And what does all that amount to? What do you get for all that suffering and disillusionment?" I pause to let them think about it. "Salvation? Liberation? Nirvana? No, it just gets you back to square one. It gets you back to the point where you went vertical instead of horizontal, where you burrowed in at the age of ten or twelve. It gets you out of the hole you've spent your life digging yourself into so you can finally start your life. We're not even talking about taking a spiritual journey at this point, we're talking about undoing the *un*spiritual journey. We spend our lives burrowing down into our own graves, like that's a clever place to hide from death. This is about climbing out of our graves and living our lives and discovering who and where we are and what we are a part of, and you can't do that from the bottom of a hole."

✧

"You say that nothing is real," says Shanti a little later. "How can nothing be real? It doesn't make sense."

"I don't know," I say. "I have no knowledge on the subject. It's the dreamstate. There is nothing else to be said about it."

"But that's so," she searches for the word, "so *unsatisfying*."

"That's a matter of perspective," I reply, "it's not that it's unsatisfying, it's that you're unsatisfied. I am lucid within the dreamstate and I don't find it unsatisfying at all. I have no questions, no complaints, no unresolved issues. I am perfectly satisfied. Everything is quite to my liking, I wouldn't change a thing."

"Aren't you even interested?"

"In what? In the fact that there's nothing to be interested in? What can you say about a dream? Do you find it unsatisfying that your nighttime dreams lack substance and solidity? That they pop like bubbles when you wake up?"

"No," she says, "of course not."

"Well, this is the same thing," I say to Shanti, but for everyone. "The only difference is that you don't know it. But you could. It's there to be known, to be seen. There is no mystery. Nothing is hidden, only unseen. These metaphors and allegories and parables we use are very powerful tools of understanding. If you wish to make any progress, you should try to trust them more, test them to see how far they'll bend before they break. Use the Spiritual Autolysis to attack them. Some are stronger than others, of course, but understanding consensual reality as a dreamstate is unbreakable. Life is but a dream. Reality has no basis in reality. With eyes closed you find it dissatisfying, with eyes open I find it delightful, magical, absurd, interactive, challenging, mysterious, playful and brief. You want answers, but there are no answers, just beliefs, and if you want to awaken, either within or from the dreamstate, beliefs are not your friends. They only hold you back. Demanding answers and explanations is an egoic stall tactic. You can just stop making these egoic demands and relax into this thing you're a part of; trust, surrender, release. You don't hear it, but there's a clock and it's ticking and you don't know how many ticks you have left. Listen for it. The game is on, whether you're playing or not."

I return to addressing the group.

"I'm not some great rocket surgeon, I'm just a guy who got serious about figuring things out. Same with Brett. There's nothing I could tell you that you couldn't figure out for yourselves. There's nothing I see that you couldn't see for yourselves. I'm like Socrates; all I know is that I know nothing. That's like the subtext of the cogito, together they form the alpha and omega of all knowledge: I know that I Am, and I know that I know nothing else. That's an easy thing to say, but it's a helluva thing to know."

✧

A casual sort of dialogue continues for a few minutes before my disposable cell phone vibrates in my pocket, informing me that Lisa and Melissa are on their way down to join us. I walk out onto the small pier and give the little phone a toss and watch it splash and disappear. That signal was the last thing I needed it for and I'm happy to be rid of it. As I watch the widening ripples, I am reminded of a long-ago night, much like this one, when I stood on a similar pier looking out at black water and threw something away. It was back at the very beginning of my awakening process, and the thing I was throwing away was a family heirloom which had been passed down to me and which, it was expected, I would pass down to my own son someday. It was a watch, old and expensive, a family treasure, and throwing it away forever was just a hell of a thing to do. I haven't thought about that watch or that night in years, and I feel a rush of gratitude and camaraderie and sympathy for that full-crazed young man that I was.

So I got to have my little moment of sentimental bullshit after all.

I walk back to the group. I have them all get up and move their chairs away and come stand in a semi-circle around me and the fire. I place one of the chairs by the fire and stand up on it.

"One of the things we're here to do tonight is say goodbye to Brett," I say. "Brett wasn't just anybody. We don't want to dishonor her memory with the trite platitudes that would serve others so well, and this raises an important question: What can we say about Brett? About her life? I won't stand up here and say things like her life had meaning or that she's gone to some better place. She'd kick my ass if she heard me talking like that, and rightly so." All laugh. "She played a good game, that's something we can say of her. She was honest in a way that is all but unknown in the world, we can say that. She had the courage to face facts. That's pretty rare."

They're silent and duly somber.

"My first idea for tonight was to bring Brett's skull for us to hold and pass around, maybe set it up on a table next to a picture of her smiling. That makes for a pretty thought-provoking tableau, the juxtaposition of the same toothy grin in life and in death, but it turns out that it's not that easy to get your hands on someone's skull, and anyway, Brett had already been cremated. It was suggested that we could have an urn down here with her ashes, and scatter them over the water of this lake while I said some meaningless crap about how she was born here, but I think that's pretty cheesy and I think Brett would have agreed. So, I asked the universe what to do and the answer was made immediately and unmistakably known to me. Does anybody know what you get when you compress a carbon-based being? Like, a *lot*?"

Some are quick to say no and ask what you get, but it was rhetorical. Over the course of a minute, while I step down off the chair and take a drink and tend the fire, the answer gets figured out and spreads through the group. When I return to my chair and look at their faces in the dancing firelight, I see that they think they know but they don't believe it.

"Who's got her?" I ask, searching among them. "Who's got the little box with Brett in it?"

✧

You can cremate a person, clean up their ashes a bit and smoosh them into a diamond. There are companies with labs that do this. When we did this for Brett, it was not a well known procedure. Of all of Brett's students, only a few had ever heard of it, and none had ever seen the results. Maybe in the future this will catch on and everyone will wear their lost loved ones around their neck or on a finger, but when we did it for Brett it was practically unheard of.

It was a pretty expensive and complicated process, but the universe supported it from all angles and Lisa and Nicole cooperated to make it happen, with the result that the large, colorless, handsomely boxed diamond was waiting for us in a hotel safe in Virginia with not a day to spare. I underwrote the project at the beginning, but much of the cost was recouped from the group and Dr. Kim and a few other sources, and the whole thing came off without any surprises, all the way up until the end.

There were no surprises from Brett's daughter. Melissa knew about this from the start. She fully approved of the plan and was directly involved at several points along the way. As soon as Lisa and I arrived today, we brought Melissa the diamond to let her spend some private time with it. There was never any thought of surprising her with it.

What *was* surprising was the group's reaction. When they realized that the diamond they had been admiring was actually the remains of their dead teacher, they didn't exactly break into wild applause. I don't know what I was expecting, but what I got was a whole lot of heavy silence.

✧

It took half an hour to explain the diamond process to everyone and to let the box be passed around again so everyone could study it in the light of their new knowledge about it. This time they took the diamond out of the box. They wanted to touch it, to hold it in their hands and think about what it was and what they themselves were, because these are the things we have to think about when we confront death and the dead and the remains of the dead. This was the desired effect I had in mind when I first thought of using Brett's skull for show-and-tell, and later when the diamond solution made itself known. What I hadn't realized was that the effect would be so moving. It took another half hour for them to process it enough for us to continue. Some were disturbed, some cried, some gathered into small groups to try to express their feelings amongst themselves. It was a full hour before shock wore off and people were settled and comfortable again.

The diamond is a pretty lie, and the group is eager to believe. They see meaning and beauty in the diamond. They see essence; a glimpse of truth, or some vague promise of immortality. They see all sorts of things that aren't there, that are being projected onto the little stone by the filters through which they view it.

Not to be a heartless bastard, but I looked at the diamond as only significant insofar as it was completely *in*significant. Its very nothingness was what I found beautiful about it. I held it up and let it swing from its gold chain and contemplated it. This was a person who walked among us, she was here, in this place, we saw her, we listened to her, she was like us, and now this is what she is, this silly little rock. Brett, the rancher, woman, survivor, teacher, daughter, mother, grandmother—now just a gaudy trinket.

Brett is not dead. There is no Brett entity to possess the status of deadness. There is simply no such thing as Brett. She's not dead, she's just nothing. In truth, she's no more or less now than she ever was, than anyone ever is. She was a face in a cloud that formed for a moment and was gone. That's all anyone or anything really is, and we can take comfort in that, not because it's comfortable, but because it's true.

✧

The next part of the evening was for Lisa and Nicole to handle. They retrieved the diamond and the box and got everyone seated and quiet. They brought Melissa to the front and said some very nice things about Brett that got everyone sufficiently weepy, and then they presented the diamond to Melissa. They did good.

Melissa did good too. She accepted the small box and studied it in silence for a long, emotional moment. Then Melissa thanked everyone and talked a little bit about her mother, and how she didn't know the Brett that we all knew, but that she wished she had.

"Mom's favorite movie was *Harold and Maude*," she said, "so I thought I should maybe come out here tonight and accept this diamond and take it straight out onto that pier and throw it in the water, like Maude did with the ring Harold gave her, and I'd say, 'so I'll always know where it is,' like Maude said. I thought that might be the right thing to do, but as I thought about it some more I realized that I really don't understand it, I don't understand *why* Maude threw Harold's gift away like that, so if I did that now it would be fake, like, just for show, so I'm not going to do it. I'm going to keep it and I'm going to try to understand my mother the way you all knew her, and if I can ever do that, then maybe I'll understand why Maude threw that ring away and maybe then I'll come down here, even if

I'm an old lady, and throw the diamond in the water and tell my mom, 'so I'll always know where you are,' and I'll know what that means. I think it will mean that I honored her and tried to understand her and didn't just throw her away to make it look like I understood something when I didn't, or like I just wanted to get rid of her. I don't know if that makes sense or not. I hope it makes some sense to all of you. Thank you for this gift and for coming here and for knowing my mother in a way I didn't."

✧

Lisa and I walk Melissa back up to the house and say good night. We say our goodbyes and take our leave. Lisa starts back toward the path to the lake. I walk toward the rental car.

"What are you doing?" she asks.

"Time to go," I say.

"Go? But everyone has more questions. You've got them all excited. They're all standing up and talking and waiting for you to come back. They have a lot of things they want to ask you."

I stop and turn toward her.

"Like what?" I ask her. "What might be an example of a valid question they might ask?"

"Why ask me? I don't know."

"Knowing what you do, what information are they lacking to make the journey out of denial into awareness? What answer do you or I have that they need to hear?"

She looks confused.

"I don't know," she repeats.

"It's time for you to stop saying that."

Her look turns hard. She gets quiet when challenged, which makes my job harder, which means I have to speak harder.

"Our relationship is almost over, yours and mine," I tell her. "A few hours on the road and that's it."

Her look softens.

"But we can still—"

"Can we? You've been sitting at that desk with me all summer. Have you seen me talk on a phone or correspond with anyone by email? You've seen the mail that gets forwarded, have you seen me answer any of it?"

"No, but—"

"Any sign of family, friends, people in my life?"

"No."

"Do you think I was hiding that part of my life from you?"

"No, I guess not, but—"

"I'm not a life coach or a guru or a surrogate parent. I don't have human relationships. *Every* man is an island, entire of itself. If my dog was a boy, I would have named her Wilson. I know where I am."

"But I thought—"

"I'd be doing you a disservice by staying available to you. Same with those people down at the lake. It's a solo thing. If a drowning person grabs onto me, I do them the kindness of kicking them in the face."

She seems saddened.

"You're an orphan," I tell her. "Even if your parents were still alive, that's what you are. That's something you have to get used to. If you write me a letter in a few years, I'll be eager to read it. I hope it will say you understood what I'm telling you right now, that you went on to develop into a mature and still-developing Human Adult, and that you're raising your children that way too. That's what I hope it will say."

"What else *would* it say?" she asks with humorless eyes.

"Dear Jed, I'm much better after my little breakdown. I'm practicing law again, the kids are doing well in school and I might be getting back together with Dennis. I've taken up golf and I'm active in local charities. No big hair and fat ass in Corpus Christi, ha ha! Thank you for helping me through that difficult time, Love, Lisa."

She looks like I slapped her.

"Is that what you think?"

I shrug. "It's up to you. Even now, after all you've been through, you have yet to open your eyes, to take your first steps, to acknowledge this new and different world you're in. You think this process is behind you, but you're still very much in it. This is your slap on the ass. *Ábrase los ojos, abogada.*"

"Jesus Christ," she shakes her head sadly, "such a beautiful night."

"It certainly is," I agree. "It's the most beautiful night in the world. So what are we doing? There's only awareness and denial, toward and away, progress and entrenchment. Those people down at the lake will either undergo the same transition you underwent, or they'll stay down in their holes. They don't need information, they need suicidal discontent. What answer do you or I have that those people need to hear? I'm asking *you* now. You're in charge. What do you want to do?"

She holds my gaze for another long moment, then nods.

"Let's go," she says.

✧

This is my bottom-line advice on the subject of spiritual awakening, whether *in* or *from* the dreamstate. Face the facts. Face death. Face your own mortality, your own meaninglessness. This applies to everyone everywhere. I touched upon the subject of death-awareness in *Damnedest*, but what I thought back then was that I was writing for a sophisticated audience, people too spiritually savvy to need so simple a lesson. I've since discovered that those who seem the most spiritually sophisticated are the most deeply entrenched and the least likely to subject themselves to the rigors of the true spiritual journey. Having gone so far the wrong way, they are the least disposed to turn around and undo all their anti-progress. Now I see that death-denial, the fear of no-self, is at the very heart of the paralysis that grips virtually all spiritual aspirants, and everyone else as well.

Death Denial, in all its many forms, is the hole at the bottom of which we sit huddled and trembling, scared to death of our own lives. Death Awareness is the act of coming out of that hole and beholding the world in which we live and the creation of which we are a part. I've said many times that all people, around the world and throughout history, look like mere children from the perspective of one who has taken even a single step, and this is that step. To venture out of that hole, to declare freedom from childish beliefs, to turn toward death, to look the unslayable arch-demons of futility and insignificance in the eye, this is where the journey begins, and no journey begins elsewhere. Everything else we do is about staying dumb and killing time and digging ourselves deeper in.

What would I do if I were in that group listening to me and Lisa tonight? Impossible to say, of course, but in an idealized sense I can say that I'd go home and draw a line. I might start by rounding up every piece of spiritual detritus and debris I'd accumulated over the years—every book and magazine, every piece of clothing and jewelry, every little statue and knick-knack and totem and fetish—and I'd make a pile and pour gas on it and watch it burn and get naked and howl at the moon and make wild, war-like vows with the stars and the moon as my witness. A big, dumb gesture? Absolutely. That's what drawing a line has to be. You have to send a powerful signal, even if it's only to yourself. No one goes into this sane and level-headed.

Or maybe I'd go the other way. Maybe I'd say that I like my life and my approach to spirituality just the way they are. I want to be happy and live a nice life. Thanks for the crazy death-rant, Jed, but I want a life-enhancing spirituality, not all this whacked out death and war business. I like my books and my meditation practice and I don't see where it makes any sense to burn a house down if all it needs is a fresh coat of paint.

After all, no matter how you play it, it's just a fuckin' game.

Passage—immediate passage! the blood burns in my veins!
Away, O soul! hoist instantly the anchor!
Cut the hawsers—haul out—shake out every sail!
Have we not stood here like trees in the ground long enough?
Have we not grovell'd here long enough,
eating and drinking like mere brutes?
Have we not darken'd and dazed ourselves
with books long enough?

Sail forth! steer for the deep waters only!
Reckless, O soul, exploring, I with thee, and thou with me;
For we are bound where mariner has not yet dared to go,
And we will risk the ship, ourselves and all.

O my brave soul!
O farther, farther sail!
O daring joy, but safe! Are they not all the seas of God?
O farther, farther, farther sail!

— Walt Whitman —

Epilogue

How did it get so late so soon?
It's night before it's afternoon.
December is here before it's June.
My goodness how the time has flewn.
How did it get so late so soon?

–Dr. Seuss

DEEPLY RELAXED AND IN A death-friendly state of mind, I sit in a magic chair and glide effortlessly through the moonlit night a few feet above the surface of a quiet planet. The Kyrie of Beethoven's *Missa Solemnis* fills my space like warm gold as the Virginia countryside streams by. It's a chilly night but I am warm in my magic chair. The sights and sounds create and define my awareness. There is no past, no future. Hills and fields and trees make room for a small town; a village of Humans on a planet called Earth. The town is asleep and we ease through and back out into the rolling countryside.

A car appears, its headlights approaching like the headlights that approached Brett in her last seconds. If these lights cross the line then I'm ready and I hope Brett was too. I hope she had a last few moments like these, time to reflect on a life well lived, a role fulfilled, a game well played. I hope she had the second and a half it would have taken her to say goodbye and thank you. Especially thank you. Thank you for having me.

Thank you for the time of my life.

✧

There are two emotions that inform and animate the human animal; fear, and a gratitude-love-awe mix that might best be called agapé. As fear goes out, agapé comes in. More accurately, a pure white light of consciousness hits the prism of self and splits outward to become the universe as we experience it. If the prism of self is gray and murky with ignorance, choked with fear, contaminated with ego, then so becomes the universe that radiates out from it. It's that simple. As the prism becomes free of such flaws, then the whole universe changes with it. It resolves into clarity, becomes brighter, more playful and magical. Because we are the lens through which it is projected, we are participants in its shape and motion; co-creators of our own universe.

That's Human Adulthood. Spiritual Enlightenment is just the same, except you take the final step in purifying the prism of self: You remove it.

The approaching car stays in its lane and passes and is gone.

I have a life and I have lived it. I have done my best. I played my part. I read my lines and picked up my cues and hit my marks. I was born a child and I became an adult, and then I went further, as far as there is to go, all the way to a weird and empty place called Done. I have written books that say the things I wanted to know back then. That's how the books and the dialogues seem to me; like it's all been one long conversation with the pre-awakened me, the one who had to go and went and is gone. That's what this book and the first two really are. What are such books worth? Whatever they're worth to the reader, I suppose. If someone had approached me back when all this began and offered me these books, I would have paid an arm and a leg for them, literally and without hesitation. *Seriously? All you want is an arm and a leg? What's the catch?* Missing limbs I could have lived with. Continued life as a lie I couldn't.

It seems like a million years ago when I stood on the end of a pier and threw my ridiculously valuable watch away, just like Melissa almost did tonight with her mom's tightly compacted remains. I could have done much smarter things with that watch, but it weighed too much so I threw it from the end of a pier. A big, stupid gesture, yes, but it was a time of big, stupid gestures. I'm happy now for those times that I was smart enough to be so stupid. When you're actually doing it, when you're actually standing there on the end of a pier preparing to throw a family treasure away forever, you know you're being dumb and that the only way it isn't dumb and horribly traitorous is if the follow-through is there. If you go all the way, if you really do what you're trying to do, then blood treason and a few ounces of metal are a small price to pay. Otherwise, it's just a hollow, foolish and unforgivable gesture. And the thing is, as you're doing it, as you're taking that watch that was given to you in trust and with meaning, and you throw it into black water, only the fool part of the equation is visible. You can only see the dumb, but you gotta go ahead and do it, because the watch is too heavy for anything else and you know that if you don't sink it, it's damn well gonna sink you.

This magic chair, this nighttime planet, this music, these hands; they're not mine, I can't keep them, but I have them now. Right now they are with me, they are mine, but only for a moment, and the lesson of the moment is that moments cannot be seized. There is no now, there is only the intersection of past and future, both of which possess the curious charm of not existing.

I think of my first friend in this life. She was, I shit thee not, an elephant. We were little kids together. I knew her name and she knew mine. I could explain that but I don't think I will. She's still alive and I know where she is. Maybe I'll go see her. Probably not.

I think of a time—and again, I shit thee not—I was racing a luxury sports car along Route 666 at twilight when I came over a rise big-air fast and had to call on all and sundry gods to avoid crashing into an emaciated white longhorn steer standing nonchalantly across the road. I busted up the car's front end and found myself stuck all night in—I shit thee not again—an Indian burial ground. On Route 666. When I looked for the unlikely animal it was, though there was nowhere for it to go, gone. I was young and that was a strangely dark and cold and long night.

Or maybe I dreamed it.

The watch, my elephant friend, that long night on Route 666, maybe this is my life passing before my eyes. Makes me wonder about the next set of approaching headlights.

Or maybe it's just that tonight gets added to that list. Saying goodbye to someone so like myself. Delivering my first and last eulogy. The haunting, otherworldly beauty of this drive. Bringing the curtain down on a big part of my own life as well. The teaching and speaking and writing thing is done now.

And then, there it is.

Click.

I am done. My work is done. This whole author-teacher gig is over. It started out twenty years ago when a diamond tipped arrow caught me square between the eyes. It became one thing, then something else, then another thing, and now it's over. I have completed my life, fulfilled my purpose, done my bit. If I haven't mentioned before that enlightenment is pointless, I apologize, I meant to. Enlightenment is pointless. In the infinite, eternal nothing of no-self, there are no points. The context that writing and teaching has given my life is over. All that's left for me now is to retire to my new home and play with my new friend, Maya.

A boy and his dog.

The *Missa Solemnis* drives through my heart like a stake. The moon is high and full and casts a surreal glow on the glistening landscape. I release all thoughts and memories and settle into the moment, immersed in beauty enough to stop a war. To outlive this moment seems a sacrilege. I look over at Lisa, wondering if she knows where we are. Tears are streaming down her smiling face as she pilots us through the eternally brief night.

She knows where we are.

Our revels now are ended. These our actors,
As I foretold you, were all spirits, and
Are melted into air, into thin air;
And, like the baseless fabric of this vision,
The cloud-capped towers, the gorgeous palaces,
The solemn temples, the great globe itself,
Yea, all which it inherit, shall dissolve,
And, like this insubstantial pageant faded,
Leave not a rack behind.

We are such stuff
As dreams are made on and our little life
Is rounded with a sleep.

— Shakespeare —

Bibliography

Adler, Dr. Mortimer J. *How to Read a Book* New York: Simon and Schuster Inc., 1940.

Bucke, Dr. Richard M. *Cosmic Consciousness* New York: University Books Inc., 1966.

Carrière, Jean-Claude. *The Mahabharata* Translated by Peter Brook. New York: Harper & Row, 1989.

Kesey, Ken. *One Flew Over the Cuckoo's Nest* New York: Viking Press, 1973.

Orwell, George. *Nineteen Eighty-Four* New York: Plume, 2003

Thoreau, H.D. *Walden* New York: Viking Press, 1947.

Voltaire. *Candide, or Optimism*, New York: Boni And Liveright Inc., 1918.

Whitman, Walt. *Leaves of Grass* New York: Doubleday Doran & Co., 1940.

Wisefool Press

THE ENLIGHTENMENT TRILOGY

Spiritual Enlightenment: The Damnedest Thing, Spiritually Incorrect Enlightenment, and *Spiritual Warfare*, are available in print, electronic and audiobook editions.

Visit us on the web to sign up for email notifications regarding news, updates, and product announcements:

www.WISEFOOLPRESS.COM

E-BOOKS & BONUS MATERIAL

E-book editions of Wisefool Press titles contain exclusive bonus materials, such as interviews and additional chapters, not available elsewhere. Visit WisefoolPress.com for more information.

CD & MP3 AUDIOBOOKS

The Enlightenment Trilogy is available on CD or downloadable MP3 format. Visit our website for details.

QUANTITY DISCOUNTS

Generous quantity discounts are available at our website.

Printed in the United States
90584LV00001B/1-90/A